Mission For Caribbean Change

STUDIEN ZUR INTERKULTURELLEN GESCHICHTE DES CHRISTENTUMS
ETUDES D'HISTOIRE INTERCULTURELLE DU CHRISTIANISME
STUDIES IN THE INTERCULTURAL HISTORY OF CHRISTIANITY

Herausgegeben von/edité par/edited by

Richard Friedli
Université de Fribourg

Walter J. Hollenweger
University of Birmingham

Hans Jochen Margull
Universität Hamburg

Band 28

Verlag Peter Lang
FRANKFURT AM MAIN · BERN

Kortright Davis

MISSION FOR CARIBBEAN CHANGE

Caribbean Development As Theological Enterprise

Verlag Peter Lang

FRANKFURT AM MAIN · BERN

CIP-Kurztitelaufnahme der Deutschen Bibliothek

Davis, Kortright:

Mission For Caribbean Change : Caribbean
Development as Theological Enterprise / Kortright
Davis. - Frankfurt am Main ; Bern : Lang, 1982.
  (Studien zur interkulturellen Geschichte des
  Christentums ; Bd. 28)
  ISBN 3-8204-5732-1
NE: GT

ISSN 0170-9240
ISBN 3-8204-5732-1
© Verlag Peter Lang GmbH, Frankfurt am Main 1982

Druck und Bindung: fotokop wilhelm weihert KG, darmstadt

ABOUT THE AUTHOR

Kortright Davis is an Anglican clergyman who was born in Antigua, West Indies, and trained for the ministry at Codrington College, Barbados. He holds degrees from the University of London (B.D.), and the University of the West Indies (M.A.), and a doctorate (D.Phil) from the University of Sussex.

He has combined continuous pastoral work in the Caribbean with an academic career (mainly at Codrington College, where he acted as Principal in 1970-71), and also with work in promoting the ecumenical movement in that region. Between 1971 and 1978 he worked with the Caribbean Conference of Churches and co-ordinated several important ecumenical gatherings including the two Assemblies of the CCC, in 1973 and 1977.

Apart from serving as consultant to several international meetings in Canada, the United Kingdom and Europe, Davis has published a number of articles and papers, contributed to collections of essays on Caribbean Christianity, and edited a few books including Moving Into Freedom (Barbados, 1977). At present he is a lecturer in Theology and Development Studies at Codrington College, and also pastor of St. Bartholomew's Anglican Church in Barbados. He is married with three children.

ACKNOWLEDGEMENT

This study would not have been possible without the invaluable help and support of so many colleagues, friends, and agencies whose interest and inspiration created a most wholesome, intellectual and spiritual environment for the writer. It would be impossible to mention all those who have shared in this exercise; yet there are some persons and agencies to whom thanks and appreciation are particularly due.

The CCC and the United Society for the Propagation of the Gospel (USPG) both provided financial assistance for travelling, and the periods of study and research in England. Professor Duncan Forrester of Edinburgh University (formerly of Sussex), and Professor Reginald Green of the IDS (Sussex) have shown remarkable patience and understanding in the supervision of this study - to both of them I am profoundly indebted.

To my wife, Joan, whose typing skill, relentless commitment and personal encouragement surpassed my own competence and determination, and who sacrificed so much in the many months of preparing this final document, I shall be eternally grateful.

I wish to thank the University of Sussex for allowing this work to be pursued under its auspices, and sincerely trust that in some small way it will have contributed to the great task of building stronger bridges of understanding between the people of the Caribbean and the rest of the global community.

Kortright Davis
August, 1980

PREFACE

"An area such as the Caribbean, which
appears to have created a new form of
armed revolution in which a government
is overthrown but which omits the
violence, hatred, chaos and repression
that every other revolution reported
in the world-wide press seems to deem
necessary, must surely be among the
most innovative and creative in the
world".

(Diana Mahabir, in EXPRESS,
Tuesday, March 20, 1979, Trinidad)

The "armed revolution" to which the writer of the foregoing quotation refers is the coup d'etat in Grenada which took place on March 13, 1979.
The Government of Sir Eric Gairy was toppled by an Opposition political
group in Grenada - the New Jewel Movement. That event signalled the
end of speculative thought in the Caribbean that such revolutions were impossible. It also epitomized the extensive winds of rapid social change
which had been blowing through the Commonwealth Caribbean since the
start of the 1970's.

Social change is possible in the Caribbean. This was the distinctive les-
son from the Cuban revolution of 1959; yet there was hardly likely to be
another Cuba in the region - so it was thought. It is too early to tell
whether Grenada will become a second Cuba, but the leaders of the Grenada revolution have claimed that they took up arms on behalf of the poor,
the hungry and the unemployed. Fidel Castro made virtually the same type
of claim. Others in the Caribbean have also come out on the side of the
poor and dispossessed of the region.

The decade of the 70's witnessed the emergence of a new spirit
of mission among the Churches in the Caribbean, which caused
them to work more closely together for the alleviation of social, economic
and political hardships in the region. This they attempted to do on an
ecumenical basis through the Caribbean Conference of Churches, (CCC)
and particularly through its Development Programme - Christian Action
For Development in the Caribbean (CADEC).

Between 1971 and 1977 a significant amount of action was accomplished
by the Caribbean Conference of Churches (in formation between 1971 and
1973), and it was pursued under the broad name of "development". The
Churches have endorsed this specific mode of engagement in the action

7

for social change in the Caribbean. Some would not be unwilling to suggest that the "new spirit of mission" demonstrated by the CCC and the change of regime in Grenada are not altogether unrelated, since the CCC itself readily assured the new regime of its "continuing interest in their future development". Further, the General Secretary of the CCC publicly stated that -

> "no one familiar with the gross abuse of
> power in this Caribbean island society and
> the extent of deprivation of a great section
> of its people, would honestly want to ignore
> the legitimate aspirations of those who have
> brought about the dramatic change".
> (THE NATION, March 19th, 1979, Barbados)

This statement was made even before any nation had officially recognized the new regime.

What, however, are the theological undergirdings for such a distinctive and unprecedented (historically) engagement of the Churches in the praxis for social change? This is the basic question that has been constantly asked both within and without the Churches themselves, and even within the CCC. The present study is therefore an attempt to suggest a theologically illuminating way of interpreting the development praxis of the CCC between 1971 and 1977. It is meant to be a contribution to the emergent process of creative theological critical reflection in the Caribbean, and to be a means of challenging some assumptions in the region concerning the historical "gaps" between Caribbean Christian thought and Caribbean Christian action.

Throughout the study, the term "Caribbean" denotes principally the English-speaking Caribbean, though many of the claims made could also apply to the Spanish, French and Dutch areas. The history of all the people of the Caribbean is almost identical, and the general aspirations for freedom, justice and well-being are not dissimilar. The present writer bases many of his value-judgements on auto-biographical experiences, and on an intimate knowledge of the Caribbean. Nevertheless, it is to be acknowledged that there are cultural and historical reflections which may not aptly apply to every Caribbean person, particularly those of Indian or European descent. Such caveats tend to underscore the difficulty of speaking of the Caribbean as if it were a homogeneous region. It is indeed a cultural mix of people who are genuinely striving to arrive at one destiny out of many people.

It has therefore been impossible to record or to include in a 'bibliography', a substantial amount of the 'material' used in this study. So much is derived from the local newspapers; the conversations on buses, in the market-places, at the dances, in the congregations, on the playing-fields. So much more is drawn directly from the innumerable encounters and friendships among those who, like the present writer, continue to search for meaning and creativity, for new paths in Caribbean life. The Caribbean is literally a hot-bed of human activity. Things are always happening. Yet, so little can ever be captured in the 'letter'; only in the 'spirit'. It is however to be hoped that the reader will recognize, at least in part, some of that search for a new spirit to which this study purports to lead.

The winds of rapid change continue unabated, and so much has happened since this study was begun, that there is already much more social activity in the Caribbean which could be theologically analysed. Yet the study ends on a note of openness towards the future, and it is to be hoped that those who read it will not be unmoved to go on to read the "signs of the times" in the Caribbean - particularly within the Christian community - which God in his good providence continues to make possible.

Kortright Davis
Barbados, August 1980

SYNOPSIS

The quality of life in the Caribbean has constantly been characterized by structured poverty and dependence, and a marked degree of cultural alienation. Any attempt to engage in action for social improvement must therefore be determined by the struggle for economic and cultural liberation.

Some Caribbean Churches have come together in the Caribbean Conference of Churches (CCC) - to promote proper growth and full human development. Between 1971 and 1977 a significant amount of developmental activity was undertaken by the CCC, which, like other agencies in the Third World, interpreted "development" to mean the pursuit of economic growth, social justice, and self-reliance towards the humanization and liberation of Caribbean people.

Development action is indeed a proper dimension of theological praxis. The CCC has yet to provide a theological framework within which to interpret appropriately the social praxis it has been promoting. It is being suggested that such a theological framework can emerge out of an in-depth reflection on the socio-historical and religious experiences of Caribbean people themselves. A theology of "achievement and fulfillment" is suggested, and the central themes of c r e a t i v i t y , c o n t i n u i t y , and c o m m u n i t y - as distinctive experiences of the Triune God of solidary love - provide a methodology for critical reflection on the development activity of the CCC.

The Church in the Caribbean will be seen to grow in maturity towards the future as it incorporates more of this innovative ministry into the very fabric of its own proclamation and witness.

This book therefore attempts to examine the nature of a theological hermeneutic appropriate to the Caribbean human experience, and to point to a theologically illuminating way of understanding why the praxis for liberation and the proclamation of salvation are inseparable for Christian witness.

ABBREVIATIONS

AMECEA	-	Association of the Episcopal Conference in Eastern Africa
ARC	-	Action for the Renewal of the Churches
CADEC	-	Christian Action For Development in the Caribbean
CARICOM	-	Caribbean Community and Common Market
CCC	-	Caribbean Conference of Churches
CCN	-	CADEC Communications Network
CCPD	-	Commission on the Churches' Participation in Development
CEYA	-	Caribbean Ecumenical Youth Action
CTRC	-	Caribbean Tourism Research (and Development) Centre
CUP	-	Cambridge University Press
DERAW	-	Disaster, Emergency Relief, and Welfare
IDS	-	Institute of Development Studies
OUP	-	Oxford University Press
SCM	-	Student Christian Movement
SODEPAX	-	Society for Development and Peace
UWI	-	University of the West Indies
WCC	-	World Council of Churches

TABLE OF CONTENTS

Chapter I

POVERTY, DEPENDENCE AND ALIENATION
IN THE CARIBBEAN

"What can we do to enable people of all
walks of life in our separate countries
to achieve a fuller life for themselves
and their families? For human life seems
to be thwarted and manipulated by those
who hold economic, political and social
power locally as well as externally."

(Inaugural Assembly, Caribbean Conference
of Churches, November 1973)

Introduction

The Caribbean presents a very unique picture in world geography in that
it is an area that links the rich North with the poor South. It is a chain
of islands which links the two continents of North America and South
America. The area itself is comprised of land masses differing quite
substantially in size and geology. The larger territories lie mainly in
the North and West - Cuba, Hispaniola, Jamaica, Puerto Rico; while
the other territories are relatively smaller - islands scattered in an arc
to the South and East, the largest of these being Trinidad on the far
South. Barbados is the most easterly of all. Added to this chain are the
three Guianas - Guyana, Surinam (both independent) and French Guiana,
which are generally regarded as being more Caribbean than South American because of their population and history. There is also Belize (formerly British Honduras) in Central America.

Most of the islands lie within the path of the Trade Winds and suffer per-
ennially from the terrors of the hurricane season. Some of them are said
to be parts of a range of summits of submerged volcanoes, and they do
not generally enjoy the benefits of high rainfall nor the fruits of rich
arable soil. With the exception of the bauxite in Jamaica and Guyana,
and the oil in Trinidad, the area can boast of no mineral or other natural resources of any great quantity. Yet the Caribbean is a densely populated area. (1)

The majority of its population is of African stock, descendants of the
slaves brought over from Africa by the Europeans. In Guyana, however,
there are more East Indians than Africans; while in Trinidad the Indians

15

account for a little less than half of the population. There are some Chinese and Portuguese who live mainly in Jamaica, Trinidad and Guyana, but they do not constitute large sectors of the population. The specific area with which we are chiefly concerned in this study therefore (the English- and Dutch-speaking Caribbean and Haiti), is populated in the main by people of African and Indian descent whose forebears were brought to the region under the economic systems of slavery and indentureship for the cultivation of sugar. None of the people with whom we will deal - African, Indian, European - are indigenous to the area. The last of the few remaining indigenous Caribs have virtually died out; and, in any case, racial purity among the Caribs ceased long ago.

The Caribbean is thus a new society, transplanted in the sixteenth century as a result of European economic, political and military policy. European capitalists saw the colonies as a source of raw materials, which could be turned into manufactured goods for the European market. A colonial society was created in the Caribbean solely for the benefit of Europe, and it was peopled by a minority of European overlords, and a majority of African slaves. It was, at its very core, a plantation society, with white European planters and black African (and later Indian) plantation workers. This novel economic and political experiment was to pay rich dividends for the material well-being of European capitalists. More than any other single factor, this serves to account for its historical movement from being an undeveloped region to being u n d e r d e v e l o p e d at the present time. Raymond Smith has written the following -

"Caribbean countries exhibit the full
effects of colonialism; here that
system of social, cultural and political domination came to full flower
through the successive stages of plantation society, creole society and now
perhaps through sponsored modernism."(2)

The Caribbean historian, Woodville Marshall, has referred to West Indian society as one which was historically artificial -

"created by imperialist objectives,
sustained by the necessities of economic exploitation, characterized by gross
social inequalities which themselves
were a product of the imperialist
creation and presence;"(3)

and he goes on to suggest that the community "was finally left to grope for a sense of community and identity when the imperialist interests had waned".

Any socio-historical analysis of the Caribbean, and of its need for social change for the better, must inevitably focus attention on at least three of the main characteristics of the underdevelopment of the region. Economic-

ally, the Caribbean is gripped in p o v e r t y ; politically, it is still in a
state of virtual d e p e n d e n c e; and culturally, it is a society which breeds
a l i e n a t i o n in a number of ways. Our aim in this chapter therefore is to
discuss these main obstacles to social change in the Caribbean and to suggest that it is the broad response to the challenges for development which
these indicate that can constitute a framework for assessing the Development Programme of the Caribbean Conference of Churches.

Poverty and Dependence

The economic and political realities in the Caribbean are so closely inter-
related that it is considered useful to discuss them in the same section. For
most people in the region, politics is essentially a question of "bread-and-
butter", so that the economic realities of poverty and the political experience
of dependence remain almost inseparable, although there are exceptional
cases of political dependence with relative prosperity in the Caribbean.
Such exceptions - notably in the Netherlands Antilles and the U.S. Virgin
Islands - tend to prove the rule.

The majority of the people in the Caribbean are very poor. The area includes the poorest country in the Western Hemisphere - Haiti, which was
also the first black country in the New World to gain its independence at
the beginning of the nineteenth century. The roots of poverty in the Caribbean are directly related to the origins of the new society. It was a plantation society in which the majority of the people were chattels, rather
than free persons producing for their own advancement. They virtually had
little else to gain than the postponement of a miserable death. Alfred Thorne
rightly suggests that the economic structure of the Caribbean islands explains "their economic levels as fully as it evidences their origins and
economic history".(4) The historical importance of these islands, particularly in the hey-day of sugar production, was the fact that they produced
so much for other people far removed from them. Adam Smith in his
W e a l t h o f N a t i o n s (1776) wrote -

> "It is commonly said that a sugar planter ex-
> pects that the rum and the molasses should
> defray the whole expense of his cultivation
> and that his sugar should be all clear profit. "(5)

The short answer to the question of why the Caribbean is a poor society lies
mainly in the historical fact that the Caribbean was meant to be a plantation and not a society as such. It was always organized for production
rather than for social life, and the owners of the means of that production,
as well as the chief beneficiaries, were not among its inhabitants. It was
an organized slave plantation society, with a rigid caste-like system that
was determined by race, and "a cultural plurality with integrative elements
deriving from the common destiny to production of the crop for everyone in
the plantation community".(6) After sugar began to decline in the late nine-

17

teenth century, diversification took place with bananas, cocoa and sea-island cotton. But the plantation remained virtually intact. The Caribbean today still survives within the shadow of the plantation, so that a brief discussion of Caribbean plantation economics should serve to illustrate the extent of the poverty of the Caribbean.

Most of the arable land in the Caribbean has up until very recently been owned by a few persons, or groups of persons. In 1931 in Trinidad just over 1% of the 47,000 farmers owned half the area under cultivation comprising units of more than 100 acres. (7) In 1935 in St. Vincent, more than half of the best land was owned by 30 plantations, while 95% of 2763 peasants owned holdings of less than 10 acres. (8) In 1944, one man in the parish of St. Elizabeth in Jamaica owned 46,000 acres, and another in the parish of St. Thomas owned 30,000 acres. (9) In more recent times, however, national governments, particularly in Cuba, Jamaica, Guyana, Antigua, Trinidad and Barbados, have assumed ownership, or control, of large areas of arable land. This development has not however altered the basic historical fact of the plantation economic reality in the Caribbean, which is that the population is comprised mainly of the poor landless peasantry.

Unemployment in the Caribbean has been steadily rising, particularly among the youth. Those who have been studying the problem very closely indicate that the rate of unemployment in the region runs between 14% and 25%. (10) When this is added to the substantial level of underemployment, and the fact that there is a serious shortage of skills among the labour force, the whole spectrum of poverty in the Caribbean assumes alarming proportions. In addition to this, there is a general lack of motivation towards increased productivity and self-seliance. There is a lack of mobility among the labouring classes, based principally on the fact that most of the migration outlets are now closed. There is also a steady growth in the population.

The basic nature of the plantation economy, however, gives rise to other serious economic obstacles to development in the Caribbean, and thereby fails to relieve the poverty situation. These may be briefly summarized as follows: -

(a) There is a fracturing of the interaction between resource supply and demand - production is exported and goods used imported
(b) The foreign ownership of the means of production drains the supply of investible funds from the income stream
(c) There is an unequal distribution of wealth and income
(d) The level of skills required is very low indeed
(e) There is a distortion in the use of resources which inhibits the flexible deployment of resource services to high-income producing activities
(f) There is a high consumer import propensity that correlates to the high export activity of plantation production

18

(g) The processing of raw materials in the plantation society is virtual-
    ly unknown. After three hundred years of sugar production in the
    Caribbean there is still no proper sugar refinery. (11)

The recent expansion in the manufacturing and tourism sectors of the
economy in the Caribbean has not yet altered the basic nature of the
plantation economy. The establishment of industries and hotels, the majority of which are still foreign-owned, has not reduced the rate of unemployment in the region. Further, there has been an all-round rise in
the cost of living; consumer tastes and values have become more costly,
and the capacity of the people to meet the high cost of living has been
sorely outmatched. (12)

Poverty in the Caribbean has therefore been structured and persistent,
and the economic history of the region has constantly revealed a "dynamic
equilibrium of underdevelopment" which George Beckford says is "endemic in plantation society". (13) The structure of poverty in the Caribbean
might be aptly illustrated by a graphic description of poverty in Jamaica -

> "In every village and town at least
> half of the young men are out of work.
> In every village and town the young
> girls have babies whose fathers are
> out of work and very often have never
> had a chance to work in their lives.
> If I could show you the old women,
> pitiful in their neglect and poverty,
> hardly able to drag one foot after the
> other; if I could show you the hordes
> of little children, underfed, barefooted,
> badly clothed, badly educated; if I
> could show you the plight of the small
> farmers struggling to make ends meet on
> hopelessly small parcels of dreadfully
> poor land; if I could show you the
> houses men and women and children
> live in, homes shabby and forlorn, bereft
> of every civilized comfort, without
> water or light or even room to live in
> peace and freedom. My friends, I do
> not invent these things. This is the
> naked state of our country. These
> are the facts that cry to heaven for
> redress. "(14)

With very few exceptions, the Governments in the Caribbean are continually faced with serious financial problems. Not only are they unable to provide jobs for the unemployed in any great quantity, but they are also unable
to provide relief for the unemployed. The following statement by Paul Singh,

19

although written about Guyana, has direct relevance to the rest of the
Caribbean -

> "The sheer magnitude of the poverty problem
> coupled with the marked failure of successive
> Governments to bring about any significant
> change in the traditional life-style of the
> poor has nourished an attitude of defeatism.
> This has been reinforced by orthodox religious
> teaching that the poor 'must always be with
> us'. Poverty has remained almost unmitigated
> for over three centuries while circulating
> power-elites have institutionalised an effi-
> cacious con-game that repeatedly drains off
> discontent by flowery-words, promises and
> propaganda designed to raise hopes."(15)

Social services are generally badly supported, and recurring Budget deficits prevent the Governments from embarking on imaginative programmes for helping the general economic situation. Most people are at the
mercy of Governments, which are themselves (in most cases) at the mercy
of the private sectors for raising revenue. The private sector depends
heavily on external commercial and industrial forces. A web of dependence is thus created by the economic, as well as the political situation.

The plantation system always requires a substantial measure of authority
and control. In the Caribbean, the management of the plantation society has
historically been characterized by a firm reliance on the colonial power.
Furnivall has suggested that there are two basic factors common to colonial practice, especially where the policy is one of colonization by exploitation. These are, first, that it is conditioned by economic laws, and
secondly, that responsibility for maintaining order is assumed by the
colonial power.(16) Caribbean society was from the very beginning of the
new era (after Columbus) rooted in the political and economic dominance
of metropolitan powers. The concept of the superiority of, and the need to
affirm dependence on, the European (and latterly the Euro-American), has
always been validated in the Caribbean. Imperialism was therefore a fairly
easy policy for the Europeans to pursue. They exercised a spiritual imperialism by inculcating a sense of duty mixed with domination. The institution of slavery and indentureship, and the effective measures of coercion
made this spiritual imperialism a natural ally to the basic preoccupation
of the people of the Caribbean to survive.

If the plantation system has been a profitable form of material imperialism
in the Caribbean, the colonial system has been an effective form of cultural
imperialism - in that it has not only engendered this notion of dependence
on metropolitan power and leadership, it has also effected the transformation and adaptation of the people by their masters. Thus, it is possible to
say with Beckford that the plantation has created an "ethos of dependence
and patronage" which has deprived the people of the Caribbean of dignity,

security and self-respect. (17) Aime Cesaire goes further and says: "My turn to state an equation: colonization = 'thingification'."(18)

Colonial society in the Caribbean therefore, based as it has been on the plantation system, has maintained a rigidly hierarchical structure, in which the dominant planter class has ruled from the top of the social pyramid from its inception. The ruling classes have been externally oriented, towards the metropolitan power, and they have depended on the colonial administration to protect their interests and their status. Constitutional developments between the 1940's and the present time, which have brought political independence to many of the countries in the region, (19) have not substantially altered the basic realities of Caribbean dependence. Indeed, one of the chief colonizing powers, Britain, had long been reluctant to cede independence for reasons which Mary Proudfoot had outlined as follows -

> "The United Kingdom government has always
> felt that it could not relinquish control
> so long as its own taxpayers had to make
> regular financial contributions. In other
> words, he who would be master in his own
> house must first be able to pay his own
> bills."(20)

Yet the granting of independence by Britain to most of its Caribbean colonies between 1962 and the present time has not radically altered the realities of economic and psychological dependence brought forward from the colonial period.

Soon after Jamaica attained its independence in 1962 the Jamaican leader, Norman Manley, complained that his people were in "the thraldom and servitude to old ideas". "Disenthral yourselves, comrades," he declared, "Be born anew for a new Jamaica".(21) On another occasion, he warned the people that they should not be fooled into thinking that they could "throw off all the patterns of behaviour and thought that colonialism brings upon a people merely by becoming free. We have tried hard in this country to overcome them, but they are not yet overcome".(22) To a very great extent therefore, the consequence of political independence for all the Commonwealth Caribbean countries that have attained it has merely been that of a shift of the locus of authority from overseas to within the territory itself. The issue of what independence should mean to the Caribbean requires discussion far more extensive than can be allowed at the present time, nevertheless it is important to agree with Gordon Lewis in principle that -

> "the central reality of independence is the
> need to convert the patterns set by those
> earlier social systems into an independent
> national society run primarily in the
> interests of its independent citizens."(23)

21

Lewis goes on to refer to it as that "traumatic transition from colonial status to freedom".(24) The fact is that Caribbean people are still caught in the grips of that divide between the freedom they are made to understand that they have, and the actual neo-colonial realities with which they still have to live. In other words, they have gained the appearance of freedom, but not its substance.

The external pressures of dependence in the Caribbean are all related to the fact that political sovereignty has in no way been accompanied by economic sovereignty. The region is still heavily dependent because of the foreign ownership and control of key economic sectors - manufacturing and tourism; through foreign aid; through trade, especially in respect of preferential and concessional arrangements; through reliance on foreign experts and imported technology; and through the importation of consumption and production patterns. In St. Lucia in 1977, a large American oil company laid down as a condition for its proposed investment in that island that the national Parliament should pass a unanimous vote in support of its proposal. Both Government and Opposition voted in favour, and the oil terminal construction has already begun.(25) Yet, on the issue of national independence both sides were sharply divided. The paranoia over investor confidence in the Caribbean constitutes one of the strongest forms of structured dependence. Added to all this is the fact that the Caribbean is in such close proximity to the United States of America.

The Caribbean is virtually the 'mare nostrum' of the United States, and the latter is anxious to protect its access routes to the Panama Canal and to prevent the build-up of any threat to its national security. Thus there are defence installations at many strategic points in the Caribbean, and the presence of American service personnel - both official and non-official - is almost everywhere in evidence. All of this is further strengthened by the keen interest which the United States of America exhibits in the internal affairs of each territory, coupled by a heavy dependence of the countries themselves on the military might of America. The United States is determined that there should not be another Cuba in the region. Neville Linton observed in 1977 that the remarkable thing about Cuba was that it had survived just ninety miles away from the United States.(26) Eric Williams made the following comment about the United States - "we have the supreme paradox of a nation born in revolution taking a consistent counter-revolutionary stand in the countries in its backyard".(27)

The stark result of the external pressures on the Caribbean is epitomized in the historical perpetuation of a politically dependent directorate in the region. For the most part, they lack the confidence in themselves, and in their own societies, to re-define the terms and conditions under which the affairs of their territories are to be controlled. "They fear that any attenuation of metropolitan links or any control over metropolitan economic and financial contact with their countries will slow down the pace of economic development".(28) This fear manifests itself quite spectacularly in

the internal situation, and it is to a discussion on the dynamics of dependence at this level that we now turn.

One of the inherent characteristics of the plantation system is that it
sustains authoritarianism. This is a definite manifestation of a relationship of dependence. Furthermore, history has made it abundantly clear
that the plantation system often requires a dependent peasantry for its
survival, since to the plantation the peasantry is always a reservoir of
cheap labour. There is also the fact of the self-perpetuating nature of the
plantation system to be noted; this clearly means that, with very few exceptions, the majority of the people in the plantation society generally
lack the social cohesion to mobilize themselves to take effective action
together.(29) The pattern of organization is thus very feeble indeed,
economic self-interests (for survival) therefore predominate, and the
trades unions emerge as the main organizational instruments in the region. They came into being, particularly in the Commonwealth Caribbean, after the social upheaval of the late 1930's. Adult suffrage was
granted to the masses in the early 1940's, and the unions were organized
mainly for the economic and political development of the working classes.

During the past thirty years, however, the region has witnessed the
emergence of a form of internal colonialism, in which the old patterns
of dependence, hierarchicalism and rigid control have persisted. Political parties without a trades union base have survived with difficulty. The
trades unions themselves have done little to better the conditions of the
unemployed, the landless, and the occasional workers, and have mainly
advanced the interests of the already advantaged wage-earners. Structured dependence remains, and a form of democracy exists which hardly
qualifies to be called by that name, since the rigid control of the many
by the few is generally the order of the day.

The claim of majority-elected governments to function on behalf of all
the people in their respective territories is generally countered by a
growing litany of complaints of official victimization in the Caribbean,
the official challenge of the right of articulate action-groups to raise
voices of dissent, and the politicization of the military and the police on
the side of the ruling party. The issue of the freedom of the press has
long moved from being an academic one - in several Caribbean territories
freedom of expression either in print, or in the spoken word, is sadly
compromised. There is one other aspect of the question which requires
comment; this relates to nationalization of industry and governmental
participation in industry.

With the exception of Cuba, the nationalization of the economic resources
of the Caribbean has not produced any significant results for the people
of the region in their state of continued dependence. Nationalization of
bauxite and sugar in Guyana and Jamaica, and majority control of several
industries in Trinidad and some other Caribbean territories have not yet
begun to produce any substantial benefits for the people. In the latter case,

foreign ownership persists with its concomitant trends of foreign management and technical processes, as well as the foreign control of the markets.
In many instances, the multiplication of local personnel in managerial
positions has served merely to overlay the old system of dependence since
such personnel are generally powerless to change the system. With respect
to nationalization, the only significant change has been that of ownership.
Effective control still remains expatriate, worker participation in decision-
making is yet to be generally accepted, and the basic need of providing
more jobs for the growing number of unemployed is yet to be met. In sum
then, the rigidity of internal colonialism remains very real, even after
the governments elected by the dependent masses have assumed ownership
of a greater part of their national economies. Clive Thomas rightly suggests that the cardinal point about meaningful participation in industry is
that it is just "one element in a comprehensive struggle to involve the
people in decision-making, ownership, and the functioning of the system".(36
This comprehensive struggle of which Thomas speaks can involve nothing
short of a collective political will.

The discussion has so far indicated that the social institutions - plantation,
trades unions, political parties and governments - are yet to promote any
genuine movement for structural change in the Caribbean. To these institutions must be added the Church.

The Spanish and the French introduced Catholicism to the Caribbean, other
Europeans introduced Protestantism. Both religious systems flourished
within the context of, and in support of, the socio-economic system - the
plantation. The Christian Church was thus established in the region principally for the benefit of the planters - first for their own religious comfort
and then for the effectual subjugation of those whose labours they exploited
for their material comfort. It was under the control of the ruling classes
and, except in a very few cases (the Moravians and Baptists), exercised a
great degree of social control over the masses. The Moravians in particular
exercised a distinctive humanitarian ministry to the slaves and the working
classes; but in general terms, the alliance between the Church and the
status quo has historically been one of the main pillars of the structure of
dependence with which Caribbean society has existed.

In almost every department of its activity, the Church in the Caribbean exhibited a firm acceptance of domination. Its hierarchical structure of leader
ship and ministry, its heavy dependence on metropolitan sources for men,
money and doctrines, its efforts to make intolerable social conditions
tolerable, its suppression of local values and native beliefs, and the non-
participating nature of its activity all made it an effective instrument of
dependence in the Caribbean. This was underlined by the fact that it exercised effective control over what most people believed, and was therefore
in a unique position to provide sanctity for the social conditions under
which it functioned. Any notion of the need for liberation in the Caribbean
therefore stood for setting the region free from economic and political

dependence on imperialism, and freeing the Church and its doctrine from foreign dependence. (31)

In spite of the emergence of an indigenous leadership in recent years, the Church still appears to be in some respects a vestige of colonialism in the Caribbean. As the major social institution in the Caribbean, it continues to retain strong links with the past, and to sustain a level of dependence and tolerance among its membership that relates harmoniously to the wider realities of economic and political dependence. James Tucker suggests that the Church in the Caribbean "has moved from a crude to a refined colonial institution". (32)

There can hardly be any doubt therefore, that, almost at its very core, Caribbean society is inherently dependent. Its major institutions continue to be effective instruments of dependence in spite of significant constitutional advancements and attempts at structural changes. Exceptions in Cuba, Guyana or Jamaica merely serve to prove the overriding rule, moreso since in these countries the major shifts have been from one form of dependence to another. In terms of the Caribbean experience, there is a poverty that results from dependence, and there is a dependence that results from poverty. The economic and political realities in Caribbean society sustain a web of dependent poverty which takes its toll on the human spirit, and which creates serious obstacles to social change for the better, and full human development. Paul Singh has commented on the "deplorable lack of appreciation of the debilitating effects of poverty and the stresses that result from a lack of adequate resources". (33) It is the experience of having nothing combined with the feeling of being nothing that has to be seriously challenged in the Caribbean. The words of David Lowenthal are partially right - "West Indians seem unwilling to begin any journey, however, unless outsiders lead the way". (34) He also suggests that each resolution in the West Indies "entails new obligations to outside sources". (35) Such a comment points to a people whose socio-economic history and cultural experience are bedevilled by a pattern of alienation. This calls for a discussion on the realities of such alienation in the Caribbean.

Alienation

The plantation system has not only sustained a great degree of poverty and dependence in the Caribbean, it has also accounted for the creation of a society, in which the ruling class has exercised a cultural domination over the rest of the society, and in which a number of social obstacles have prevented the realization of human dignity among the majority of the people. Like other plantation societies, Caribbean society manifested some of the typical characteristics. These included a weak community structure (horizontally), but a rigid social stratification (vertically) based on race and class; a general absence of social responsibility because of poorly developed educational systems; a high degree of social instability due to the great divergence of intersectional interests in the society; and a pervasion of 'great house' values and aspirations (the great house on the plantation constituted the centre of value and the height of social status). Keith Hunte, another Caribbean historian, has contended that in the Caribbean historical experience "the plantation has proved something of a stultifying influence on the development of free community".(36)

Historically, the Caribbean has moved through slavery, the plantation system, colonialism, to neo-colonialism. In each of these stages social cohesion was possible only through social control and the economic system. At no stage had it been possible for the majority of the people either to participate effectively in the control of their social, political and economic affairs. Even today, mechanisms are lacking in the Caribbean which would attempt to promote wider participation of the people in the decision-making process. Roy Neehall has commented that in the Caribbean "democracy is caricatured as five minutes in a polling booth every five years".(37) The distribution of real political power is largely based on the pattern of distribution of economic and social power. In any event, plantation society carries a rigid pattern of stratification, thus rendering social status quite ineffectual for labouring classes.

The socio-historical process of creolization, which had its inception simultaneously with slavery, ensured that the cultural patterns of the people were subjugated to those of the dominant planter class, who themselves drew all their cultural strength from the European source. Thus, people of African stock were "drained of their essence",(38) their native culture was trampled underfoot, Negro peasantry had to surrender to the overt acceptance of their inferiority and to come to believe that "the white man's culture is the only culture that is considered worth having, or, indeed that exists".(39) There thus existed in the Caribbean personality the spiritual dependence on other men and on alien cultures, and the notion of 'society' in the Caribbean was fixed by reference to the dominant group within it, and every group accepted the norms and values of that group while retaining an ethnic identity.

The question of ethnic identity in Caribbean society has given rise to a considerable amount of discussion among social scientists over the years. The debate has been led mainly by scholars such as Herskovits,(40) M. G. Smith (41) and Raymond Smith (42) about issues concerning the survival of Africanisms among the people of the Caribbean, and also about the nature of the pluralism in Caribbean society. This latter issue is of relevance to our present concerns about alienation.

M. G. Smith had based his analysis of West Indian society on Furnivall's theory of the plural society.(43) Furnivall had developed his theory from a study of Far East societies notably Burma and Indonesia. He said that the plural society existed where there was a predominance of Western superstructure over native life, where there were distinctions in language, religion, culture, ideas and ways, where there were separate castes and racial sections, where there was a feebleness of the social will (especially in its inability to control economic forces), and where each section was an aggregate of individuals rather than an organic whole. "Each section in the plural society is a crowd and not a community", wrote Furnivall.(44) Although the socio-cultural, and economic histories in Burma and Indonesia were different from the Caribbean, M. G. Smith applied this theory to the West Indian situation, showing that there were institutional differences relating to marriage, family, education, property, religion, economic institutions, language, and folklore. Smith showed that these institutions were incompatible, and that the cultural domination of the minority ruling group made the social problems in the Caribbean more acute. Of particular significance for our study, however, was Smith's insistence that the differentiae within the plural society of the Caribbean were cultural and not racial, and that it was this that accounted for the basis of the 'white bias'.(45)

Many have taken issue with Smith's thesis - Brathwaite, Lowenthal, Lewis, and Raymond Smith (46) - and the debate covers a number of areas, such as class-stratifaction, common underlying values, and conflict, with which we cannot deal here. On the question of race, however, both Raymond Smith and George Beckford insist that the issue is crucial to the proper understanding of West Indian society. Raymond Smith says that in the Caribbean race must be stressed "since it was characteristic of creole society to deny value of any racial identity except 'whiteness'".(47) While Beckford accepts the principle of pluralism in the society, he insists that in the plantation society of the Caribbean, where there has been a rigid colour stratification of whites at the top, the mixed in the middle and the black at the bottom (with virtually little mobility) race has continued to be the important factor in the division of the classes.(48) Thus, in the Caribbean, it has been possible to speak of an 'elite of skinocracy' - the lighter the skin, the greater the status. Furthermore, Cesaire has said quite categorically that with blacks "we are dealing with the only race which is denied even the notion of humanity" (49)

The question of race can therefore never be shelved if we are to understand the fact of alienation in the Caribbean, and if we are to understand that the cultural difference between the ordinary folk and the elite middle-classes are "the consequences of racial segregation and of inequalities of power, status, and rewards, which stem from slavery and social pluralism".(50) For it was the middle-class in Caribbean society which constituted one of the chief engines of alienation. In their drive to gain upward social mobility, they always looked outwards to Europe for their reference of values and upwards to the white ruling classes for their economic and social survival. Raymond Smith has suggested that they have resulted in a creole elite who have perceived themselves as being qualitively different from other non-Europeans because of their 'refinement'; they distinguished between local whites and 'true' whites in Europe - preferring cultural whiteness to a nationalist image. Smith says that they have -

"..... continued to think of themselves
as being profoundly different from the
masses of the population. Sometimes
this shows itself in the form of a fear
of the supposed hostility of the lower
classes and sometimes in the form of a
conviction that the lower classes are
'culturally impoverished', mentally
twisted or basically inferior to the
middle and upper classes in some way". (51)

Alienation among the middle-class is also described by Beckford who says
that "the deculturated blacks have as much contempt for the 'unrefined'
masses of black people as the dominant group". (52)

It is precisely because the people of the Caribbean have had no alternative
but to imitate European (and lately North American) culture that the rigours of alienation have had such a cultural effect on them. They have had
no native language to use among themselves, and have therefore remained
open to the dominating force of European languages; (53) the effects of the
communications media have been overwhelming in inculcating alien values
and generating a set of rising expectations which the society has not been
able to fulfill; and, with centuries of persistence, the educational system
has produced a people with aptitudes unsuited for their own environment.
Kathleen Drayton says, "Colonial education separated people from their
own environment, taught them dependence and destroyed their self
worth". (54) Demas suggests that in the schools pupils received "an orientation towards the metropolitan rather than the local environment". (55)
Eric Williams diagnosed that -

> "The educational system of the Caribbean
> violated the fundamental principle that
> education should proceed from the known
> to the unknown, from the village to the
> great wide world, from the indigenous
> plants, animals and insects to the flora
> and fauna of strange countries, from the
> economy of the village and household to
> the economics of the world". (56)

The situation has virtually remained unchanged, and the skills and values
instilled in the pupils are hardly suited to the social and economic development of their societies, for the struggle for any form of genuine independence, or the search for a Caribbean identity. It is this search for a Caribbean identity that exemplifies the depth of alienation in the region. It runs
like a common theme throughout and is exacerbated by the fact that most
of the economic and cultural lines of communication run from each territory to outside the region, and that fragmentation between the island states
exists at a very intense level. Most of the ventures at regional cooperation

have been beset by either failure, or serious difficulties. At the beginning of 1978 no fewer than four Prime Ministers of Caribbean countries were bemoaning the fact that the Heads of the Commonwealth Caribbean had failed to meet together since 1975. The words of the Secretary-General of the Commonwealth Secretariat are apt on this point -

> "The natural state of our Caribbean is
> fragmentation; without constant effort,
> without unrelenting perseverance and
> discipline in suppressing instincts
> born of tradition and environment it
> is to our natural state of disunity that
> we shall return". (57)

Ramphal has always been a strong proponent of the theme that it is mainly in the struggle for Caribbean unity that the search for a Caribbean identity will bear fruit. (58) In the final analysis, therefore, the fact that Caribbean people are engaged, however feebly, in the search for their identity (or "pedigree" as Philip Mason says) indicates the extent of the cultural alienation with which they are beset. (59)

Suggestions for Change

The student of Caribbean society encounters great difficulty in locating literature which does not describe the Caribbean in terms negative and gloomy. This is mainly because the study of the Caribbean is essentially a study of colonialism at its worst. As late as 1954 Mary Proudfoot could write, "'Civis Britannicus sum' is still the proud boast of white, coloured and negro alike". (60) Norman Manley would have called this, not a proud boast, but the effects of the 'dead hand of imperialism' which in 1938 he described thus -

> "The dead hand of imperialism is made
> manifest in the dearth of our culture, in the
> paucity and poverty of our arts, in the
> drying up of the sources of charity,
> in the decay of faith and the licentious-
> ness of morals, in the dishonesty of our
> escapism, in the malice of our leaders,
> in the cowardice of government, in the
> narrow circumscription of all our horizons". (61)

Manley was speaking at a time when the masses of the Caribbean were rising up in their first full-blooded and riotous protest against the social and economic oppression in the region. He went on to say -

> "One touch of creative intensity and
> a veritable desert would quicken into
> life with rank weeds jostling the

flower shoots striving for living room.
There would be life and trouble, blossom
and fruit, but the dead hand, quietly with
blind efficiency, closes on it all". (62)

Thirty years later, another Caribbean leader, Eric Williams, wrote that
Caribbean history "can be viewed as a conspiracy to block the emergence
of a Caribbean identity - in politics, in institutions, in economics, in
culture and in values". (63) Williams went on to call for a psychological
revolution among Caribbean people and for metropolitan empathy with
Caribbean aspirations. It is this need for a psychological revolution in
the Caribbean that constitutes a fundamental imperative for social change.
Drexel Gomez, the Anglican Bishop of Barbados has made the following
observation -

"Among the peoples of the region there
is a definite desire to correct the im-
balance and deficiencies of the colonial
past which created societies crippled by
inequality of opportunity and disparity
of wealth in which the masses, largely
black, were both deprived and socially
dispossessed". (64)

There are a number of areas which must be effectively dealt with by the
Caribbean people themselves; for in spite of the poverty, dependence and
alienation - Caribbean people have survived with a rich emotional life,
with wit and gaiety, with rhythm and colour, and much more. They have
a tremendous capacity for survival - it is only this that can explain the
rich elements of native religions that have continued to flourish in the
Vodun in Haiti, the Shango cults, the Spiritual Baptists. It was this which
produced Marcus Garvey (65) as a twentieth century counterpart to the
leaders of resistance during the Slavery and post-Emancipation periods,
and from whom the late Martin Luther King (Jr) derived much inspiration
for his civil rights work in the United States of America. (66) J. Michael
Dash suggests that the only thing which Caribbean people could possess
(without being tampered with) was their imagination "and this became the
source of their struggle against the cruelty of their condition". (67) Dash
also posits the existence of a 'counter-culture' of the imagination among
the oppressed Caribbean people. Thus in the Caribbean, discontent is always below the surface, but overt manifestations are spasmodic, subtle
and often short, since the need to survive in a poor dependent situation
has continued to override the expediency of constant demonstrations of
discontent.

There have been many suggestions about how best the Caribbean might
tackle its economic, political and cultural problems. Some of them have
been more radical than others. Apart from Cuba, no Caribbean country
has been able to bring about a radical revolutionary break with the past,

30

to get rid of the 'curse of the Caribbean' - the plantation system, to get rid of unemployment, or to mobilize the whole population towards national reconstruction. The likelihood of a repetition of the Cuban performance is generally regarded as remote at the present time in other Caribbean countries. Yet the possibility can never be entirely ruled out. Other less spectacular attempts at social change are however more feasible. We can do no more than list them at this point. Such changes that have been suggested include the following -

1. Regional economic integration - this has been attempted in recent times through the establishment of the CARICOM arrangement, (68) and regional financial institutions such as the Caribbean Development Bank.

2. Re-negotiation with metropolitan enterprise - in order to ensure that greater benefits are secured for the Caribbean as a raw material producing area. The establishment of the ACP arrangement, (69) and the IBA is a step in this direction. A revision of investment incentives is also involved. (70)

3. Re-distribution of land and income - this entails several facets such as the rediscovery of agriculture as an industrial activity from which the peasantry can profit with dignity, the re-orientation of crops for domestic and regional markets, the re-orientation of financial and market activity to the benefit of the peasants, and the equitable distribution of the ownership, control and production activities among the pluralities of the plantation society. In fact, some economists insist that the plantation system must be destroyed. (71)

4. The maximum use of local raw materials in industrial production - this refers not only to the traditional plantation products such as sugar and bauxite, but also the use of new raw materials such as bagasse, pith (from the sugar cane), sand and clay. The development of cottage industries in the crafts sector, with the use of local materials - skins, straw, cotton, fruits and vegetables has also been widely recommended. (72)

5. The encouragement of more labour-intensive methods of production has long been recommended. This would obviously have the effect of reducing the number of unemployed. Yet the region continually accomodates a number of capital-intensive industries with a greater reliance on machines rather than on manpower resource - of which there is an abundant supply. (73)

6. The development of a programme of divestment of foreign-owned enterprise in the region, in order to effect the transfer of power to take major industrial decisions to within the region. This would bring about a gradual localization of all prominent foreign-owned assets. This in its broadest sense (and most radical) amounts to the nationalization of all foreign assets. Nationalization itself, however, can also include the state take-over of all key sectors of production and distribution - as in the case of Guyana. (74)

31

7.   The reconstruction of political systems in the Caribbean
     to ensure that power effectively remains in the hands of the people,
     that the political directorate becomes more accountable to the people,
     and that the institutional framework guarantees a much closer rela-
     tionship between the people and the public decision-making machin-
     ery. (75)
8.   The dismantling of the old, and the establishment of a new,
     educational system that renounces elitism and alienation,
     and that meets the needs of the people in their own environment. (76)

The foregoing list, far from being exhaustive, represents a small consensus of opinions of what is required for social change in the Caribbean. Because it is a region with very limited resources, its options are extremely limited. The problem is further exacerbated by the fact that it is comprised of small societies which are susceptible to the assimilative process
of more atrractive and richer societies. It is because of this easy assimil-
ation, made even easier by foreign-oriented communications media, that
the need for a socio-psychological revolution, a decolonization of the
mind, a radical change of values, is always of top developmental priority.

Social change will only be possible in the Caribbean when there is a collective effort made to confront the social, political and economic realities
of the region. With the exception of Cuba, only conflict-avoidance strategies have so far been employed - and the need for economic and cultural
liberation still remains acute. As far as economic liberation is concerned,
nothing short of a revolutionary transformation of the existing system will
do, and the will to initiate such a transformation must be essentially political. The political will must be mature enough to acknowledge the continuing power and presence of the United States of America, while at the same
time adopting a process for developing the effective participation of the
adult population on a basis of equality. This means radical changes in institutional structures to facilitate effective participation in the ownership
and control of the forces of production. People's creative and productive
energies are released when they have a stake in the productive process
and greater confidence in themselves. The need for greater self-confidence
is directly related to the need for cultural liberation.

Culture denotes the sum total of the creative human spirit. It must also be
borne in mind, however, that the very essence of being human derives
much from one's attachment to the land, the earth, the soil, the place
of one's birth or domicile, one's habitat. Humanity cannot be alienated
from that with which it is most familiar, that which is most authentic to
it, and still claim to be liberated. Cultural liberation in the Caribbean
therefore involves the full affirmation of the common manifestations of
the creative spirit - language, song, art, beliefs and so forth. It involves
an orientation away from the preference for foreign values because they
are foreign. It involves a re-orientation of the roles of all popular institutions towards the promotion of greater self-reliance, self-awareness,
and responsibility through participation. It involves the conscious dis-

32

covery of the dignity and value of all racial identities in the region. It involves the mutual acceptance of each other in the society, since self-con-
tempt and mutual conflict were constant factors in the relationship of
plantation society. Cultural liberation entails the necessity of the poor
to transform themselves as they attempt to transform their alienating
and oppressive conditions. Edward Brathwaite is right when he suggests
that the basis of culture for the Caribbean lies in "the folk", and he goes
on to describe 'the folk' as -

> "A people who, from the centre of an
> oppressive system have been able to
> survive, adapt, recreate; have de-
> vised means of protecting what has been
> so gained (miraculous, precarious
> maronage), and who begin to offer to
> return some this experience and vision". (77)

At the turn of the 1970's then, the Caribbean society with which we are
primarily concerned was gripped in the experience of structured poverty
and dependence, and cultural alienation. The socio-economic and political
apparatus was placed above the majority of people, and there was an
urgent need for economic transformation and cultural liberation. In 1971,
Roy Neehall stated thus -

> "Without liberation from enslavement
> to the values which perpetuate exploitation,
> dependence, adaptation and powerless-
> ness, we cannot expect that transforma-
> tion of political, economic and institu-
> tional structures will bring in a new
> day". (78)

Neehall was at the time delivering the opening address at the Consultation
on Caribbean Development in Trinidad, at which representatives of the
Churches in the region had met to determine what was to be the role of the
Church in the movement for social change and human liberation. That
event represented the turning-point in the history of the Church in the
Caribbean, since it not only outlined for the Church what was to be the
nature of its prophetic praxis but also ushered in a new era of the Church's
participation in the development process. It is therefore to a description
of the work of the Church in development, through the Caribbean Conference of Churches, that we turn in the next chapter.

Chapter II

ECUMENICAL ACTION FOR CARIBBEAN DEVELOPMENT

"We, as Christian people of the
Caribbean, separated from each
other by barriers of history,
language, culture, class and
distance, desire, because of
our common calling in Christ,
to join together in a regional
fellowship of Churches for
inspiration, consultation and
co-operative action. We are
deeply concerned to promote
the human liberation of our
people, and are committed to the
achievement of social justice and
the dignity of man in society.
We desire to build up together
our life in Christ and to share
our experience with the universal brotherhood of mankind."

(Preamble to the Constitution of the
Caribbean Conference of Churches,
November 1973)

Introduction

The Caribbean area has historically been the scene of great missionary
enterprise. The establishment of the major Christian denominations over
the last three centuries has not only been the result of religious zeal in
metropolitan countries, but also a demonstration of that desire on the
part of metropolitan peoples to extend the realities of empire beyond the
political to the social and religious dimensions as well. The Caribbean
has reflected quite faithfully much of the religious controversy and dissent that has arisen in Europe, and more recently in North America. Religious denominationalism has been transplanted into Caribbean society
with a great deal of vigour. The profileration of religious groupings in
the Caribbean during the twentieth century has however served to make
some Caribbean people more aware of the need for community and joint
co-operation, since such proliferation has often tended to create further

divisions among a people whose past has not been blessed with any high degree of solidarity.

Most of the former British colonies have been predominantly Protestant, while Roman Catholicism has predominated in St. Lucia, Dominica, the French Antilles, Trinidad, the Netherlands Antilles and Haiti. In Trinidad and Guyana, where there is the heaviest concentration of the Indian population in the Caribbean, Islam and Hinduism are prominent religions. Judaism is practised by a small minority in the Netherlands Antilles and Jamaica. Many Pentecostal groups around throughout the region and some of them are directed from North America. Others have arisen among groups of religious dissidents who have broken away from one or other of the main-line denominations. Caribbean society as a whole therefore presents a varied picture of Christian groupings, but in the main the majority of the people claim allegiance to the historic denominations whether Protestant or Catholic.(1) Apart from some intellectuals and returned migrants, hardly any Caribbean person would profess to have no faith. It is against this background that a brief attempt will now be made to trace the emergence of ecumenical action in the Caribbean.

The Development of Ecumenism

Ecumenical co-operation in the Caribbean goes back to the early decades of the twentieth century when theological training was combined between the Methodists and the Baptists at their Colleges in Jamaica.(2) The joint training of ministers for several denominations of the Non-conformist tradition made it easier for them to acknowledge each other in the fraternity of the wider pastorate and also to share ministrations between them. The birth of Councils of Churches in Trinidad, Grenada, Guyana, Jamaica and the Netherlands Antilles up to the beginning of the 1960's (3) also marked significant steps forward along the road to greater ecumenical action; but there was still no Caribbean-wide movement formed up to that time.

The Councils of Churches held out great promise for a more systematic and coherent policy on the part of the Churches to work closer together for the common good. The Councils could at least attempt to do together what individual denominations could not do well on their own. There were serious problems of finance and manpower, however, and busy clergymen found themselves having to support young inter-church structures, and programmes of social welfare and community development, in addition to their parish duties. The Councils therefore embarked on a very uncertain road bedevilled by a lack of financing, organization, efficiency and expertise.

Caribbean-wide ecumenical action began in the late 1950's following the initial surveys which were carried out in the region by Mr. E. J. Bingle for the International Missionary Council and the World Council of Christian Education. (4) A Carribean Consultation met at San German in Puerto Rico in May 1957 to discuss the feasibility of establishing a Conference of Churches in the region. It was attended by 51 persons, 15 of whom were from outside the Caribbean. One of the participants at the Consultation, Professor G. Baez-Camargo of Mexico wrote about the meeting in these words -

> "It was in a sense an experience
> of mutual discovery, of looking
> at each other at a much closer range
> than ever before ..... There was a
> realization of the emergence of
> common ethnic, economic, social,
> cultural and religious situations,
> resulting in common needs, problems
> and opportunities". (5)

The Consultation agreed on five areas of need for joint ecumenical action - Christian Education, Theological Education, Home and Family Life, Evangelism (with a particular focus on Hindus and Muslims), and special problems facing the Church in the Southern Caribbean. Churches and Church Councils were urged to work for closer co-operation with their neighbours in their respective areas. The region was grouped into two areas - Cuba, the Dominican Republic and Puerto Rico were grouped as Area I, while the rest of the Caribbean were designated as Area II. Correspondents were appointed for both areas.

Two years later, in 1959, the Caribbean Christian Education Curriculum Conference was held in Jamaica, and out of this meeting was formed the Caribbean Committee on Joint Christian Action (CCJCA). Its immediate objective was to create an indigenous curriculum for Sunday Schools in the Caribbean. The Board of CCJCA appointed Dr. David Mitchell, a Grenada-born Methodist minister with specialist training in Christian Education, to be its Executive Secretary and Editor. The training of Sunday School teachers and the production of appropriate Sunday School materials soon began on a co-operative basis, so that between 1964 and 1969 four of the six grades of the "Caribbean Christian Living Curriculum Series" had been published. David Mitchell himself writes - "For the first time in Caribbean history Churches were co-operating across the whole area and in their own respective countries". (6)

It is instructive to note that up to this point the Anglicans and the Roman Catholics were not participants in what was at the time the only Caribbean ecumenical body in existence. CCJCA however served as a catalyst for other fields of ecumenical endeavour. These included the establishment of a loosely structured Home and Family Life programme in 1964, the inauguration of the Caribbean Christian Communications Network (CCCN) in 1966, and the launching of the Youth Commission - The Caribbean Ecumenical Youth Action (CEYA) - in 1970. (7)

During the month of July 1967, Dr. James Hackshaw, who was then
Professor of Community Organization of the Columbia University
School of Social Work, visited the Caribbean at the request of the Committee on Middle America and the Caribbean of the Latin America
Department of Church World Service of the National Council of Churches
of the United States of America.(8) The purpose of his mission was to
undertake a brief survey of the Leeward and Windward Islands within the
following terms of reference -

> "1. To prepare an analysis of economic
>   development program opportunities
>   in the Islands in Consultation with
>   local church organizations.
> 2. To prepare recommendations on the
>   feasibility of Church World Service
>   cooperation in a specific develop-
>   ment program."(9)

Hackshaw visited Trinidad, Grenada, St. Lucia, St. Vincent and Antigua,
having cancelled a proposed trip to St. Kitts because of political difficulties
there at that time. His primary objective was to consult with a wide cross-
section of persons in these communities in order to determine "what might
be strategic points at which Church World Service could intervene to provide appropriate assistance if necessary and feasible".(10) Not only did
he speak with Church leaders (both clerical and lay), politicians, civil
servants and social workers, but he also held 'informal conversations'
with cane-cutters, dockworkers, shopkeepers, peddlers, teen-agers and
taxi-drivers.

Hackshaw came to the conclusion that the Leewards and Windwards were
actually "pockets of poverty" existing in a "relatively rich continent". He
stated -

> "The paradox of consistent economic growth
> in the USA and the widening gap of its
> continental neighbor, the Eastern Carib-
> bean, makes mandatory some responsibility
> to help toward the reduction of these in-
> equalities. In essence, poverty is
> sufficiently great to justify technical
> and material assistance on these grounds
> alone".(11)

He outlined the serious economic and social difficulties facing all the
Islands he had visited. He was particularly impressed by the expressed
willingness of the local Churches to work together on community development programmes - "the mechanisms exist for a vital planned joint
approach to church involvement in the problems of the social and economic
well-being of the Island residents".(12) He found that each Island government was willing to work with Church Councils on developmental program-

mes, and that what was essentially lacking was "the supply and utilization of the necessary planning and organizational skills that can combine the various resources in the Church and Voluntary sector into viable action programs for the entire region". (13) Hackshaw therefore emphasized the need for regional programming for the Eastern Caribbean instead of "Island-by-Island projects".

Together with this regional programming, Hackshaw suggested that one of the "outstanding West Indian Church ministers who had the organizational ability, the intimate knowledge of the Islands and their institutions, as well as the political sophistication necessary to initiate and sustain the momentum in the Church", (14) whom he had met, could be freed from pastoral responsibilities for at least three years to initiate the regional plan. Such a person would be charged with the following responsibilities:-

"a) Consulting with church councils on each Island to help strengthen their organization and program.

b) Arranging exchanges of opinion between each Island Council to eventually develop a regional approach on the part of Councils.

c) Developing liaison between the regional planning authority and Church Councils or Church projects.

d) Identifying components of the Island Five Year Plans that necessitate close work with Church bodies; e.g., community development, agricultural demonstration programs, public and denominational school planning.

e) Identifying and recruiting in co-operation with Church World Service Voluntary U.S. technical aid, personnel and equipment that could relate to regional approaches to farming and fisheries improvement programs.

f) Working closely with the departments and schools of the University of the West Indies to expand training programs in agronomy (Trinidad School of Tropical Agriculture), community development (School of Social Welfare, Jamaica), co-operatives, etc., at the Church parish level.

g) Serving as a focal point of contact between current voluntary assistance programs on the Islands and Church Councils". (15)

It is necessary for one to grasp the full import of Hackshaw's seven-point suggestion for the functions of the "planning technician" whom he recommended, since it constituted the earliest agenda of what was to become the Development Programme of the Caribbean Conference of Churches. It was significant that he recommended that a pastor, ordinarily trained in theological disciplines and very little else, should be the person to pioneer the work. It seemed to be crucial that such an innovative ministry in the Church would need an ordained Churchman to accord it some measure of authenticity or acceptance in the eyes of the Caribbean Church itself.

Hackshaw also specifically recommended that a "Data Bank" should be established in the region to provide useful information for Church Councils on the availability of technical aid resources and personnel outside the region, the requirements that were to be met, methods of application, and duration of aid. He felt that external aid programmes might also find such a data bank helpful for assessing their own priorities in the light of requests from the Islands.

Following the submission of the Hackshaw Report to Church World Service, CCJCA was requested by them to convene a special consultation to discuss its implications, and also the broader issue of the participation of the Churches in Caribbean development. A member of the Executive Committee of CCJCA, the Rev. Robert Cuthbert a Moravian minister organized the Consultation. Cuthbert was born in Jamaica, but had been recruited from New York for pastoral work in the Moravian Church in Trinidad. The Consultation was held in St. Vincent in November 1968. Representatives from Christian denominations in the Leeward and Windward Islands participated. The Consultation endorsed the recommendations of the Hackshaw Report, and called for the establishment of a regional co-ordinating agency under the aegis of the Churches. Thus it was that "Christian Action For Development in the Eastern Caribbean" (CADEC) (16) was proposed, and the process was immediately set in train to secure the services of the Rev. Robert Cuthbert as its Co-ordinator. (17) ·

After making a familiarization tour to St. Kitts, Nevis, Montserrat, Antigua and Barbados in March of 1969, Cuthbert was released from pastoral duties in the Moravian Church of the East West Indies Province in May of that year. He proceeded to the United States of America the following month for a three-month orientation course arranged by Church World Service. The nature of the orientation in North America seemed to indicate that the Co-ordinator was expected to familiarize himself with a number of funding bodies in the United States, as well as develop a certain type of developmental sensitivity by visits to co-operatives, community development projects, and other programmes related to agricultural development. Cuthbert himself claims that the orientation programme afforded him the opportunity to work closely with Professors at Columbia University in New York (where he had previously been a research student), and that this made it possible for him to become involved in "some of the projects of the current anti-poverty programme in the U.S.A". (18) He also claims that throughout his orientation programme he used every available opportunity to publicize the new ecumenical developments in the Eastern Caribbean. Cuthbert took up residence in Barbados in September 1969, and began the co-ordinating function of the newly-established CADEC with offices in his home.

Between 1969 and 1971 CADEC was engaged in supporting a number of small projects in the Eastern Caribbean, in arranging seminars and courses in Agriculture and Cooperatives, and in promoting the establishment of Councils of Churches on the Islands.

The demand for social and economic development at the end of the 1960's was certainly not a problem for the Eastern Caribbean alone. As soon as the Church had opened up new possibilities for its own engagement in this sphere of Caribbean activity a programme of much greater proportion had to emerge. It was in the year 1971 that this expansion of the programme took place, but not before certain key issues had been agreed on by churchmen in the region.

Three significant events preceded the historic Caribbean Ecumenical Consultation on Development in Trinidad of November 1971. First, the Ecumenical Steering Committee had been set up early in 1970 to work towards the establishment of a regional ecumenical structure. This followed closely on the appointment in 1969 of the Rev. David Chaplin, an Anglican and former Dean of Holy Trinity Cathedral, Trinidad, as the World Council of Churches Caribbean Secretary for Inter-Church relations. The Steering Committee comprised two representatives each of the Anglican, Methodist, Moravian, Presbyterian and Roman Catholic Churches. It was at this point that the Anglicans and Roman Catholics began to take a more formal and active part in ecumenical development in the Caribbean as a whole. The Committee met in Jamaica in October 1970 and consulted with a number of persons for five days. The report of that meeting clearly indicated that the modest structure of the newly-formed development agency (CADEC) would need to be expanded. It stated thus -

> "In organizing Christian action for
> development, which represents a com-
> paratively new field of ecumenical
> activity in the region, immediate
> collaboration among all Caribbean
> Churches is desirable and seems
> possible. Therefore efforts must
> be made to ensure full cooperation
> among the Churches of all language
> areas in the Caribbean in the planning
> for and participation in the proposed
> Consultation for Development and the
> commission which will carry out the
> decisions of the Consultation". (19)

The Steering Committee agreed on the first draft of a Constitution for a Caribbean Conference of Churches, and took a decision to convene the Inaugural Assembly of the Conference in the latter part of 1971.(20) It also called on CADEC to draw up proposals for a development programme in the English- and Dutch-speaking Caribbean, to "establish immediate liaison with the French- and Spanish-speaking areas", and to investigate the possibility of establishing "through local and external contributions ..... a development fund which could be used to stimulate local involvement in development".(21)

It was at that meeting that the Rev. Roy Neehall, a Trinidad-born Presbyterian minister, who was at the time the Associate Secretary of the Committee on Society, Development and Peace (SODEPAX), introduced the formal discussion on the proposed Consultation on Development. The proposed Consultation was to include all the major language areas in the Caribbean. In their deliberations on the proposed Consultation, the Committee members agreed that the field of development was the point where -

> "immediate contact might be established
> between all the language areas of the
> region and this could lead eventually to
> negotiation for a Conference of Churches
> which would do full justice to the name
> 'Caribbean'".(22)

They also felt that although the term 'development' had as yet defied all attempts at a proper definition, it still remained for them "the all-inclusive word which spells social justice, peace, and human dignity".(23)

The second event of significance was the Consultation an "The Role of Women in Caribbean Development" which was held in Jamaica in July 1971 as a preliminary meeting to the November Consultation on Development. The fact that the Churches in the Caribbean were beginning to pay particular attention to the role of women in the development of Caribbean society was significant for at least four reasons. First, the Churches were acknowleding the fact that Caribbean society was essentially matrifocal, and that the woman played a determinative role in the moulding of the character of Caribbean personhood. Secondly, women comprised the vast majority of the visible and active community called 'Church' in the region, and it was crucial that the discussion on the role of women in Caribbean development in general should precede the specific debate on the role of the Church in Caribbean development. Thirdly, Caribbean community life had not yet made adequate provision for women to lead more self-fulfilling lives - women were still over-domesticated and socially exploited. It was necessary for the Church to begin to identify more avenues for women to develop talents other than those which made them good wives and hardworking mothers. Finally, the Church needed to look at itself in order to discover the ways in which it had pursued the false myth of the inferiority of the woman. Its structures, policies, and organizations called for careful scrutiny if it were to promote social justice, human liberation and dignity among the majority of its own membership.

The July 1971 Consultation on the Role of Women therefore called for the establishment of a Caribbean Ecumenical Service for Women, with a staff of three co-ordinators strategically located throughout the region and charged with the responsibility of "injecting into existing women's organizations the perspectives developed at this Consultation with regard to the new Caribbean woman".(24) The co-ordinators were expected to travel extensively throughout the region promoting co-operative action among Church women in meeting their expressed needs; to provide suitable educational material for their use; to train Church women for community development; and stimulate awareness on the concerns of women by making available relevant resource material. (25) It is very instructive that in the case of the proposals for the establishment of the Women's Programme on a regional and ecumenical level, specific language about "women's liberation" was not used. The concerns of the Consultation were further discussed at the November 1971 Consultation of the Planning Committee of the Caribbean Conference of Churches (information), and the recommendations for the establishment of the Women's Programme were approved.

The third significant event was the Consultation on the Role of Tourism in Caribbean Development, which was held in Barbados in November 1971. By the turn of the decade of the 1970's Tourism had already made a conspicuous impact on the lives of Caribbean people in their own homes. It had become a far more attractive industry than agriculture, and its effects on the value systems of the host societies were not being carefully measured. Studies had already indicated that the Caribbean was losing far more than it gained from this glamorous industry, that there was a need for careful planning at the national level, and that more attention should be paid to the life-long needs of the local people than to the transient desires of the pleasure-seeking tourists. (26) One leading Caribbean Economist, William Demas, had described the Tourism issue in this way -

> "The dominance of tourism in small islands
> such as the West Indies also has certain
> undesirable social effects. Large tracts
> of land have been permanently alienated
> to foreigners. Some of the best beaches
> in some of the islands become exclusive
> preserves of foreign (and local) Whites.
> Consumption habits (food, drink and
> recreation) of tourists influence the as-
> pirations of the local population. Casinos,
> with their obvious dangers, may be intro-
> duced". (27)

Demas estimated that only between 20 % and 40 % of the gross earnings of Tourism remained within the Caribbean. (28)

The Consultation therefore looked at the effect which Tourism was having on Caribbean society as a whole. It examined the role which the Church in the Caribbean should play in promoting the highest values and dignity of the people of the region. It suggested ways in which Tourism might be better managed in order to serve a more useful role in the development of Caribbean society.(29) Two significant actions emerged out of the meeting, which was attended by over 40 representatives of Churches, Governments, Tourist Boards, and Universities. The first was a letter which was drafted by the Consultation and sent to the World Council of Churches for onward transmission to the Churches in metropolitan countries from which the tourists generally came. The letter asked the Churches to plead with their members as 'prospective tourists' to the Caribbean to visit the Caribbean as guests and to pay ample deference to the local mores and customs in the host communities.(30) One direct result of this letter was the formation of a concerned group in Ontario, Canada called "TWIN" (Tourism With Insight).

The second significant action was the proposal for the establishment of a Tourism Research Centre to study the effects of Tourism in the Caribbean, and to continue to suggest ways of protecting the higher interests of the host community while promoting the harmonious interaction of tourists with locals. The process was speedily set in train for the establishment of such a centre, and the result has been the emergence of a viable research unit located in Barbados - first known as the Caribbean Tourism Research Centre (CTRC) (31) The CCC has joined with Caribbean Governments and other Tourism-related bodies in sponsoring the operations of the CTRC. Yet the impact of Tourism on the values of the society continues to be of considerable concern to the CCC.

The Caribbean Ecumenical Consultation for Development began in Trinidad on November 15, 1971 and lasted for six days. It was sponsored by the Steering Committee of the Caribbean Churches, the Christian Council of Trinidad and Tobago, SODEPAX, and the Pontifical Commission on Justice and Peace. There were approximately 260 participants from 16 Caribbean territories, and from a number of metropolitan countries as well. They represented 25 religious traditions, and also some Caribbean organizations committed to social change in the region. The objectives of the Consultation were stated as follows -

"1. To witness to the will and the determination of the churches to carry their share of the responsibility for participating in the process of human fulfilment, and social and economic development.

2. To study under the direction of experts in various fields (theology, sociology, anthropology, economics and politics) the problems and possibilities of development of our Caribbean people.

3. To define ways of expressing Caribbean participation in and commitment to the development of the Caribbean in terms of human freedom and justice.

4. To plan strategies of ecumenical action for these ends in co-operation with national programmes, international agencies and institutions". (32)

The Trinidad press hailed the Consultation as being an event of great importance. The Editor of the Trinidad Guardian wrote -

"The Caribbean Ecumenical Consultation
for Development is perhaps the most important conference ever to take place
in the West Indies.
It is important not because of its
ecumenical significance ......
but because of the total involvement
of the Church in the people of the area -
to help them to be educated for their own
self-development.
What comes out of the Consultation will
most likely alter the role of the
Church in the Caribbean for the next
decade or two". (33)

The resolutions and recommendations which were adopted by the Consultation may well be summarized in five principal points -

a) The Caribbean should develop its own appropriate life-style.
b) Caribbean people should participate fully in their own affairs.
c) Development in the Caribbean requires radical structural change.
d) The Churches must be totally engaged in Caribbean development.
e) Every effort must be made to work for Caribbean unity.

These points require some elaboration and discussion.

a) In calling for a more appropriate and relevant style of life in the Caribbean, the Consultation urged that the social goals and structures should be suited to the needs and capacity of its own people and land. Such a renewal required that the imported values should be diminished, since they currently determined the direction of development in the region. There was a call for the local ownership of land and other resources, and for a decrease in the dependence on foreign aid and personnel. The participants declared -

"We feel that the Church should seek
to create a new image which is Caribbean, and
be more closely related than formerly to
the aims and objectives of the Caribbean

insofar as these serve to promote the
work of Christ". (34)

b) The Consultation called for the maximum participation of the people
in the making of decisions which affected their lives. Such participation
was not only to be at the political level, but also at the cultural and
economic levels as well. Thus there was a need for programmes of
awareness-building "conscientization"; more adult education and literacy
programmes; closer collaboration with, and understanding of, the Black
Power movement and other radical movements; and greater participation
of women in the affairs of Church and society. It called on the Churches
to provide guidelines for "education in social justice of persons especially in the context of the present and future social situation in the Caribbean". (35)

c) There was need for fundamental changes in the existing patterns of
Caribbean development, the Consultation felt, with the emphasis being
placed on personal and humanizing values rather than on economic growth.
The current pattern of economic development increased the disparities
of wealth in the region and also the misuse of resources. The call was
therefore for an end to the plantation system in the Caribbean, and for
the promotion of co-operatives of workers and peasants; for the development of technological models in agriculture and small industry suitable
for the capacity of the people; the subjection of Tourism to criteria suitable for local cultural, social and spiritual development. It is interesting to note that the Consultation rejected the notion that there was in
the Caribbean a "simple dialectic of conflict between the capitalist class
and the proletariat class", and it called on trades unions, "largely in-
fluenced by practices in the North Atlantic areas" to avoid the development of an elite worker class in the Caribbean. (36)

d) The Consultation felt that the role of the Churches in Caribbean development should be unmistakable and total. The Churches were being called
upon to identify themselves with the poor and dispossessed in the region,
and to take up their struggle for economic and social justice. "The participation in human development was seen not as an added responsibility
of the Churches, but as an inseparable part of the Churches very life". (37)
Thus the Churches were expected to reduce ostentation in all its forms;
to make more of their land and buildings available for use by the poor
people; to disengage themselves from the promotion of an elitist and ex-
clusivist type of formal education through schools; to assist in the
teaching of agricultural, technical and craft skills; and to encourage
their Governments to reassess and redeploy their human and material
resources for the better development of the rural areas. The Consultation recommended that the CCC should appoint an agricultural economist
as a matter of priority "in the interest of rural and agricultural development throughout the region". (38)

e) There was a strong call for deeper and more effective Caribbean unity
that would nurture a spirit of co-operation rather than competition, and

that the human and material resources could be used for the benefit of the entire region. The Consultation called on Caribbean Governments to end speedily their isolation of Cuba, and deplored the fact that the Cuban delegation -

> "had to suffer the inconvenience of
> going all the way to Madrid in Europe
> in order to get to a sister Caribbean
> country separated from it by a few
> hundred miles". (39)

The Consultation also called on Churches to increase their links with the Church in Cuba.

The role of the communications media as an effective instrument for development was constantly emphasized throughout the Consultation, and the "hard-sell" advertising and "brainwashing" techniques of the foreign-owned media in the region was deplored. It therefore called on the Churches to -

> "seek to represent a voice of the public
> concerning national programming and
> advertising policies, which criticisms
> ought to be based on positive cultural
> and moral values" (40)

The Churches were challenged to make better use of the existing communication media; to plan programmes of cultural value to the region; to promote the training of local communicators; and to express their concern for, and to try to prevent, "the erosion of the freedom of the press and of free expression" which was said to be taking place in the region. (41)

Immediately following the Development Consultation at Chaguaramas in Trinidad, there was a second Consultation in Port-of-Spain. This Consultation was held from November 22 to 24, 1971 and was attended by the members of the Steering Committee of the Caribbean Conference of Churches (in formation) and 71 other persons (mostly representatives of Churches) who had just attended the Consultation on Development. The projected plans for holding the Inaugural Assembly of the Caribbean Conference of Churches in September or October of 1971 had not materialized. (42) The WCC Secretary for Inter-Church relations had already announced his intention to return to his home in Britain. (43) The final preparatory stages for establishing a strong and viable regional Conference of Churches appeared at that time to be losing momentum. It therefore fell to the lot of the two-year old CADEC to assume a wider range of ecumenical responsibilities far in excess of its original mandate. The Port-of-Spain Consultation therefore identified new areas of responsibility for the Development Agency, and also stipulated a much wider mandate for ecumenical action.

The report of the Consultation indicates that the participants were keenly aware of the historical significance of the just concluded Consultation on

Development. The report notes that participants had agreed that -

> "the Consultation for Development had
> brought the CCC out of the realm of
> theory and idealism and face to face
> with the practical application of the
> resolutions coming from that Consulta-
> tion. The necessity of a regional
> Conference of Churches was made clear,
> in order that the Churches, through
> ecumenical regional co-operation,
> might be able to play a significant role
> in the development of the region". (44)

In its "Message to the Churches" the Consultation claimed that the Development Consultation had provided a clear and challenging message for the
Churches and that the Church had "come alive to its responsibilities and
has been given direction for the step forward". (45) It therefore called
on the Churches to set about implementing the resolutions of the Consultation by joining in the proposed Caribbean Conference of Churches (which
it hoped would be inaugurated in 1973), and by providing support of manpower and money.

The Consultation endorsed the four basic goals which CADEC had set itself over the past two years. These were -

> a) the promotion of a spirit of self-dependence
>   by enlarging the people's capacity to generate
>   and sustain indigenous development efforts;
>
> b) providing catalysts for development efforts in
>   the region;
>
> c) making contributions to the material growth of
>   the poorer people in the society;
>
> d) the promotion of wider participation of the
>   people in the social process and greater re-
>   conciliation among estranged groups in the
>   society. (46)

To these were added four other principles of action which the Consultation
suggested would be indispensable if the Churches in the region were to
accomplish a programme of implementing the resolutions of Chaguaramas.
The principles were fundamental guidelines designed to assist CADEC in
its expanded role as the Development Agency of the Churches in the
English- and Dutch-speaking Caribbean. It is necessary to quote them
in full -

> "(a) the Churches to be exercised continually
>   in the forging of a basic concept of
>   development for the Caribbean,

(b) a commitment on the part of the Churches
to this concept and its follow-up in
terms of personnel and funds,

(c) an immediate project to raise funds
within the Caribbean for the support of
the total programme, and

(d) a set of criteria by which international
agencies can contribute to, and participate in, Church-initiated development
projects in the Caribbean, and contribute
also towards the development fund". (47)

The foregoing quotation requires some comment. First, it should be noted that the Churches were being called upon to determine what "development" should mean in the Caribbean - a call for an appropriate definition. This was to mark a radical break with tradition in the Caribbean where the Churches generally accepted and responded to definitions from abroad. That the Churches should be called on to define their own terms of action was indeed a signal that a major aspect of their dependence was likely to be interrupted. Secondly, the new development programmes were to be funded initially by the Churches themselves, and to be supported by the secondment (at least) of some of their personnel. This meant that institutions whose very survival had historically depended on the supply of men and money from abroad were now being expected to make a specific contribution to Caribbean development by sharing their scarce yet valuable resources. Thirdly, the Consultation insisted that the as-sistance from abroad should respond to the rules of taking determined in the Caribbean itself rather than the rules of giving which were generally applied by the donor agencies in metropolitan countries. This very innovative and radical departure from current patterns of develop-ment assistance was to serve the Caribbean Conference of Churches in good stead over the next six years, and it ushered in a new era of re-lationships between those who had to give and those who had to receive. (48)

The Consultation gave full endorsement to CADEC as the agency authorized to work on behalf of the Churches in implementing the objectives and prin-ciples outlined above, and changed the meaning of "CADEC" to "Christian Action of Development in the Caribbean". The word "Eastern" was there-fore dropped from the original title. CADEC was mandated to work close-ly with the Women's, Communications and Education programmes of the CCC (as it was already being called), to work with a specially-appointed Advisory Board, and to establish not only a central Development Fund but also a Caribbean Community Appeal. (49)

When the Inaugural Assembly of the Caribbean Conference of Churches met in Kingston, Jamaica, in November 1973, it gave final and formal approval to the resolutions of Chaguaramas, and called on the CCC, through its Development Agency (CADEC) to implement these resolutions

as a matter of priority. (50) No further endorsement could be expected,
since the Conference was now a legally constituted body, representing
sixteen member Churches throughout the English-, French-, Spanish-
and Dutch-speaking Caribbean, and since five of the six CADEC Offices
to be located throughout the region had already been established by this
time. (51)

With the basic infrastructure firmly established, it was possible for
CADEC to attempt to interpret to the Caribbean what the Churches had
said at Chaguaramas. Not only from the point of view of the history of
the Church in the Caribbean, but also from that of the historical development of the Caribbean itself, November 1971 marked a very important
turning-point. The largest and most influential network of non-Govern-
mental organizations in the Caribbean - the Churches - decided to come
together on a common agenda, and to work more effectively and systematically for liberation and social change in the region. They placed the highest value on the need for a radical break with the historical patterns of
the Caribbean, and decided to engage more seriously in the struggle for
human liberation, social justice, and greater self-reliance. They acknowledged all this to be an essential part of their mission, and therefore essentially adopted a programme of ecumenism that was to be
liberation-oriented. This focus of liberation was to be central to the
Development Programme of the CCC. It is therefore, with an overall
description of the Development Programme of the CCC between 1971
(the Chaguaramas Consultation) and 1977 (the Second Assembly of the
CCC) that the rest of this chapter will be mainly concerned.

CADEC 1971-1977

The Constitution of the Caribbean Conference of Churches provides for
the functioning of two Commissions - one on Renewal and the other on
Development. The Renewal Commission functions through its Programme
Agency called ARC (Action for the Renewal of the Church). ARC is responsible for eleven programmes of the CCC, (52) some of which have
a very clear developmental component. For example, the programmes
relating to Women, Youth, Caribbean Identity, and Home and Family
Life Education are directly related to the principal aims and objectives
of the Development Programme of the CCC as they were defined in
November 1971. Indeed, the programme priorities outlined in these
areas reflect quite accurately the basic objectives and goals of CADEC
itself. (53) The distribution of such programmes under the Renewal
Agency therefore can only be explained in terms of the need to provide
adequate supervision and co-ordination for the twenty-one programmes
of the CCC. (54) The General Secretary in his report to the Second General
Assembly in Guyana, in November 1977, explained that "development and
renewal are projected as two sides of the same coin and as having an
inter-relationship within the framework of the mission of the Church". (55)
He commended the Directors of ARC and CADEC for the "conceptual
integration" that had been achieved within the CCC.

The more immediate concern of this Study, however, is with the programmes which are co-ordinated under the Development Commission through its Programme Agency, CADEC. These can be broadly listed as follows - Project Development, Education for Development, Communications, Caribbean Community Appeal, DERAW (Disaster, Emergency Relief and Welfare).

Project Development

One of the main goals which had been set for CADEC was the provision of material assistance to the poorer people of the Caribbean in projects which would stimulate self-reliance and also improve their economic well-being. The Chaguaramas Consultation had issued a clear call for the Churches to identify and make available more resources for the self-development of Caribbean people. (56) It had also called for the establishment of a Development Fund through which groups of persons could be assisted. While a few small projects were supported in 1972, the main work of project support assumed systematic and major proportions after the Fund was eventually established in March 1973. The majority of its resources had to be requested from outside the region, mainly from donor agencies in Europe and North America. (57) The Fund was stated to be a major financial resource for the work of the CCC, and "a tool in a wider programme of education for development", which "seeks to uncover Caribbean man's opportunity and potential for his complete liberation". (58) The Development Fund is administered by a special committee and served by a group of technical staff.

Specific criteria were laid down for the guidance of the Fund in its response to requests for support from persons throughout the region. These included

(i)   a determination for greater social and economic justice;
(ii)   the promotion of community co-operative action;
(iii) the use of local resources;
(iv)   a wide participation of project-carriers in the leadership and decision-making;
(v)   the increase of productivity and the reduction of unemployment;
(vi)   the increase of awareness-building and the participation of the local Churches.

These criteria guided the administrators of the Fund as they supported nearly 250 projects with financial, technical and material assistance. The official reports indicate that up to the end of 1977 some BDS$ 3,897,268 had been made available to these projects. (59)

The major sector of support has been provided for agricultural and agro-related projects and fisheries, while other categories of projects have been listed as small industry, cultural, crafts, educational and vocational training. Support has been provided both in the form of loans and grants, and loans have either been at very low interest rates (e.g. 1 % - 5 %) with generous conditions of repayment, or without interest at all.

In 1975 the Fund instituted a policy of limited decentralization in which local committees were established in territories throughout the region to take decisions on projects not exceeding a limited sum of money.(60) This pattern of decentralization, although not diminishing the power of control by the Central Committee of the Fund, enabled the representatives of Churches at the local and national levels to share in the work of responding to developmental needs as expressed by the people themselves in their respective territories.

The range of projects varied quite considerably. The following table attempts to put together a sample of project descriptions in summary form, in order to illustrate the range of CADEC-supported projects.(61)

No.	COUNTRY	SPONSOR	PURPOSE	AMOUNT
				BDS $
1.	Antigua	Rev.S. Eardley	To provide a Revolving Loan Fund for Fishermen	2,200
2.	Barbados	Mr. James Husbands	To manufacture solar water heaters	20,000
3.	Belize	Rev. Martin Avila	Establishing a Co-op among peasant Bee-keepers	17,050
4.	Dominica	Rev. P. Wyatt	To provide assistance to small home-owners in a Revolving Self-Help Project	4,000
5.	Grenada	Grenada Inter-Church Council	For assistance to youth agricultural projects	14,000
6.	Haiti	Methodist Church	For the control of rats in Petit Gouave	10,000

No.	COUNTRY	SPONSOR	PURPOSE	AMOUNT
				BDS $
7.	Jamaica	Rev. A. Smith	To train and employ young school drops-outs	24,960
8.	Trinidad	Mr. F. Gajar	Promotion of Steelband Music through production of LP Record	12,500
9.	St. Kitts	Mr. E. Morton	To support training Course in Leathercraft and Tanning	8,700
10.	Regional	CADEC	To discover attitudes of people to working in Agriculture in Leeward Islands	2,050

One of the largest amounts disbursed over the period was provided for a Workers' Co-operative at Dangriga in Belize.(62) The report on that project suggested that the area represented "much of the history of exploitation, oppression and colonialism to which the region had been subjected".(63) The area had a population of 9000, 2000 of whom were directly employed in the citrus industry which was owned and controlled by foreign corporations. After a series of industrial disputes the industry was abandoned and the workers were left destitute. "The already poor conditions were aggravated, with malnutrition and starvation becoming the order of the day".(64) A major grant from CADEC enabled the workers to join co-operatively in farming, fishing and carpentry, and to engage in a programme of education. A recent assessment of the Dangriga project stated -

> "its success or failure should not be
> measured only or solely in terms of economic
> returns or viability, important as these
> are, but by the impact and effect of the
> project on the community, and its poten-
> tial for developing change, not only material-
> ly, but also attitudinally".(65)

Not only has CADEC been engaged in responding to requests for project support from the people in the Caribbean, but it has also provided liaison services for several groups and Churches in channelling financial support from agencies outside of the region. The Project Development Programme has also prepared project proposals on behalf of local groups for submission to agencies abroad. (66) In these cases, however, CADEC has attempted to apply the criteria of the Development Fund to such proposals and to endorse them as if they were suitable for support from its own limited resources.

In a few instances, CADEC has taken the initiative in developing projects and programmes throughout the region. These have tended to relate directly to the specific mandate of Chaguaramas with respect to the re-deployment of Church lands for the use of the poorer people of the region. In this regard, the "Land And Food For People Programme" was launched in Jamaica in 1974, in which Churches were encouraged to bring their unused arable land under cultivation, under the supervision of a CADEC-appointed Agronomist. (67) This programme was extended to the Eastern Caribbean in 1976 with the appointment of a second Agricultural expert. (68) The Anglican Church in St. Vincent turned over 20 acres of land for the development of a self-help housing scheme at Barroualie. CADEC has been mainly responsible for the implementation of this project. (69)

The work of CADEC in the field of project development, therefore, was quite extensive during the period under review. The ecumenical basis of its operation gave it a flexibility to respond to requests from groups of persons who were either connected with the Churches, or else had no connections at all. The reports of the work of CADEC in this field indicate that it has been implementing the mandate of Chaguaramas by means of a wide range of project activity, and that it has attempted to initiate a new concept of mission in the Caribbean through an active and concrete engagement with the people's expressed determination to liberation and self-development. Together with this concrete action was coupled the programmatic attempt to reflect on what Development in the Caribbean should entail. This complementary objective has been pursued by CADEC through its Education for Development Programme.

Education for Development

The Chaguaramas Consultation had outlined what it called the "Aims of Caribbean Education". (70) The fourteen aims included a variety of aspects of the process of "Conscientization" which had by this time (1971) become very familiar in the Caribbean after the work of its chief protagonist Paulo Freire of Brazil. (71) One of the leading speakers at the Consultation, Bishop Roque Adames of the Dominican Republic, had delivered an address on this subject. In general, therefore, the Consultation suggested that the process of education in the Caribbean, if it were to liberate the people rather than to domesticate them any further, should "enable people to be critical, to choose, to be articulate, to take part in decision-making". (72) People, it said, should be enabled to develop a capacity to communicate with their fellows, to co-operate with them,

to be creative and responsible subjects rather than passive objects.
They should also be motivated to -

> "Develop a restlessness of spirit that
> is not satisfied with mediocrity, that
> accepts change, lives with it and seeks
> continuously for excellence". (73)

The Education for Development programme of CADEC was therefore
based on these objectives and was said to be aimed at "the transformation
of society" including a change of "systems irrelevant today and changes
of roles played previously by the expatriates and power structures overseas". (74)

The development debate was carried forward in 1972 and 1973 by specially appointed teams of resource persons, some of whom were full-time
members of the CCC staff. (75) Their main task was to interpret through
seminars, conferences and meetings the principal concerns expressed
at the Chaguaramas Consultation and to motivate Churches and Church
groups to change their styles and priorities in accordance with the new
directions being suggested. One resource person was Mr. Owen Baptiste,
the Editor of the new CCC newspaper, Caribbean CONTACT, the
principal organ of the CCC strategy of Education for Development, and
which had been published for the first time at the close of the Chaguaramas
Consultation. Special attention will be paid to Caribbean CONTACT
later in this chapter. (76)

CADEC secured funding for scholarship assistance to Caribbean persons
who wished to be trained in such fields as Social Work, Community Development, Industrial Relations, Agriculture, Crafts, Nursing and Health Education, as well as Applied Theology. During the period 1972 to 1977 over
120 scholarships and bursaries have been awarded by the CADEC Scholarship Committee, and in the majority of cases the training facilities available within the Caribbean have been utilized. (77)

One of the techniques which CADEC employed in 1973 to draw the attention
of the wider Caribbean to some issues, which it considered were seriously
affecting the pattern of development in the region, was the convening of a
number of major Consultations. Four such Consultations were held in
1973, two of which were preceded by technical surveys to provide up-to-
date material for the respective participants to consider. (78) In April
1973 a Consultation on the "Patterns of Urbanization in the Caribbean"
was convened in Guyana. The role of the Church in two of the poorest
territories of the region was also the subject of attention during that
year - and Consultations on "The Church and Development" in Haiti, in
July, and on "The Church in a New St. Vincent" in St. Vincent in September dealt with these issues. The immediate result in both cases was the
establishment of an ecumenical development body in each territory to
carry out the resolutions of their respective meetings, and also to pioneer
the work of the Churches' participation in national development on an

ecumenical basis. This made it easier for CADEC to relate to a central co-ordinated unit in these countries on which the concerns of its participating Churches were represented.

The fourth Consultation was held in Antigua in September of 1973, and dealt with the most pressing problem in the economic development of the Caribbean - Unemployment. The Unemployment Consultation looked at the main constraints affecting the possibilities for self-employment in the region, and drew up a five-point strategy which it suggested that CADEC might consider implementing in its programmes. Such a strategy pointed to the need for a concerted assault on the economic structures in the region, and indicated modest ways in which CADEC could motivate particularly the unemployed youth in the Caribbean. (79) The subsequent programmes of the CADEC Development Fund and of the Youth Department of the CCC both identified this as an area of high priority. For example, a recent CEYA Report indicated that the Programme had been attempting "to bear witness to christian justice in the Community" by tackling the unemployment problem in the Caribbean (where "over 50 % of the unemployed in the region fall between the ages of 15 - 19; 80 % of that number are unskilled") (80) in three major ways. These were through Seminars on Unemployment; a regional survey on Unemployment covering 18 territories; and a multiplicity of projects for self-employment. The Report outlined that the projects were not only to "ease the burden of unemployment", but also to train young people in co-operative practices, to stimulate greater self-reliance among the young, and to generate more income. (81) Many of these projects are already under way in Grenada, St. Kitts, Antigua, Jamaica and Belize.

From 1974 onwards the trend moved away from the major regional (and more formal) Consultations to smaller and more informal Workshops, Seminars and meetings. This strategy enabled the CADEC staff, (and the resource persons whose expertise and interests have been the mainstay of the Education for Development programme) to implement their work at a level much closer to the on-going Church programmes. Not only have member Churches of the CCC made provision in their Synod agendas for development issues to be debated, but in a number of cases the staff of the CCC have been specially invited to initiate the dialogue on the new developmental challenges which the Churches in the region have set themselves.

Two other aspects of the Education for Development Programme require brief mention. First, there was the attempt on the part of the CCC to carry forward the implementation of the Chaguaramas resolution which called for an end to the isolation of Cuba. The Caribbean Governments of Trinidad and Tobago, Guyana, Barbados and Jamaica had all established diplomatic relations with Cuba in 1972, less than a year after the Chaguaramas Consultation. Although the causal relationship between Chaguaramas and the action of the Governments might be difficult to establish, the prophetic voice of the Church in the Caribbean was unmistakable on this issue. It was therefore left to the Churches to play their own part in increasing links with the Cuban Church.

The General Secretary of the CCC had paid an official visit to Cuba in November 1974. He reported that he had recognized in Cuba many signs of "deep commitment to Jesus Christ and of equally deep commitment to the process of revolutionary change as an act of obedience to the will of Christ". (82) Two delegations of churchpersons - one each from Jamaica and Guyana - visited Cuba in 1976 to see at first hand what it meant for the Christian Church to witness and work in a society which had in fact been transformed along Socialist lines. It is interesting to point out that both Jamaica and Guyana have in recent years been led by Governments which espouse a Socialist model of national re-construction.

The CCC went even further in 1976 and appointed a Cuban Baptist minister, the Rev. Uxmal Livio Diaz, ordinarily resident in Cuba, as a special Consultant in its Education for Development Programme in the Spanish-speaking Caribbean. In 1977, Diaz became responsible for the publication of a special bi-monthly CCC newsletter in Spanish thus expanding the contact between the CCC and the Churches of the Spanish-speaking Caribbean and Latin America. (83) During the Second Assembly in November 1977, two Cuban Churches, two Churches in the Dominican Republic, and one in Puerto Rico were admitted into membership of the CCC. (84)

The second aspect relates to the efforts of CADEC in its attempt to implement the Chaguaramas resolutions, which called for the maximum utilization of all the resources in the Caribbean in the development process. It was mentioned earlier that the Development Fund had adopted as one of its criteria the principle that the projects it supported should be based on local resources, local cultural patterns, and local life styles as far as possible. (85) In addition to its programme of project support CADEC initiated in 1976 a programme in Appropriate Technology in an attempt to make available to groups of workers in the region, techniques and ideas, research findings and expertise suitable for the exploitation of local resources particularly in the areas of Agriculture, Housing and Energy. In July 1976 CADEC sponsored an Appropriate Technology Workshop in Barbados, which was attended by 34 persons from the Caribbean and an expert from the Intermediate Technology Development Group (ITDG) in London. Some representatives of regional Governments and the Caribbean Development Bank were also present. Among other recommendations, the Workshop called for an integrated approach in the Caribbean to the tasks of providing more local employment, of using local materials and of promoting the greater consumption of local products. (85) It called for the establishment of a regional resource centre thr(86)h which information on appropriate technology could become readily available. It also stated that Caribbean people needed "to be encouraged to think more appropriately". (87) CADEC therefore proceeded to expand its Documentation Service in Barbados to include a wide range of material deemed to be useful in this connection.

CADEC's programme of Education for Development has therefore been an attempt to implement the broad mandate given at Chaguaramas in 1971. The results of such a programme, geared as it is to attitudinal change and social transformation, are perhaps among the most difficult to measure. Perhaps one useful way of assessing it is to identify how far it has managed to maintain a pattern of consistency, and the extent to which it has helped to shape the content of the other programmes for which CADEC has direct responsibility. These other programmes include Communications, the Caribbean Community Appeal and the Disaster Emergency Relief and Welfare (DERAW).

Communications

Reference has already been made to the concerns expressed at the Chaguaramas Consultation about the role of the communications media in process of development, and to the part which the media was expected to play in emphasizing values consistent with Caribbean culture and human dignity. (88) The Consultation had also endorsed the work of the Communications Programme of the CCJCA as the nucleus of that which was required to carry out its mandate. The CCCN (Caribbean Christian Communications Network) was expected to provide information about the CCC, to undertake training programmes for local communicators, and to liaise with other groups engaged in communications in the region.

During the period under review, the Communications Programme, which had its name changed to CADEC Communications Network (CCN) in 1974, attempted to implement its work in several ways. These included an innovative course in Communications called "Communicarib" at the Anglican Theological College in the region, Codrington College, in Barbados. There were four such courses between 1973 and 1977. Students in training for the ministry and workers in the media had the opportunity of sharing in joint reflection on, and training in the use of, the media as an important tool in the development process.(89) CCN has also been engaged in the training of clergy and church-workers in the use of the media, in many Caribbean territories. It has produced many taped programmes for use on radio and television throughout the region, and these programmes have reflected the concerns of the Caribbean Conference of Churches on a wide range of issues. Its most recent and regular service has been RADIO CONTACT, a half-hour radio magazine programme, broadcast on most stations throughout the English- and Dutch-speaking Caribbean.(90)

In 1974 the CCC established under CADEC its own publishing unit called CEDAR (Christian Engagement in Development and Renewal) Press. Its mandate was to produce the CCC materials and those of the member Churches, together with other materials promoting a greater awareness

57

of regionalism and integration in the Caribbean. It was also to produce materials "which develop the potential of Caribbean artists, writers and poets especially of the grass-roots, in reaching the Caribbean people". (91) The Report on its activities to date suggests that it has achieved limited success because of serious financial and administrative contraints. Nevertheless, the CCC and some of its member Churches have availed themselves of its services, and a number of books relating to the issues of development and renewal in the Caribbean have been published.(92) Two factors appear to militate against the survival of CEDAR Press as a viable economic unit. The first relates to the fact that the CCC has experienced considerable difficulty in locating new sources of funds to keep it going. Secondly, the Caribbean public has not yet developed reading habits substantial enough to support a market of specialized material. This means that such material has to be produced in very limited quantities, and at costs too high to make their price attractive enough for the ordinary reader. At the close of 1977, therefore, the future of CEDAR Press appeared to be facing grave uncertainty.

Within the cluster of Communications programmes, CADEC in 1974 also established CADEC Audio-Visual Services (CAVIS). This was centred in Guyana and placed under the leadership of a Guyana-born Methodist minister, the Rev. Edwin Vandeyar, who had received specialist training in Audio-visuals in the United States of America and Britain. The CAVIS programme was generally engaged over the period in training a number of Church-related and other persons in a variety of audio-visual techniques, including the effective use of the cartoon. The construction of a centre on lands belonging to the Methodist Church in Georgetown, Guyana, in 1977 enabled CAVIS to commence on a systematic scale the production of cassettes, slide sets, study-kits, posters, charts, flip-charts, flannelgraphs and photographs as aids to the overall work of the CCC in its programmes of education for development and renewal. These services were made available to the entire Caribbean, but in Guyana itself CAVIS acquired a mobile audio-visual unit for promoting the educational work of the CCC in the rural areas of the country.

The programme of the CCC which has without doubt had the highest visibility, the widest appeal, and the most significant impact on the Caribbean, however, has been Caribbean CONTACT, the regional newspaper. It was designed to be a principal instrument of communication to transmit ideas and contributions which could help to "reshape the Caribbean into a single nation for the development of the masses who share a common history of deprivation". (93) It was to stimulate dialogue in the Caribbean on development issues, promote regional unity, sensitize Caribbean people on new perspectives in development, and serve as a medium of information about, and for, the CCC and its member Churches.

The newspaper started out as being a free give-away, but went on sale from February 1975. Its content has always been a source of heated con-

troversy and strong debate. This is illustrated by the following
quotations -

> "My main criticism is that the issues I
> have read and circulated were too political
> and economic in content to have any real
> appeal to the man or woman in the new
> .... Let us have more theological
> content". (94)

> "Whereas the CCC is especially committed
> to the defence of the oppressed and the
> underprivileged in our region; and where-
> as this commitment together with the practi-
> cal means for carrying it out need to be
> communicated as widely as possible through-
> out the region; be it resolved that top
> priority be given to the continuing pub-
> lication of CARIBBEAN CONTACT and that the
> paper express the public voice of the
> Church in a forthright and fearless manner
> and be it further resolved that the mem-
> ber Churches of the CCC tangibly support
> CONTACT by paying for the copies issued
> them in the future". (95)

The former quotation represents the typical reaction of some Churchpersons to the style and content of the newspaper. The latter is the text
of the resolution on the newspaper which was passed by the Inaugural
Assembly of the CCC. The newspaper has concentrated on the following
areas - culture, theological concerns, politics, communications, ecumenical affairs, development issues, economic issues and Latin America-
Caribbean issues. It has taken a very strong line on a number of political
issues in the Caribbean, for example the question of political oppression
in Grenada in 1974. (96) Some Governments in the Caribbean have reacted
sharply against its contents, as in the case of French St. Martin where
in January 1976 the Prefect accused the Methodist minister, the Rev.
John Gumbs, of "political interference in France's affairs by distributing
to Church members copies of Caribbean Contact" and also for preaching
what was deemed to be a 'political sermon'. (97) In response to such
attitudes to the newspaper the General Secretary of the CCC once asked -

> "If our programmes reflect an interest
> in persons, their total life, on earth, as
> in heaven, their hopes, fears and problems,
> their social, economic and political life,
> then are we not following in the footsteps
> of the master? Our interests are the
> interests of Jesus' ministry, set within

the context of today's realities in the
region to which we belong". (98)

At the close of our review period, the newspaper was still the only
regional newspaper in the Caribbean, and was increasing its sales
particularly in territories of which it has been most critical - notably
Guyana and Grenada. The most recent report on the paper indicated
that it had a minimum readership of approximately 150, 000, with a
monthly print-run of 52, 000 copies. (99) Steps have recently been taken
to deal with the problems of distribution and advertising which the
paper has experienced over the first four years of its existence. The
newspaper continues to be a very important instrument for regional
communication and integration in the Caribbean.

Caribbean Community Appeal

The Port-of-Spain Consultation in 1971, which followed that of Chaguaramas, had suggested that if the Churches were to implement the resolutions
of the Development Consultation they would need to raise funds immediately within the Caribbean for the support of such a programme. (100) The
Consultation therefore proposed that a Caribbean Community Appeal
should be launched, and that a full-time director should be appointed. (101)
An Anglican clergyman, Barbados-born the Rev. Andrew Hatch, was
appointed the Director of the Appeal in April 1972.

Over the past five years, the Appeal has developed into a public relations
programme for the CCC, in which the Churches have been kept informed,
by a number of devices, of what the CCC has been doing. The use of a
monthly newsletter Christian Action, and the promotion of an
annual fund-raising Campaign in each Caribbean territory during "Christian Action Week" have been the main mechanisms. Although the actual
financial returns have been relatively modest, (102) in terms of what is
possible through the Churches in the region, the Caribbean Community
Appeal has been a very useful programme for three reasons.

First, the fact that 75 % of what is raised annually is required to remain
in each respective territory, for the support of local development and
renewal work, suggests that the Churches have a type of thermometer
with which to measure the extent to which they have been able to com-
mend the development and renewal programmes to their people. Secondly, the programme provides a very useful link between the regional
ecumenical movement and the local congregations, since there is a
wealth of information which is shared during the promotion of the
Appeal, and opportunities for stimulating a better understanding of
CCC programmes and activities are afforded. Thirdly, it provides a
common agenda for the local councils of Churches, since the Appeal is
generally promoted on an ecumenical basis. The usefulness of such a
common agenda can hardly be overstated, since one of the major difficulties experienced in the growth of the ecumenical movement has been

60

relative inactivity of the national councils of Churches. It might also be stated that the Appeal signifies an effective method of assessing the true nature of the involvement of the member Churches in the total working of the CCC.

Deraw

In November 1975 CADEC launched a new programme to deal with disasters, emergencies and welfare situations. This was in consequence of a number of situations in which CADEC had been called upon to provide assistance in disaster situations such as earthquakes and hurricanes. Indeed, the earthquake which shook the Island of Antigua on October 8, 1974 had left a vast amount of damage officially estimated to have been in the vicinity of US $ 50,000,000. The first major efforts at rehabilitation after the disaster were started by CADEC on the Island, with emergency supplies being flown in from the United States of America, and teams of builders being recruited to repair or rebuild houses for distressed families. Twenty-two houses were repaired and 14 new houses were built. The report of the Rehabilitation Programme (103) in Antigua makes very interesting reading for the student of Caribbean development, if for no other reason than that it describes the interlocking patterns of the development scene in a situation that is determined by obvious needs rather than by pre-conceived priorities. It also depicts the possibility of community participation in a crisis situation when it is animated by a Church-related agency like CADEC.

CADEC had responded to other disasters in Honduras, Guatemala, Nicaragua, St. Vincent and Belize. Yet it became obvious that there was a need to systematize its mechanism of response in some programmatic form that could meet the challenge for on-going emergency and welfare services, without detracting from its development work. It had also been engaged in some projects of the welfare type - in St. Vincent, Grenada, Montserrat and St. Lucia - and had attempted to relate such projects as closely as possible to its concepts of development.

The DERAW Programme has therefore been working through a number of counter-part committees at the national level; in most cases these committees are sub-committees of the National Councils of Churches. The programme continues to serve as a channel for resources of food, clothing and other material supplies from external sources (and some internal) to the places where extreme cases of need have been identified. Although the programme, by its very nature, tends to have a fairly low visibility, it does provide the Churches in the region with yet another opportunity for joint ecumenical action, since individual Churches are constantly being requested to respond to the welfare needs of the very poor and indigent members of their communities. It helps to provide the Churches with part of an answer to the problem of what to do about those people who cannot become active participants in the development exercise.

Second Assembly Hearings

The Second Assembly of the CCC which met in Guyana, November 16 to 23, 1977 provided an opportunity for the Churches in the region to review and evaluate the Development Programme of the CCC, over the period 1973 to 1977. The report of the "CADEC Hearings" indicated that there existed in the minds of many Church members a gap between the work of CADEC and the acknowledgement of that work as an essential mission of the Church in the Caribbean. The report suggested, inter alia, that "some have yet to catch up with the mandate given to CADEC at Chaguaramas".(104) It called for a greater improvement in the links of communication between CADEC and the Churches. There was a strong call in the Hearings that "the process of conscientization for pastors and lay persons should continue".(105)

A separate group at the Assembly constituted the "Hearings" on Communications. The report of this section of the Assembly issued a call for the preservation of the several strands of the CCC communications mechanism, "so as to keep open as many communications channels as possible amid the pressures and constraints varying from country to country in the region".(106) It was the regional newspaper Caribbean CONTACT which attracted the most attention in this Hearing, at the end of which a resolution was sent to the full Assembly, and ratified, which referred to the newspaper as one of the few existing means available for the regular "critical analysis of issues pertinent to full human development".(107) The resolution therefore called on the member Churches of the CCC to re-affirm their confidence in the editorial policy of the newspaper, and "to commit themselves to active support, promotion and distribution of 'Contact' in their respective territories".(108)

The Response of the Churches

There has been some indication, over the period of review, that the Churches have been attempting to make their own individual responses to the challenges extended to them at Chaguaramas in 1971, and re-affirmed in 1973. It was virtually impossible to expect that institutions which had been created out of a colonialistic and dependent ethos could almost immediately begin to make radical breaks with their past without any major disruptions. The only possible course open to the Churches in the Caribbean in 1971 was to "pour new wine into old bottles" in the hope that they would not break, but rather be renewed. Between 1971 and 1977 there has been a significant attempt by the Churches to participate in the new process of Caribbean development, along the lines which were suggested at Chaguaramas.

In 1976, the CCC through its Assembly Planning Unit, launched two investigative projects in which some effort could be made to ascertain the level of the response of the Churches to the 'Call' of Chaguaramas and Kingston. One project was called "Operation Outreach" and the other was known simply as "Project Five". The reports of the projects suggested that although there was still a "clash of agendas between the CCC and its constituency",(109) the Churches appeared to be much more aware of, and responsive to, a commitment to renewal and development. Under "Project Five", a study of the Synod reports of seven of the member Churches had shown that, in such areas of concerns as Liberation, Social Justice and the promotion of human dignity, only limited reference had been made to any "active lobbying or participation in any action designed to promote changes or even to promote some awareness of the necessity for change".(110) It was also reported that the member Churches were showing some awareness of the need for generating employment, particularly among the young; that there were attempts being made to "develop community life", although there still existed a need for "training for development among the clergy themselves, many of whom recognize this need".(111) The continuing gap between the agenda of the Development Programme of the CCC and the pre-occupations of its member-Churches with preserving their own structures and denominational programmes is of major concern to the ecumenical movement in the Caribbean. We shall have occasion to discuss the programmes of the Churches in the last chapter of this study.

Conclusion

The foregoing account of the rise and development of ecumenical social action in the Caribbean attests to the fact that a considerable amount was accomplished in this field, particularly between 1971 and 1977. There are, however, a number of significant observations to be made by way of a conclusion to this account.

It should be clearly noted that the CADEC initiative really started outside of the region - the CWS-sponsored survey on conditions in the Leewards and Windwards was the major start. Some would argue this in itself was typically a Caribbean phenomenon, where catalysts always appear on the scene from outside - it closely reflects the criticism made by Lowenthal to which we have already referred.(112) Outside initiative is not necessarily a bad thing, however, since the physical and resource limitations of the region very often make necessary, (or at least useful) that catalytic impulse from others who are not so restricted. The correlation between limited resources and limited initiatives is unmistakable, but it should not be used as an excuse for lack of any initiative at all.

It is also of interest to note that the coming together of the Churches in the Caribbean paralleled quite closely the building of functional links between Caribbean Governments for economic and political purposes. Common areas of action and joint co-operation were agreed on. Nevertheless, the Churches stayed clear of any action that spelt the bringing of themselves together into a union. Co-operation and ecumenical action stopped well short of union, although they acknowledged a common history and a common destiny. Furthermore, nothing in the action taken by the Churches necessarily signified a radical liberating thrust away from their dependence on the outside world, or from the entrenched historical patterns to which they had all been subjected. Indeed, a study of the rise and development of ecumenical social action in the Caribbean during the period does not clearly reveal the extent to which such activity was meant to usher in prophetically a form of psychological, or spiritual, revolution - a revolution of the inner Caribbean person.

With particular reference to the CADEC project activity, it was clear that it did not in every respect have the appropriate political and economic context necessary for catalytic growth in accordance with the principal objectives it set itself. It more easily became yet another funding source to spring up in the region, than an agency whose programmes and projects were geared to initiate significant social change. This factor has been of grave concern not least to the personnel within CADEC, since they have been anxious to promote their work as open demonstrations of the call for practical approaches to indigenous theological reflection and action, and also to greater efforts for self-reliance and social justice.

It was generally easier for Churches to agree on an agenda of a political economic nature, and to sponsor the establishment of an agency to carry out this agenda on its own, than for them to make any radical modifications to their own respective denominational agenda and concerns. Thus there still existed, at the end of 1977, a stark contrast between the work of the Churches and that of the ecumenical body that functioned on their behalf. Institutional constraints in denominational traditions create difficulties for individual Churches, from which a new ecumenical agency would largely be free. On matters of theological interpretation and reflection, therefore, the Churches would experience grave difficulties in identifying common ground. This is precisely what has happened in the ecumenical movement in the Caribbean. 'Doctrine' still divides while 'service' unites.

Ecumenical action has preceded any systematic and concerted attempt at ecumenical theological reflection on what that action entails. The work of the Renewal Agency of the CCC - ARC - has not devoted much attention to this fundamental prerequisite for change among the very Churches which are themselves attempting to promote change in the Caribbean. Chaguaramas had articulated very cogently the ways by which the Churches should proceed to change the Caribbean, but it seemed to assume too lightly that the Churches were capable of changing themselves without any clear signposts of where they should begin theologically. It failed to suggest what were the necessary connecting links between the Gospel, Development and Theology.

The need still exists in the Caribbean for the theological sub-stream of the Churches in the region to be appropriately affected. The rest of this study is therefore meant to be a contribution to the debate on how that theological sub-stream can be so affected, in order that the Church's understanding of itself and of its mission can be reflected more concretely in its engagement in social praxis generally, and in the development process specifically.

Chapter III

FOR FULL HUMAN DEVELOPMENT

> "The social and psychological needs
> of the human person must be considered
> to be as important as technological com-
> petence. Only so will the much bruited
> virtues of service, productivity, creati-
> vity, economic sufficiency and social
> commitment make sense as necessary means
> of meeting the problems of the society". (1)

These words of Rex Nettleford, (2) of Jamaica, provide for us the focus
for our discussion in this chapter. They represent the type of concern
for the development of man and his society which began to gain prominence
at the beginning of the decade of the 70's, in the context of the development debate. The concern for development was not merely an urge for
material progress, it had to relate to other dimensions as well. These
dimensions included mainly the demands for social justice, and the importance of self-reliance as an essential component of full human development. Our discussion will thus be concerned with the three main aspects
of the development debate - economic growth, self-reliance and social
justice - together with the meaning of human development as a goal of
developmental action. We shall look first at the global scene, however,
and outline the extent of the great divide between rich and poor countries,
and also describe briefly what the basic concept of "development" has
been taken to mean.

Countries rich and poor

It would be true to say that countries are neither rich nor poor, but that
there are people in countries suffering from hunger, illiteracy, poor
health and abject misery, while there are others who are not. Poor
countries are identified by their low income-per-head. Indeed, there
are poor people in rich countries, but nevertheless the seriously poor
in Europe (at US $ 500 per head per year) are five times better off than
their counter-parts in Asia (at US $ 100 per head per year). (3) The vast
majority of the people in Asia, Latin America, Africa and the Caribbean
exist in poverty. It is estimated that there are at least 800 million people
who are still living in absolute poverty; and they represent more than
one-third of the total population of the developing world. (4) Between the
rich and the poor countries, there are a number of factors which place
the latter at a continuing disadvantage.

The best way to fight poverty is to create a structure in which productive and fairly remunerated employment (including self-employment) is available to all. The rich countries had been able to develop a type of society in which most people were employed, and in which there could really be said to be a scarcity of labour. The industrial technology which therefore developed in the rich countries was evolved in conditions of labour scarcity. Such technology is generally unsuitable for poorer countries where there is a surplus of labour. Thus, first of all, the technological gap seriously affects the fight against poverty in the Third World.

Secondly, there is often a flight of capital and skills to the richer industrial countries away from the poorer regions. Opportunities for securing an attractive return on capital invested in the rich countries are usually substantially greater than in the poor, and political stability and security is guaranteed to a much greater extent in the former. People normally prefer to invest where the political climate is stable. With regard to skills, professional men attract much higher rates of remuneration in industrial countries and are easily attracted to such places - thus drawing away the most important factor of production from the poor to the rich countries. In addition, the existence of an international market of professional skills means that the poorer countries will scarcely be able to attract many professionals from this source, if their scales of pay are not competitive. In order to keep their professionals, the poorer countries are generally forced to pay them comparatively high salaries, thus creating internal inequalities. It is pointed out by Streeten and Seers, that "international inequality has an impact on internal income distribution in underdeveloped countries".(5)

Thirdly, Streeten has pointed out that technical progress in the rich countries has tended to reduce the need to import staple products from developing countries.(6) This has been due to the increased substitution of synthetics for natural products, an increasing economy in the use of raw materials, and a shift towards a demand for services and products which have a low primary import content. Thus systematic scientific research has a heavy bias towards insulating "a rich and comfortable society from the disturbance of change, even at the cost of some reduction in the benefits derived from international specialisation".(7) By the end of this century, the increased use of solar energy in the rich countries of Europe and North America may well create a different economic picture for the oil-producing countries of the Third World.

Fourthly, the role of foreign private enterprise in the development of poorer countries has not always had a positive effect. The rates of interest at which capital is borrowed has steadily increased in recent years - especially long-term private capital. The repatriation of dividends and profits to the rich countries seriously aggravates the balance of payments problems in the poorer countries, and reduces the amount of capital available for re-investment.

Fifthly, the efforts at national consolidation in the rich countries - in creating a welfare state, in working towards full employment, and in trying to insulate the national economy from external pressures - have severely reduced the export of capital and skills to poorer countries, as well as restricted immigration to the rich countries themselves.

Sixthly, there is the question of how much the poor can profitably learn from the rich. Western concepts and theories of economic development are largely inappropriate to deal with the serious problems of underdevelopment among the poor. Furthermore, the demonstration effect of the material progress in the rich countries creates a sense of urgency among the elite in the poorer countries, and significantly reduces the patient attitude and sober adjustments which the development process requires.

As a seventh point of attention, the question of foreign aid and its effect on the poorer countries needs to be considered. While it is true that aid from the rich countries does bring some measure of relief and development to the poor, it is also true that aid policies are generally aimed at complementing the trading policies of the donor countries and less at encouraging social reforms in the receiving countries. Very often it is social reforms in the poor countries that are most urgently needed to promote national progress and development. Progressive regimes are generally less likely to be added by the rich than are reactionary and conservative ones. (8) In any event, foreign aid provides more substantial gains for the donor than the recipient in the long run - this continues to be one of the major anomalies of international economic relations.

Eight: the matter of international trade raises a number of issues about the real political strength of poorer countries, about the organizational capacity between them in negotiating with the rich, and about their technical and diplomatic skills in acquiring the information they need to make substantial gains in this sphere. Further, the increased prices of goods which poor countries usually have to import from the rich, are often in excess of the price incomes which the former receive from the sale of their raw materials to the latter.

A ninth factor concerns the dilemma of the poorer countries' inability to make any substantial difference to the policies in the rich countries. They have relatively little power to effectively influence desirable changes of policy in their favour in the rich countries. Such changes would relate to the lowering of tariffs, reductions in freight rates (since rich countries virtually own the shipping trade), strict immigration controls on professional personnel from the poorer countries, and a more sympathetic and open attitude towards the overall problems of underdevelopment in the poorer countries.

The gaps between the rich and the poor countries of the world are enormous. Seers describes them as "immoral"(9), and John Cole depicts them as "obscenities". (10) There are not only gaps between rich and poor countries, there are also gaps between rich and poor within the poorer countries. Indeed the most unequal distribution of wealth and power is to be found in the poorer countries of the world. It is the stark realization of this complex situation between countries and within countries, and the increasing capacity of poorer countries to determine and pursue such policies as would be more favourable to their own national and economic interests, that has given rise to a global concern about "development" since the late 1950's. (11) We turn now to a brief discussion on the concern for development.

Development

The growth of awareness about the problems of development in the poorer countries was inevitable, since the poorer countries recognized that poverty was not their inevitable fate after all, and that something more could be done about it, not as a matter of course, but as a matter of right. Further, as a result of the so-called Cold War, the super-powers began to take a much greater interest in the poorer countries. This gave rise to the three-world categorization of the global community - the Western countries, the centrally-planned economies and the under-developed or Third World economies.

In addition to this, many of the former colonial territories had achieved political independence during the last thirty years. India, for example, gained independence in 1947. Political sovereignty was however limited by economic sovereignty. The aspirations for national development, and the growth of nationalism as a focus of development, would thus be increased. In any event, the growing awareness of the structures of international injustice which enabled the rich countries to achieve rapid economic growth at the expense of the poorer countries - through political and economic domination - was becoming more and more evident within the rich countries themselves to sectors of the societies (Churches, universities, pressure groups), who felt that historical imbalances needed to be corrected.

Development thus became a cause for international concern, since there was within the poorer countries widespread poverty, growing unemployment and underemployment, and grave inequalities of wealth, power and privilege. The immediate target for the development process therefore, was for the realization of the means to acquire the basic necessities of life - food, clothing, footwear and shelter. In order to acquire these, people needed to find a job for themselves, rather than to be dependent on the productive capacity of other people. It was only within the framework of growing equality, however, that more of the necessities of human life could be secured. If poverty, unemployment and inequality were to be seriously tackled, the development process would need to consist mainly of an increase in productivity.

In its broadest sense, development has been seen as a generic process in which the social, economic and political aspects of human life are all interdependent. These three aspects have been used as the classifications of the resources available for the productivity inherent in the development process. It has been rightly claimed that productivity "represents capability over time to satisfy basic human needs and desires, not only materially with goods and services, but in other respects as well". (12) We are therefore dealing with a process that is greater than mere production and growth. Development always involves changes in structure, while growth involves only changes in scale. Any structural change within the development process, therefore, will always involve changes in the pattern of the possession and use of resources in a country. The development process also links rich countries to the poorer ones (particularly in matters of trade and aid), and structural changes are therefore necessary both in the developed as in the developing countries.

Thus far, it is possible to say that in its basic form the process of development requires an increase in productivity and changes of structures for the better realization of social, economic and political equality. It involves what S. L. Parmar called a "dynamic equilibrium between persons and structures". (13) Dr. Kenneth Kaunda stated that it involved a total transformation of society, "the birth of new values and beliefs in relation to life and new institutions which give expression to new ideas and principles". (14) Lauchlin Currie recently suggested that development also involved having a better control and dominance over the physical, social, political, economic and demographic environment. He was of the opinion that not only should development imply the "satisfaction of physical wants, a comfortable living and a lessened sense of deprivation which entails less inequality in styles of living", but also "a better degree of control over the environment, nationally and internationally, as a necessary condition of survival". (15)

Development has also been understood by some to mean a process of modernization - but it is difficult to maintain that social transformation in poorer countries and the process of modernization can mean the same thing all the time. Great harm is done to a country where, in the interests of modernization, traditional social values are indiscriminately abolished, and where there is a naive transfer of alien tastes, techniques and values without studied and careful adaptation. Peter Berger rightly asserts that "policies that ignore the indigenous definitions of a situation are prone to fail". (16) Duncan Forrester contends that -

> "A developing country is not a tabula
> rasa to be filled in according to the
> whim of the development expert. It is
> a society and a culture with its own
> soil, its own riches of tradition and
> human resources, its own values and a-

bility to choose its goals, its own
particular capacity for change". (17)

Development therefore implies p r o p e r growth and d e s i r a b l e modernization.

Most of the literature on the issues of development, however, has tended
to deal with the subject under three general aspects - economic growth,
self-reliance, and social justice. The Montreux Consultation, sponsored
by the Commission for the Churches Participation in Development (of the
World Council of Churches) in 1970, described human development as
"enabling both persons and societies to realize the full potential of human
life in social justice, self-reliance and economic growth". (18) It was not
without significance that economic growth was mentioned last. Our discussion on these three aspects of development will however take economic
growth first, since it is that aspect on which there is least disagreement
in the development debate. We shall later have occasion to outline the
perceptions and priorities for development action which were evident in
the ecumenical debate, particularly on human development itself, up to
1977. (19)

Economic growth

There is no doubt that one of the basic objectives of development is that
the poor should have more than they do at present. It is not simply concerned with helping the poor, but also with helping them to help themselves and others. The motivation is essentially an economic one, but
it is fundamentally related to social and political factors as well. During
the 1950's and 1960's, however, it was mainly with economic growth that
most groups and agencies connected with development were primarily
concerned.

Benjamin Higgins had suggested that in the process of economic growth
no increase in output would be possible without "capital accumulation,
resource discovery, population growth, technological progress, or improved organization". (20) It is difficult to resist the observation that
apart from population growth the developing countries have hardly qualified
for growth according to Higgins' prescription. W. W. Rostow insisted that
the poor countries should be able to benefit from the experience of the rich,
and should follow their example in achieving high rates of growth in Gross
National Product per head. They should be able, thought Rostow, to
"take off" into self-sustained growth. Rostow went further -

>"There may not be much civilization
>left to save unless we of the democratic
>north face and deal with the challenge
>implicit in the stages-of-growth, as they
>now stand in the world, at the full stretch
>of our moral commitment, our energy, and
>our resources". (21)

The notion that economic development in the underdeveloped world should mirror that of Western countries was widely supported. Sir Arthur Lewis, for example, agreed that rapid economic growth in the poorer countries was possible as it had been realized in some European countries like Germany. (22) There were writers such as Bator, Hagen, Lerner and Millikan who suggested that underdeveloped countries were facing what developed countries had faced in the past, but that the former could begin to look like the latter once growth was built in as a central feature of their economies. (23) It was felt that the Western rich countries should provide help to the underdeveloped countries because of the latter's peculiar problems of population, technology and politics, and that the Western countries should exert their influence in order to help them to advance along lines which were harmonious to their (Western) interests. Social stability in the underdeveloped countries was crucial, it was felt, and development assistance from the Western rich countries should "help to make the evolution to modernisation successful enough so that major groups will not struggle either to repress change entirely or to promote it by ruthless and extremist measures". (24) Such concepts assumed a unilineal path of development, and firmly held to the belief that the Western rich countries could not, and would not, be overtaken. The balance of power, and control of the global resources, would remain fairly fixed. Furthermore, very little obligation was placed on the rich countries to make substantial adjustments and sacrifices as a significant pre-requisite of any worthwhile process of global development.

The Pearson Report of 1969 re-stated the basic concept of increased growth rate in GNP. The Report had observed that although there had been a widening gap between the developed and developing countries, there had been economic growth in several developing countries "at faster rates than the industrialized countries ever enjoyed at a similar stage in their own history". (25) In the face of the modest growth realized during the 1960's, there were still increased populations, growing unemployment and underemployment, poor educational facilities, poor trading arrangements, increased foreign debts, and decreased foreign aid. The Report suggested that aid from the rich to the poor countries was a moral obligation on their part, as well as an exercise of enlightened and constructive self-interest. It suggested a ten-point strategy of international co-operation for development which would be directed towards "a durable and constructive relationship between developing and developed nations in a new and interdependent world community". (26)

Lord Balogh has recently suggested a number of reasons why strategies of aid against poverty in underdeveloped countries have not been outstandingly successful. He has pointed to the emergence of restrictive monetary and fiscal policies in developed countries, following the rise of oil prices in 1973/4, to the decline of the capacity and the willingness of the rich to aid the poor countries - coupled with increased corruption among the ruling elites in the latter. Further, he suggests that the new ruling classes in the poorer - yet independent - countries have demanded

exorbitant incomes based on high productivity levels in metropolitan
countries, that the rich land-lords have benefitted from rural development schemes. Lord Balogh agrees that with the great differences
between developing areas - cultural, technical, environmental -

> "it is questionable whether a standard
> development model of general applicability
> can be constructed. Nor is it plausible
> to assume that rapid success can be achieved
> by the sequential application of 'packages'
> of pre-selected and identical composition". (27)

He strongly contends that the absence of political factors in development
aid strategies has militated against the professed aims and ideals. He
states that "the passionate pleas of UN officials and others for a non-
political, stringless, 'leverage'-less, automatic allocation of aid contributions appear naive, indeed tragically ironic". (28) Lord Balogh's
paper provides unwittingly an illustration of development aid as a strategy
of the rich against the poor rather than against poverty itself. Development as growth alone weakens the poor. (29)

The difficulties involved in regarding development as being synonymous
with growth in GNP per head have been outlined by many writers. Charles
Elliott has indicated that first, there are technical problems in using
the figures of GNP per head since they do not measure the 'subsistence
income' of the majority of the population which is engaged in subsistence
agriculture. (30) Secondly, says Elliott, GNP per head does not reflect
the actual levels of income of individuals. (31)

Parmar suggested that the drive of the poorer countries to 'catch up'
with the rich countries through an increase in GNP per head was beset
with many problems. Parmar said that the quest for development should
not be for a 'catching up' but rather for a 'standing up'. The drive in
poorer countries to 'catch up', he said, lacked realism and generated
frustration and defeatism; it involved a great deal of subservience, and
called for high-consumption patterns. (32) Parmar went on to suggest
that progress should not be measured in terms of having more, but
rather in terms of stronger social and economic structures to produce
more. Innovation was more important than imitation and adaptation.
With particular reference to his native country, Parmar showed that
India had faced severe problems in the decade of the 1960's when development was being measured by growth in GNP per head. There had been
an increase in the extent and intensity of poverty in spite of an increase
in GNP per head. Industrial progress had been accompanied by industrial
unrest and unemployment. The Green Revolution, he said, had been
technically successful, but there had still been serious shortages of
food grain and higher prices for agricultural products. Although the value
of exports had increased, balance of payments deficits had continued.
Education facilities had expanded, Parmar stated, but with 70 % of the

population still illiterate there were more persons in that category than five years previously. (33)

James Grant of the Overseas Development Council of the United States of America pointed to Mexico as a good case in point for the argument against the use of GNP as an index for development. Grant indicated that in Mexico GNP per head had risen annually at a rate of 5-6 % over a fifteen-year period, but that the rate of unemployment and the disparity of wealth had also risen. Grant claimed that in the early 1950's "the total income of the top fifth of the Mexican population was ten times that of the lowest fifth; by 1969, it was sixteen times as great". (34) He also claimed that similar examples could be drawn from the experiences of the Philippines, Brazil, Pakistan and Ghana. (35)

It is in this respect that the Caribbean presents a very distorted picture if it is measured in terms of GNP per head. The region can boast of high figures of income per head which would tend to suggest that it is not among the poor regions of the World. For example, in 1972, the U.S. Virgin Islands, the Bahamas, and Puerto Rico each had a GNP of over US $ 2000 per head, (36) but these figures said nothing of the heavy dependence of these economies on the United States of America, neither did they indicate the considerable gap between the "haves" and the "have-nots" in these territories. Similarly, in the Commonwealth Caribbean, Guyana is classified as a more developed country (MDC), and Belize is regarded as a less-developed country (LDC). Yet in 1972 Guyana showed a GNP of US $ 400 per head, while Belize showed a GNP of US $ 670 per head. (37) Owen Jefferson has shown that in Jamaica in 1968 the GNP was US $ 420 per head - the top 5 % of households had a figure of US $ 2,500 per head (about the same as Sweden), the next 5 % averaged US $ 1,100 per head (about the level of Italy), the lowest 50 % averaged US $ 110 per head (about the level in Kenya). Jefferson stated that such approximations as GNP per head "should make us wary of laying too much stress on increases in per capita income as a measure of economic welfare". (38) He went on to point out that the "growing integration of the economy into the North American complex has been accompanied by a form of perverse growth involving a growing polarization of the society". (39)

Bishop Benjamin Vaughan states that if the increase in gross national income is not related directly to an actual increase in the consumption of goods per head in a way that the poor might have more to eat, better houses and clothes, then the criterion is misleading. (40) Vaughan points to a number of "economic fallacies", as he calls them, and asserts categorically that "growth alone is not enough". (41)

Throughout the Third World in general, there was considerable agreement with the arguments against GNP as a measure of development by the beginning of the 1970's. In India, the focus changed to a strategy for self-reliance and the removal of absolute poverty by providing employment opportunities and basic minimum needs in health, housing, education, drinking water, roads and electrification. In Tanzania, the Arusha

Declaration had already been proclaimed in February 1967, in which the pattern of economic development based on urban-based industrial development (aided by foreign technology and finance) was heavily criticized. It deplored the heavy reliance on money as the major instrument of development in a poor country like Tanzania, and espoused the course of development through growth in self-reliance and the improvement of human and land resources. Thus in that country there has been the establishment of Ujamaa villages in which co-operation, participatory democracy and common ownership of land have been sought to be made the main principles of organization. Educational reform, health care, sanitation and drinking water have also been provided for in the new development strategy. (42) In Latin America, the emphasis in the development debate in more recent time has been on such questions as marginalisation, income distribution, and poverty. The Latin American experience has been that of a peripheral economy in which capital-intensive investment patterns have failed to absorb the growing labour force. The emphasis is therefore being placed on achieving greater collective self-reliance among Third World countries by delinking the periphery from the central economies of the United States and Europe. Several scholars have also been advancing theories of transnationalisation and dependent development. (43)

In the Caribbean, the Cuban model of revolution was not adopted in any other country. The main debate at the end of the last decade was about nationalization of the productive resources in the countries which had them in considerable abundance - Guyana, Trinidad and Tobago, and Jamaica. In Jamaica, Norman Girvan called for the nationalization of the bauxite industry. He suggested that this was necessary in order to "secure e f f e c t i v e national ownership over the industry; and e f f e c - t i v e control over decision-making, especially as regards pricing and marketing, the purchase of supplies, processing and expansion, and the use of profits". (44) In Trinidad, the Prime Minister Dr. Eric Williams, had outlined a model of development which allowed for reliance on outside investment and trade, Government and local control of the economy, racial harmony and social equality, and a conscious development of a national and cultural identity. (45) Williams had declared -

> "The Trinidad and Tobago Government and
> people have sought, and believe they have
> found, a middle way between outright nation-
> alization and the old-fashioned capitalist
> organization backed by the marines and the
> dollars of the United States of America.....
> The inefficiency of much more modest efforts
> in the field of public ownership of public
> utilities is, in any case, an inauspicious
> beginning to public ownership of basic
> industries". (46)

In Guyana, the process of nationalization has been accelerated since the Government's take over of the bauxite industry at the end of the 1960's. Today the State owns the sugar industry and controls most of the distribution services in the country.

By the turn of the decade of the 70's, there was already a growing body of opinion among development experts that perceptions which were primarily constrained by GNP growth alone were unsatisfactory. Indeed, the ILO-sponsored missions on Employment in Colombia (1970), Sri Lanka (1971) and Kenya (1972) all underlined the continuing need for unemployment, poverty and inequality to be tackled by a different set of developmental priorities. In November 1973 Albert Hirschman wrote about the "drastic transvaluation of values" that was occupying the minds of those who were engaged in the study of economic and political development, about what was being referred to as "the bankruptcy of the 'old' development economics", and about the call for greater emphasis on a "new doctrine that would emphasize income distribution, employment, and self-reliance". (47) Owen Jefferson had already been calling for a re-definition of development goals in Jamaica, based on a full employment of all resources, an equitable distribution of income, and an approved minimum standard of living for every individual - "based, of course, on what is possible from full exploitation of our resources". (48)

In 1974 a new strategy of "Redistribution with Growth" was being suggested by a group of experts. The proponents of this strategy noted that, in spite of the general increase in GNP in most underdeveloped countries during the First Development Decade, the lowest third of the population in these countries had received little or no benefit. This meant that the whole idea of aggregate growth as a social objective was to be seriously questioned. They therefore called for a strong combination of growth strategies with redistribution strategies. Such a combination should focus on increased growth in GNP, per head savings, and resource allocations in such a way as would benefit all groups in the society; the redistribution of existing assets - particularly land; the redirection of new investments for the creation of assets generating income for the poorest; and the transfer of income to support consumption among the poorest. Nothing could be achieved in this direction, the proponents argued, unless there was the political will to use the necessary policy instruments and planning models which were required. They estimated that there should be an annual transfer of 2 % of GNP per head from the rich to the poor over a 25-year period if such broad strategies of growth-plus-redistribution were adopted in underdeveloped countries. (49)

The Dag Hammarskjold Foundation (50) and the ILO, (51) in 1975 and 1976 respectively, were mainly responsible for promoting yet another strategy for development which shifted the emphasis away from growth. This strategy was called the "Basic Human Needs" strategy, and may be summarily outlined as follows -

a. "universal ability to secure basic personal consumer goods - food, clothing, shelter, household furnishings;

b. universal access to basic communal services - primary and adult education, preventative and simple curative medicine, pure water, transport and communication, environmental protection;

c. full employment (including self employment) productive enough and fairly enough remunerated so that all families have the income to purchase (or the ability to produce) their basic personal consumer goods;

d. universal participation at all levels in the taking as well as the implementation and review of decisions directly affecting individuals and communities";(52)

e. "the physical, human and technological infrastructure and the capacity to produce the capital and intermediate goods necessary to provide the consumer goods and services". (53)

Reginald Green says that this is neither a "soft strategy" (since it requires not only greater equality but ceilings on individual consumption, wealth, power, and status), nor is it an illusory strategy which ignores material constraints (since it recognizes the need to raise output in order to reach basic goals). (54) The ILO recognized that the satisfaction of such basic human needs required "action on all fronts, both redistribution and growth together". (55) It also pointed out that the sooner there was necessary redistribution, the shorter would be the period necessary to reach basic human needs targets; nevertheless, it said, the strategy implied high levels of investment - "without which there would be neither growth nor meaningful redistribution". (56)

It is of significant interest to note that in the Caribbean the Government of Guyana, in 1972, had embarked upon a national programme over a four-year period to feed, house and clothe all its people (FHC) by 1976. This FHC programme could be said to have been a small attempt to pursue a minimal basic needs strategy for development. The fact remained, however, that in Guyana as in all other developing countries food, housing and clothing were not enough. Man does not live by bread alone, and much more than material advance (economic growth) is required. To quote from Bishop Vaughan again -

> "economic growth may be accelerated
> by different kinds of stimuli, but if
> this is at the expense of basic human
> values of dignity, freedom and equality,
> there is no guarantee that it will be
> maintained". (57)

It has increasingly been recognized that growth in self-reliance is an essential component of the development process. This aspect of the debate on development requires our attention.

Self-reliance

Helene Castel wrote that the development process was one in which people who were powerless were freed from "all forms of dependency - social-cultural-economic and political - so that they can create a personal sense of history for themselves and thereby express their full potential as human beings". (58) This attempt at a definition is much more comprehensive than one which places the emphasis mainly on a growth-plus-change concept. There can certainly be growth and change without real development, but there can be no real development without growth in self-reliance. This is the theme which has been taken up in most of the Third World in the present decade, especially in the wake of the Arusha Declaration of 1967 in Tanzania.

Charles Elliott rightly points out that a rationale of self-reliance is the increase of growth itself since economic dependence and domination inhibit the rate of growth of the economy "by building in distortions in the pattern of investment and a chronic surplus of imports over exports". (59) Parmar defined self-reliance as "the ability of a country to maintain a desired rate of growth through its own resources". (60) Yet the concept of self-reliance is much more than an economic rationale, it is an attitude, an approach to human, community, national and international development. Its central principle is the necessity, the right, the capacity and the freedom of each people to define, and to struggle to achieve, their own goals of development through policies, programmes and institutions chosen by themselves. Self-reliance can be seen both as a means and as an end. When self-reliance is perceived as an end, Reginald Green says that it is critical to self-respect and self-fulfillment. He goes on the state -

> "Copying, begging and dependence
> are neither materially nor humanly
> effective or desirable (and nor are
> their mirror images arrogant offering
> of models to copy, niggardly manipula-
> tive alms 'giving', dominance)"(61)

The emphasis on self-reliance therefore points to the need for social and political ends to dominate and inform economic means. Economic activity and the need for self-reliance must always be closely intertwined within the development process. There is, however, another level of interaction which is implicit in the concept of self-reliance. It has to do with levels of human consciousness and practice as they develop towards greater self-fulfillment, it has to do with the interaction of persons and communities, since the perception of self-reliance focuses on the human person as a being-in-a-community, and it has to do with the interaction of different communities.

In 1969, Dudley Seers wrote an article in which he attempted to deal with the question of the meaning of development. (62) In 1977, Seers wrote again, this time on what he called "the new meaning of development". (63) Seers admitted that "development" though tarnished, had to be retained but redefined. He therefore suggested that the element to add to a re-definition of "development" was that of self-reliance. This involved reducing dependence on imported necessities, changing patterns of consumption, increasing relative capacities for production, re-distrib-uting incomes, increasing the national ownership and control of sub-soil assets, improving the national capacity to deal with multi-national corporations, reducing cultural dependence. Seers suggested that the key to all this was to adapt a selective approach to external influences of all types. Such a course, he said, would appeal to the strong feelings of 'nationalism' which is in itself "a stronger force than social con-science". (64) On the issue of cultural independence, Seers suggested that its increase had direct economic effects and that it also strengthened the motivation of the political leadership "to make further reductions in dependence" while weakening the internal opposition to these reductions. (65) Seers therefore saw development as being a world-wide problem and sug-gested that theories and experiences from the so-called 'developing' countries could be transferred to the so-called 'developed' world. (66)

Self-reliance involves the selection of a strategy of development that is appropriate, and one that inspires self-confidence. In many cases it implies that the alienated man in the industrial world should recover his humanity. It requires that the "extension of the dictates of consumerism to the poor countries" be rejected. (67) Thus the rich would need to curb their consumerism, if the poor were to "opt for production related to their needs", (68) since the aim of a strategy of self-reliance is to "re-late the pace of material growth to actual human needs". (69) No one would seriously wish to contend against the suggestion that the rich in the present world consume too much.

There are a number of cautionary notes which must however be observed in the debate about development as self-reliance. First, because we live in an interdependent world, it is important to insist that self-reliance does not mean autarchy, it means that the nature of the external relations of a country is determined by that country in accordance with its national goals for self-reliance. Secondly, it does not imply the total rejection of foreign aid. Parmar rightly said that "aid is considered good if it leads to no aid, i.e. it helps to increase the production and export capacity of recipients to the point where they can finance their development efforts". (70) Minhas has commented that the policy makers of a country need to be quite clear about the terms and conditions on which they are to accept aid "and not overdraw the singular virtues of self-reliance in personal behaviour into national policy". (71) He goes on to contend that there can be no special merit in a strategy of development "which is aimed at reducing aid requirements even if larger aid were available on terms and conditions acceptable to a country". (72)

The third cautionary note relates to the question of growth. Self-reliance does not mean zero growth on the one hand, but it does not necessarily ensure rapid growth or a 'catching up' with richer countries either. Development can sometimes be a rather slow process, and, in the words of Elliott, "a steady maturation and integration of growing points". (73) Fourthly, self-reliance is radically opposed to a spirit of domination and exploitation since "preventing the self-reliance of others denies the self-reliance of its authors". (74) Fifthly, it is crucial to state that self-reliance is not a strategy "concerned solely with minimum physical human needs". Green says that it is unreasonable to suppose that "a uniform, static, minimum level would be consistent with human development". (75)

Perceptions of self-reliance are re-inforced by perceptions of collective self-reliance. President Nyerere of Tanzania referred to it as "co-operation against poverty". (76) Green sees it as both a means and an end - as a means it enjoins the struggle against material obstacles which are faced by the peripheral economies, and as an end it liberates a country from self-centredness and promotes the transcendence of self. "Without it", says Green, "the only bond is that of self interest and that alone has never proven a stable, satisfactory or satisfying cement for any society whether at village or at global level". (77) President Nyerere also referred to it as the "Trade Union of the Poor". (78) Thus with collective self-reliance we are dealing not only with the relationships between the poorer countries themselves (South-South relationships) but also with joint activity by the poorer countries to secure alterations in the relationships between themselves and the rich countries (South-North relationships).

There can be no doubt at all that co-operation among the poorer countries can lead to a faster growth of trade and exports. But this faster growth in exports, if it is to pay for an increased cost of imports based on imitative and foreign-oriented consumer values, militates against the central meaning of self-reliance. Nothing would be gained by economic advancement in the poorer countries if there were not a radical diversion away from an imitative and elitist thrust of their strategies of development and modernization.

With particular reference to the Caribbean, several persons have been promoting the doctrine of collective self-reliance through regional integration. Alister McIntyre, William Demas, Norman Girvan and Owen Jefferson, among others, have long been writing in support of Caribbean regional integration. (79) The integration of Caribbean and Latin American economies had been suggested by Girvan and Jefferson in 1968, (80) following the establishment of the Caribbean Free Trade Area (CARIFTA) in 1967. CARIFTA gave way to a more consolidated regional grouping - Caribbean Community and Common Market (CARICOM) - in 1973. (81) Thus far, the regional integration movement in the Caribbean has been steadily growing, and the list of achievements up to 1976 was proudly recited by William Demas (a former Secretary-General of CARICOM) at the Sixth Annual Meeting of the Board of Governors of the Caribbean Development Bank in May 1976. (82)

Except for the lack of the very important factor of a common policy on foreign investment in the region, the CARICOM arrangement has become the major instrument of collective self-reliance within the region. (83) The inclusion of the Caribbean countries among the ACP (African, Caribbean and Pacific) Grouping in the Lome Convention, also indicates the region's wider participation in the global thrust for collective self-reliance. Demas underscored his promotion of the cause of collective self-reliance in the Caribbean by asking the following question in his Presidential Address to the Caribbean Development Bank Governors Meeting in 1977 -

> "Yet what can be simpler than the
> proposition that the development
> of neighbouring countries - each with
> a small national market, an insufficient
> range of human resources and a narrow
> range of natural resources considered
> individually, but collectively endowed
> with a much bigger market, a reasonably
> balanced pool of human skills and a
> fairly good natural resource base in
> relation to their population -
> can only be meaningfully promoted
> within a framework of close colla-
> boration and co-ordination rather
> than one of individual effort com-
> bined with wasteful and unhealthy com-
> petition and very expensive duplica-
> tion of economic activities and in-
> frastructural facilities? "(84)

Ten years earlier, another Caribbean leader - Mr. Forbes Burnham, Prime Minister of Guyana - had spoken in a similar vein:

"Either we weld ourselves into a
regional grouping serving primarily
Caribbean needs, or lacking a common
positive policy, have our various territories and nations drawn hither and
thither into, and by, other large
groupings where the peculiar problems
of the Caribbean are lost and where
we become the objects of neo-colonialist
exploitation, and achieve the pitiable
status of international mendicants".(85)

Social justice

Emmanuel de Kadt suggests that in one area the Church has been ahead of
the development specialists in the development debate, in that Churchmen
have discussed development in terms broader than 'growthmanship', and
have related it to social justice and social participation.(86) A note of
warning about socio-economic inequalities and the danger of not including
all classes of citizens "in the increased productivity" had already been
sounded by Pope John in his first major encyclical, "Mater et Magistra"
in July 1961. The Montreux Consultation in 1970 affirmed that -

"Development should be seen as the
process by which both persons and
societies come to realize the full
potential of human life in a context
of social justice, with an emphasis
on self-reliance; economic growth
being seen as one of the means for
carrying forward this process".(87)

The ecumenical debate on development has indeed been insisting that the
three objectives of economic growth, self-reliance and social justice
must be seen as interrelated components of the central goal of development.

David Miller has contended that "an egalitarian conception of justice will
be preserved in a community in so far as it manages to maintain close,
solidaristic relationships among its members".(88) But social justice
should not be seen merely as the result of such relationships, for to a
very large extent we are dealing in fact with distributive justice. The
principle here is based on the equitable distribution of the national product, incomes, and access to the means of production; it is concerned
with the question of social status for all members in the community;
and it is also concerned with the question of power, and the extent to
which this is shared among all sectors of the community.

Distributive justice should focus attention on the way in which members of a community are allowed to share in the community's wealth. Such a notion is usually countered by suggestions that in poor countries poverty cannot be distributed, and that it is better to have production first and then distribution afterwards. Yet it is important to the development process that the poverty of the poor countries should be 'shared' by all, chiefly by general agreement on absolute minimum levels of living, and on permissible maximum levels as well, in any society. Thus what is distributed is not really poverty but the available wealth in a general environment of poverty. Further, distributive justice entails a better and more efficient use of all available resources. The notion that production should precede distribution strongly suggests that there should be a postponement of the dissolution of the structures of social injustice, that there could be consensus about w h e n would be the appropriate time to begin the distribution, that control of the resources should remain in the hands of the rich and the powerful only, and that distribution would not lead to greater productivity. All these suggestions are inimical to the central goal of human development.

It should be clear from the preceding discussion that the attainment of social justice is impossible as a central goal of development without structural change. Indeed, as Erhard Eppler asserts, underdevelopment is "primarily due to the inadequacy of the social structures in the countries concerned, as well as in the industrialized countries and in international society". (89) Parmar insisted that without radical changes in social and economic relationships, and the diffusion of political power, development cannot take place. Parmar went on, "such changes are accompanied by instability, disorder, upheaval". (90) In close agreement with the principle of change and popular participation, the ILO made the following comment -

> "It is essential that the people whose
> basic needs have to be met should parti-
> cipate in the determination of these needs,
> rather than having them handed down from
> above". (91)

The right of people to participate actively in the political and economic processes of their country is intrinsic to the principle of social justice. The question of peoples' participation, therefore, requires some discussion.

Samuel Huntingdon and Joan Nelson published a study in 1976 about political participation in developing countries. (92) In it they defined political participation as "activity by private citizens designed to influence governmental decision-making". (93) They made a distinction between "autonomous participation" (activity originated by the actor) and "mobilized participation" (activity originated through someone other than the actor). The usual forms of political participation, they said, consisted of electoral activity, lobbying, organizational activity, contacting, and violence; and they noted that the common bases from which participation sprung were usually class, communal group, neighbourhood, party, or faction. Huntingdon and Nelson suggested that the political elite seldom promoted participation as a primary goal, and that they regarded it more as an instrumental valve. (94) They said that -

> "The extent to which political parti-
> cipation does expand reflects in large
> part the extent to which it is either
> a means to the achievement of other
> goals or a by-product of that achievement". (95)

They also suggested, however, that groups in developing countries prefer to concentrate on improving social status and material well-being rather than value political participation as a goal, and that these other goals may increase political participation.

With particular reference to the political participation by the poor, the writers noted that the poor took little part in politics and were mostly unaware of government policies and programmes. They suggested that the reason for this was due to the following factors - the poor generally lacked the resources of information, contacts, time and money; there was a lack of co-operation among them because of divisions of race, tribe and religion; there was a general fear of victimization and repression by the power elite and thus they lacked confidence in their capacity to induce change. The poor therefore regarded political participation as a difficult and ineffective way of advancing their interests or of coping with their problems. (96)

On the side of the government, however, and its responsibility to promote popular participation, the former Prime Minister of Jamaica, Mr. Michael Manley, suggested that when there was popular involvement in the decision-making process of government, "a government may find itself emboldened to call for sacrifice". (97) Mr. Manley asserted that the principle of popular participation -

> "involves the attempt to make government
> the beneficiary of institutional advice
> and responsive to popular need. Its
> tools are communication and dialogue,
> its method involvement, and its purpose
> mobilization". (98)

Social justice must thus be seen to be impossible without popular participation. The spectacle of a small elite controlling the power in a community is generally a strong suggestion of social injustice as the reality, allied quite often to a regime of corruption. The principle that justice must not only be done but must also be seen to be done remains quite operative in the field of social justice. Social justice remains an important component of the development goal, and it is imperative that the persons involved must be, and be seen to be, the subjects, agents and goals of their development. The following words of Michael Manley are relevant here -

> "One, then, might summarize social
> justice as being concerned with the
> organization of access. There must be
> equal access to jobs, to food, clothing
> and shelter; to social security; to
> the decision-making process; to the sense
> of belonging and being of equal value; to
> creative leisure; to the processes and
> remedies of the law, and to education.
> Men are not equally gifted but they are
> severally endowed and to each there must be
> accorded access to society's opportunities". (99)

Full human development

The following words from the Inaugural Assembly of the CCC are pertinent not only for this section, but also for the entire chapter -

> "We, as Caribbean people and as Christian
> communities, must seek ways whereby we
> may ensure a more just use of power in the
> area that will lead toward the full human
> development of all persons and communities". (100)

We have been maintaining that development seen as growth alone is not enough, since there can be growth without development; and that development only becomes valid and meaningful if it promotes social justice and, in the process, strengthens the forces of self-reliance, and thus accelerates the rate of growth. The core of development is the concern for the human, and it is essential that the concern for development itself does not take precedence over the concern for the human. C.I. Itty has rightly affirmed that "development is for man and not man for development". (101) Action for development must be guided by the moral imperative that the struggle for human dignity and freedom is crucial for the global demands for change, and that the right to self-development is to be ceaselessly promoted in human society everywhere.

It is along these lines of full human development that the ecumenical debate on development has been pursued continuously since the 1960's. The Papal Encyclicals - "Mater et Magistra" (1961), "Pacem in Terris" (1963), "Populorum Progressio" (1967) - underlined this central concern. The Uppsala Assembly of the World Council of Churches in 1968 had stated unequivocally that "the central issue in development is the criteria of the human". (102) Two years earlier, the World Conference on Church and Society had stated that the task of Christians was to conserve what was "truly human in the present but, alert to the many existing in-

justices, to seek to realise fuller possibilities of human life through
the processes of economic growth and social change". (103) At another
World Conference in Beirut, in 1968 (sponsored jointly by the World
Council of Churches and the Roman Catholic Church), the following
statement was issued -

> "Our task in the twentieth century - the
> task of all men - is so to develop and
> share the riches of the world together
> that all men may benefit and come to their
> full human stature. True human develop-
> ment is the aim; economic and social
> development is a necessary part of human
> development. What we search for is the
> enrichment of the human spirit at all
> levels - in ourselves as in others". (104)

A major concern for the human was continually expressed in the ecumenical gatherings - at Montreux in 1970, (105) New Delhi in 1970, (106)
Kenya in 1970, (107) Chaguaramas in 1971, (108) Beirut in 1972, (109)
Bossey in 1974, (110) and at the Fifth Assembly of the World Council
of Churches in Nairobi in 1975. (111) By 1975, however, there had already been a growing debate on the concern about human rights. The
Nairobi Assembly gave much attention to this problem, and the call
which it issued was taken up in many parts of the ecumenical world,
not least among them being the Caribbean itself.

At the Second Assembly of the Caribbean Conference of Churches in
1977, the Prime Minister of Guyana, Mr. Forbes Burnham, declared -

> "There are rights of human beings far more
> important than those which have been given
> emphasis and repeated over and over. There
> is the right of the people to eat; there
> is the right of the people to be clothed;
> there is the right of the people to have
> decent shelter; and there is a right to
> have free education, as the people in
> Guyana do now". (112)

Mr. Burnham said that he considered these to be "the most vital and
important human rights". Many would disagree with Mr. Burnham, however, since the more fundamental and structural rights to freedom of
expression, and to participation in the political process, are essential
to the provision of the basic needs of human livelihood - food, clothing,
shelter, education. The political debate in Guyana at present (1978)
centres around the basic right of all the people to participate effectively
in the decision-making process; there is no dispute about whether or not
people are entitled to be fed.

The General Secretary of the World Council of Churches, Dr. Philip
Potter, (himself a West Indian), also spoke at the Second Assembly.
He suggested that human rights were a much broader issue than Mr.
Burnham had tried to emphasize, and that the six specific human rights
which had been outlined at the Nairobi Assembly in 1975 were of particular
relevance to the Caribbean. These were -

1. The right to basic guarantees for life.
2. The rights of self-determination and to cultural identity, and the
   rights of minorities.
3. The right to participate in decision-making within the community.
4. The right to dissent.
5. The right to personal dignity.
6. The right to religious freedom. (113)

Dr. Potter insisted that the action for the development and renewal of
Caribbean society had to include the full recognition of these basic human
rights. Towards the end of his address he said -

> "Finally, we must never forget that we are
> not alone. All peoples are now engaged in
> the struggle for human rights. The forces
> which violate and abuse human rights are
> one across the world. The economic and
> political forces which operate here in the
> Caribbean are at work all over the world and
> especially in the Third World. The struggle
> is a global one and we in the Caribbean are
> part of it". (114)

It has been suggested by C.T. Kurien that development is itself a developing concept which has to be re-examined and evaluated constantly. (115)
Kurien goes further to say that "the content of development is what we
put into it". (116) This statement merits a substantial measure of agreement since the process of change usually requires that methods and
definitions are validated by the realities of concrete circumstances and
experiences. The Caribbean experience, as it was discussed in our first
chapter, is characterized by poverty, dependence and alienation. Any
valid and effective attempt to define the structure of the development
process for the Caribbean must take these realities into account. It is
instructive to argue that the emphasis on economic growth attacks the
dimension of poverty, while that on self-reliance attacks dependence,
and the objective of social justice seeks to eliminate the traumatic
experience of alienation. Nevertheless, there is a danger that such a
paradigm might tend to undermine the wholistic and integrated nature
of the human dilemma in the Caribbean.

It is not incorrect to affirm that the needs of Caribbean people for self-
development are greater than the sum of the three basic aspects of
development which we have been discussing in this chapter - economic

growth, self-reliance and social justice. There is the need for full human development in areas both material and spiritual. It is a need which they share with others across the globe, but which they feel more acutely because their very claim to humanity has been historically in doubt - by considerations of race and class. There is a need for the development of the relational capacity in Caribbean people, which would not only hold the material and spiritual dimensions in fertile tension, but which would also promote the development of true community in the Caribbean with its own self-generating dynamics of integrity, mutual respect and human achievement. For the christian at least, human development thus becomes the possibility of the sign of divine fulfillment - the working out of man's response to God's action. This means that there exists the need for a theological framework which would complement and inform the basic aspect of the development process we have been outlining. This need has been recognized in the general theological debate on social change. We shall therefore discuss the broad outlines of this aspect of the theological debate, as a prelude to our own explorations into the Caribbean experience, and to our suggestions for a theological interpretation of the development work of the Caribbean Conference of Churches.

Chapter IV

THEOLOGY FOR CHANCE

"I believe in God, Creator of an unfinished
world Who does not decree an eternal plan
of development in which we cannot participate.

I believe in God, Who has not divided people
into the poor and the rich, specialists and
the ignorant, owners and slaves.

I believe in Jesus Christ, Who saw the world
situation and Who took a stand in it.

Taking Him as my example, I see the precaution
with which we must organise, the extent to
which our intelligence is atrophied, our imagination impoverished, and our efforts neutralised.

Each day I fear that He may have died in vain
because we do not live as He lived, because
we betray His message.

I believe in Jesus Christ, Who rises for our
life so that we may be liberated from the pre-
judices and presumptions of fear and hate,
so that we may transform the world into the
Kingdom of God.

I believe in the Spirit Who came with Jesus
into the world.

I believe in the community of all peoples.
And in our responsibility for making of our
world a place of misery, hunger and violence
or the City of God.

I believe that it is possible to build a
just peace.

I believe that a life full of meaning is
possible for all and in the future of this
world of God.   AMEN."(1)

This quotation is taken from a Latin American Mass, and forms the
"Credo", the expression of faith, which arises out of a particular socio-
historical and liturgical context in Latin America. It articulates in
credal form the response of a particular people whose daily experiences
of oppression, exploitation, alienation and underdevelopment do not
represent for them what they believe to be the will of God. To incorporate
such an expression of faith into the very core of their formal and collective

liturgical activity, an expression that speaks of their desire for change and liberation, is to give practical illustration of the fact that no experience of theirs can be free from the interaction of ideology and faith, of theology and a concern for development, and of the importance of faith in the realm of social praxis. Such interactions are the continuing realities in the human experience, and they have a direct bearing on the nature of the human response to the need for social change as a Christian concern. Our main concern in this chapter therefore, will be to explore the implications of a search for a theological method, by illustrating the interrelationship between ideology, theology and praxis, by surveying the debate on development as a theological concern.

Ideology, theology and praxis

One of the most important goals of human existence is to develop and sustain a high level of responsibility and maturity in human behaviour. Human praxis has to be responsible and purposeful, and it has to contribute to the better ordering of human society. In fact, human praxis is paradoxically the cause and effect of human society - the society very often determines the praxis, and the praxis also creates (or re-creates) the society. Human praxis is however the result of responses to two basic questions of living - "why", and "how". A person's behaviour is normally determined by what he considers to be appropriate, or most expedient, in a given situation. Thus praxis is often the result of reflection. Human reflection on praxis determines further (or future) praxis, just as human praxis has a direct bearing on human reflection itself. At the level of human reflection on praxis, however, we are dealing with activities of thought such as ideology; and for religious man theology also has its origins here. Theology and ideology are both reflections on praxis, as well as motivations for praxis. We shall therefore discuss the inter-relationship between ideology, theology and praxis, with particular reference to our search for understanding the nature of theological method. We first need to distinguish ideology from theology as distinct patterns of human thought.

Karl Marx insisted that there was no such thing as "pure theory". He suggested that such 'ideologies' as morality, religion and metaphysics did not have any autonomous existence, but were "necessary sublimates of men's material life-process". (2) Marx said that these ideologies had "no history, no development; it is men, who, in developing their material production and their material intercourse, change, along with this their real existence, their thinking and the products of their thinking. Life is not determined by consciousness, but consciousness by life". (3) Marx believed that "the mode of production of material life determines the general character of the social, political, and spiritual processes of life". (4)

Karl Mannheim has, in this century, carried forward the work on the sociology of knowledge, with particular reference to the issue of ideologies. Mannheim regarded ideologies as conscious disguises of the nature of situations. He suggested that it was becoming increasingly evident that -

> "(a) every formulation of a problem is
> made possible only by a previous actual
> human experience which involves such a
> problem; (b) in selection from the multi-
> plicity of data there is involved an act
> of will on the part of the knower; and
> (c) forces arising out of living experience
> are significant in the direction which the
> treatment of the problem follows". (5)

The notion of the 'act of will' is central to Mannheim's thought on this issue. Systems of ideas should not therefore be taken at face value, but should be interpreted in the context of the life situation of the person who expresses them.

Ideology is basically an attempt to explain present realities, to project a future state that one desires, and to link the present to that desired future by means of a transforming process. Althusser describes ideology as a "system of representations". He says that it is an "essential struc-ture in the historical life of societies", and can also be called an "in-strument of reflective action on history". (6) Ideology can also become the embodiment of the ideas of a particular social grouping, a system of social thinking in which the trans-empirical categories, and the choice of empirical material, is determined by special attitudes and interests. To that extent, ideology can be an instrument of deception, obscuring reality, treating man as a stylized being, and promoting a gravely defective image of man. (7)

Ideology can however have a determinative function in social praxis. It can be the main collective instrument through which social roles are determined. For human beings, however, the choice of ideals, and of the roles through which such ideals are pursued, takes place at the trans-empirical level. There can never be any means of knowing in advance whether such ideals will be satisfying or not, or whether they are even attainable. The element of risk is clearly involved. This element of risk is a continuing factor of one's commitment to a particular picture of reality, and to its inherent demands for hope and praxis. Ideologies generally involve the belief in the value of one's analyses and predictions as conveying the implications for immediate praxis. Ideo-logical response therefore includes the risk of faith in truth - not in abstract truth, but rather in transforming truth.

Faith must be seen as the totality of human praxis in response to what is perceived as ultimate reality. It gives direction to one's life, and that direction is constantly relativized by faith itself. The experience of religion in the Third World in particular has led us to recognize that the ideological content of one's behaviour should constantly be re-evaluated in the light of one's response to ultimate reality. Faith changes ideologies, but it does not change the n e e d f o r ideologies. The witness to one's faith, and the pursuit of ideological goals both take place within the same concrete socio-historical situation. There is a close correlation between ideology and faith. St. Augustine and St. Thomas Aquinas were just as ideological as Luther and Calvin were in their religious perceptions. Segundo speaks of faith as "maturity by way of ideologies, the possibility of fully and conscientiously carrying out the ideological task on which the real-life liberation of human beings depends". (8)

Theology always follows faith, and should never be confused with faith itself. Theology essentially attempts to express systematically the experience of an encounter with ultimate reality in such a way that this experience can be explained, justified, and made accessible to other persons. It does not treat faith as an atemporal universal body of divine revelation that is totally free from any ideological connection. It is always a dynamic attempt to validate the response of faith in a given historical situation. (9) James Cone rightly asserts that "theology arises out of life and thus reflects a people's struggle to create meaning in life". (10)

The Geneva Conference on Church and Society in 1966 agreed that the role of theology was to reflect not only on the action but also the inter-action between God's revelation and "man's ideological understanding of his own condition and desires". (11) The Conference stated that Christians were affected by secular ideological perspectives like all other human beings. Elliott has suggested that although theological insight sometimes causes discontinuities in the manner in which Christians look at their world, it would be a mistake to treat theology as an independently determined activity reacting upon the ideological presuppositions of the Churches. He insists that the "inter-relationship between ideology, theology and praxis is a good deal more subtle and the streams of causation run in both directions". (12)

Theology must therefore be seen as critical reflection - man's critical reflection on himself as a man of faith, and on his basic principles. It involves a measure of response that relates clearly to his attitude to the social, political and economic realities in his experience. Such critical reflection and response should lead to definite patterns of social praxis within a definitive framework that relates creatively to human liberation. Gustavo Gutierrez writes -

> "Theological reflection would then necessarily
> be a criticism of society and the Church in
> so far as they are called and addressed by
> the Word of God; it would be a critical theory,

worked out in the light of the Word accepted
in faith and inspired by a practical purpose - and therefore indissolubly linked to
historical praxis". (13)

Gutierrez goes on to show that such a critical attitude requires an openness to the world, since it is in this way that theology can play the role
of an ideology which attempts to rationalize and justify, or criticize
and overthrow, a given social or ecclesial order. Such theology not
only helps the pastoral activity of the Church by putting it in a wider
context, but it also fulfills for man a liberating function in that it
preserves both him and the Church from idolatry and fetishism as well
as narcissism. Such a theology has a necessary and permanent role of
liberating man from every form of religious alienation. Yet, says
Gutierrez, it also grows and changes; for any theology which only has
so-called "truths" as its reference points - "and not the Truth which
is also the Way - can be only static and, in the long run, sterile". (14)
It is only in this way that theology can fulfill a prophetic function, says
Gutierrez, as it interprets historical events and points to their profound
meaning. Gutierrez does say, however, that the other traditional functions of theology such as rational knowledge, and wisdom, are given
greater significance in ecclesial praxis when theology itself is seen as
critical reflection. (15)

Christian theological reflection can only be meaningful if it has a basic
threefold purpose. First, it has to be faithful to what is involved in
being a Christian - individual commitment as a disciple of Christ and
membership of the community of faith as the people of God. Secondly,
it has to discern very clearly what Christians should initiate or promote.
Thirdly, it has to bring judgement on what Christians should attack,
remove, or change in so far as it prevents people from being human.
Dr. Shoki Coe has contended that theology has to be contextualized -
contextualization is a process involving both word and action, theory
and practice. Coe goes on to insist however, that authentic theological
reflection must also be a "theologia viatorum", a theology of a people
who understand themselves as a pilgrim people, subject to change, and
ready to receive new revelation. (16) The following words of Wolfhart
Pannenberg are most pertinent here -

"By relating the particular content of the
Christian tradition to questions regarding
the truth about nature, man, society and
history, theology explores the field for
possible contributions of Christianity to
mankind, and therefore to the public structure of social life in a particular society".

He goes on to suggest that such a function entails the uncovering of the
"religious implications in human existence" and the relating of the Christian tradition to the religious implications of present experience. (17)

It is therefore possible to affirm that 'ideological man' and 'theological man' are one and the same person. The historical and social context within which he functions, and through which he has to interpret an understanding of himself and his possibilities for the future is identical. Ideological analysis and theological reflection both take place within the same mind, within the same historical and existential situation, and both play a significant role in the process of taking decisions for human praxis in society. Although it is true to say that ideology and theology are both analytical structures of human thought, and are directly related to the nature of human response to socio-historical reality, it must also be borne in mind that while all theologies are ideologies all ideologies are not theologies. The concern for development is basically an ideological concern, but it also involves a great deal for theological critical reflection. Development as a focus for human action must certainly concern the man of faith. If theological method is to radically affect the human attitude to society, it follows that it must relate substantially to social attitudes for change and purposeful praxis. We therefore need to move on to a discussion on the search for a theological motivation for action by the Churches towards developmental change.

Theology and development

The literature on the relationship between theology and development has been increasing rather rapidly during the last twelve years. The work of SODEPAX (Committee on Society, Development and Peace) - a joint committee which was launched by the Roman Catholic Church and the World Council of Churches in 1967, and which was hailed at the time as the "world's most practical ecumenical venture" - has been of immense value in this connection. In 1969, Fr. Gerhard Bauer drew up for SODEPAX an annotated bibliography entitled T o w a r d s A T h e o l o g y o f D e v e l o p m e n t, (18) and this is still regarded as a basic source book in this field. In more recent time, the work of CCPD (Commission on the Churches Participation In Development) of the World Council of Churches has also been of great value, and its system of network relationships throughout the Third World has enabled it to monitor the debate on Theology and Development on a much wider scale than had been possible during the previous decade. (19) The reader will therefore find a wealth of information and insights in referring to the works of SODEPAX and CCPD. For our immediate purposes however, we must merely summarize the debate, and identify the points of impulsion which might create new perspectives for critical reflection and action by the Churches in the Third World towards the goals of full human development.

The Beirut Conference of 1968 acknowledged that the simple appeal to the law of Christian brotherly love was grossly inadequate when dealing with the Christians' response to the complex challenges of development. The "projects of here and now" were more challenging, since, for many, the world beyond had virtually disappeared, and the traditional understanding of salvation worked little commitment. The Conference asked "does an essential discontinuity exist between the eschatological future and the present of man in his city?"(20) It was felt that salvation was explicitly tied to developing this world, and that development in all its dimensions was God's will since man was destined to be more fully human. "Insofar as having more is necessary to being more," the Conference suggested, "material progress is good". It was also good because it could be a manifestation of that "specificity of man as 'imago Dei', which is to be spirit, free, responsible, and creative".(21)

The Geneva Conference of 1966 had urged that Christian theology could only be considered prophetic in so far as it attempted, "in full reflection, to declare how, at a particular place and time, God is at work, and thus to show the Church where and when to participate in his work".(22) It called on the World Council of Churches to convene a special consultation of theologians to make a special theological evaluation of its report and to give special attention to certain aspects of Christian social ethics such as contextual ethics, and the "dialectical relationship between a rigorous ethic of purity and the ethics of effective and compromise".(23) The Consultation was called by the WCC, in March 1968 in Zagorsk in the USSR, and it examined in close detail the meaning of the 'humanum' as a criterion in ecumenical social ethics. It was at that consultation that there was an attempt made to think theologically about development, by use of a christological approach. This method of a christological approach was also adopted in the following month at the Beirut Conference to which we have referred above.(24) At Beirut, the approach was spelt out in the following principle: "But if Christ is the finisher, he is also the beginner of this work of man's development".(25) Beirut said that it was through Christ that men would arrive at that measure of human development which was embraced in the term "the fullness of Christ" (Ephesians 4:13). The christological approach requires further discussion.

Nikos Nissiotis suggested that there was a real need for a theological sense of development that would precede a theology for development as such. This theological sense requires that we look at development through faith in Christ and his incarnation as a prelude to the social involvement of the Church, for "after the incarnation of the Word of God", says Nissiotis, "our word cannot remain an abstract philosophical reflection about God".(26) He insists that authentic theology of development is different from a natural theology, or a humanism, in that it attempts to discern the signs of the times according to God's saving judgement, acting in Christ and present in the Spirit. Nissiotis says that because God is not an abstract ethical principle, but he is the heart of the events in history, involved in a dynamic action for the progress of all creation, and because Christ is the raison d'etre and purpose of the creation, we should not be speaking of a theological phenomenology of development but of a christological one. Thus the basic premise of a christological phenomenology of development would go like this -

"Development is a God-given possibility to
man for making him a collaborator towards
the completion of God's creation, through
man's link with God in Christ. This struggle
of humanity towards its full dignity reveals
that man and the world are created with a
specific purpose, with a goal to be attained
through a continuous process of change and
renewal. That goal is the reality which has
been revealed by God in this world in the
person of Jesus". (27)

Jurgen Moltmann also adopted a christological approach to the theology of
development. In Moltmann's case however, there was a close connection
drawn between his 'theology of hope' and 'theology of development'. He
said that the primary and fundamental event for Christianity was the
Christ event, that is, the Cross and the Resurrection, which must also
be the ground of the "theology of hope and of development". Moltmann
speaks of the anticipation of the future (the Resurrection) and
the vicarious representation (the Crucifixion) as christological concepts which have profound meaning for the Christians' engagement in development. He says -

"The truth that God's future began with
the crucified, a truth which is fundamental
to the Christian faith, brings Christians
into radical conflict with technocratic
views of development. This conflict is not
waged in the name of the ultimate super-
natural hope against penultimate earthly
hopes, but in the name and on behalf of
"those who, now and in the future, are
neglected, oppressed, and excluded by the
development process". (28)

Moltmann's thoughts were contained in a working paper which was used
at a special consultation at Cartigny in Switzerland in November 1969.
It was sponsored by SODEPAX, and it brought together a number of
theologians to discuss the search for a theology of development. The
report of that Consultation, entitled In Search Of A Theology
Of Development is perhaps the most important document on the
subject that is available today, from a technical, as well as a global
point of view.

The Cartigny consultation heard from Rubem Alves that it was the task
of a theology of development to "develop by means of clearer images,
the ideas already present in a more or less latent form in the praxis and
spirit of communities". (29) It caused Charles Elliott to write that there
was a danger that the word 'development' was being used in such wide
and varying terms - "from spiritual conversion to the establishment of

a more just international economic structure" - as to be almost meaningless. (30) He proposed that it should be used only in its technical
sense denoting "the transformation of economic and social structures
of an individual country accompanied by quantitative and qualitative improvements in general welfare and the generation of forces within the
society for the sustaining of those improvements". (31)

Paul Loffler summarized what he considered to be the four possible
methodological approaches to a theology of development which emerged
from the debate at that Consultation. The first approach was to explore
the pastoral, ethical and prophetic insights being discovered by Christian communities engaged in development, and to attempt to reconstruct
a theology from their perspectives. Secondly, there could be an effort
made to communicate and compare theological reflections relating to
different societies, different sectors of society, different centres of
power, and different cultural environments. A third approach would be
to identify the theological resources - both in Scripture and Christian
tradition - which could help towards a critical involvement in, and a
deeper christian understanding of, development in relation to the issues
which it posed. Finally, there could be an attempt to engage in dialogue
about the longterm goals of development, with those whose religious
and ideological presuppositions differed, in order to articulate the Christian hopes and horizons for the future. Loffler stressed, however, that
these four approaches pointed to different emphases which were needed
in relating development to theology. (32)

Charles Elliott, who was responsible for the co-ordination of the Cartigny
consultation, has elsewhere been engaged in exploring the theological
bases of a concern for development. (33) Elliott suggests that the three
sources of theological reflection are Scripture and Church Tradition,
the worshipping community, and the facts of the actual situation. He
says that God as the Creator and Lord of history reveals some truth
about himself in the world and its history, and "if we want the churches
to be serious about development we must at least be serious about the
facts". (34) Elliott contends that theology has to continuously review and
challenge the normative premises of the ideological matrix so that we
might be able to see the facts of man in the light of God. He goes on
to say that there is no theology of development as such, but only a
"theologically illuminating way of looking at different concepts of development". (35) Elliott suggests that the major themes in Christian theology -
the Person of Christ, the nature of man, the fact of the Church, and
the possibilities of the future (eschatology) - should be regarded as the
starting-points. It is his view that the hopeless and the poor have to be
taken seriously, and that the resources available should also be used for
the benefit of those without them. Pointing to the disparties in the world,
Elliot says that they indicate that God has provided an opportunity for
human response. For Christians, this means radicalism, a radicalism
that involves putting one's care where the world's relationships exclude
care. (36) In more recent times (1975) Elliott has amplified this radicalism

by speaking of 'radical contemplation' and 'radical action'. This radical restructuring, he says, involved a more critical attitude to wealth, a more critical approach to the relationship between Churches and liberal-capitalist regimes in the First World, a determined skewing of the social involvement of the Churches towards the poorest and the alienated, and "a liturgy that does not start from the assumption that a fundamentally unjust and exploitative social structure is ordained by God and therefore immutable". (37) Elliott's work in this field constitutes a most valuable and important contribution to the debate on theology and development.

There can hardly be any doubt that the basic connection between theology and development rests in the actual living experience of the community of faith, the day-to-day experience of the Christian community. It is here that they respond existentially to the living promises of God. Added to this is the fact that the community is itself a living memorial of faith, a faith characterized by a struggle against poverty and oppression. It is a faith characterized by a prophetic witness against injustice, or to put it another way, a determined effort to struggle for the realization of God's justice in their actual situation. Justice is a fundamental characteristic of God's nature and activity in the Bible, and the search for God's justice was not merely for an inner certainty of a right relationship with God but also for an outward social manifestation of God's intrinsic nature. Justice was also relational, a mutual affirmation of a right relationship between human beings. But there was also another element connected with the concept of justice in the Bible. Justice (or righteousness) showed particular favour to the poor, the weak and the oppressed (Amos 5). The search for justice should thus become fertile common ground for both theology and development. Furthermore, the need for liberating praxis, the need to challenge the social and political structures of sin - which cause oppression and underdevelopment - should also be of common concern to theology and development.

The General Secretary of the World Council of Churches, in his annual report in 1973, had this to say -

> "There is the further charge that theology
> is too often an instrument of the rationali-
> zation of existential decisions rather than
> a necessary element of action. At least it
> seems that whatever we may assert to the con-
> trary, we have failed in the World Council
> to communicate the relation of what we are
> doing to the message of the Gospel. We are
> not sufficiently interpreting our actions
> theologically so that they may be understood
> as actions in faith, which indeed they are,
> nor are we helping those, in all the movements
> and groups with which we are in touch, who

act in faith to articulate theologically the
new insights they are undoubtedly receiving". (38)

Dr. Potter's observation was of more than passing significance, coming
as it did some five years after the Fourth Assembly at Uppsala, and
with such a strong plea for more intensive theological reflection on
praxis in actual situations. The Uppsala Assembly had already pointed
out the urgent need for a theological undergirding of the Church's
activity in social praxis -

> "Theology has also to come to grips with
> the meaning and goal of peoples all over the
> world who have awakened to a new sense of
> the human. Indeed the interaction between
> technology and social justice is a crucial
> issue of our time". (39)

The Third World theologians who met in Tanzania in 1976 affirmed that
a new vision of a theology "committed to the integral liberation of persons
and structures is now being developed in the very process of participation in the struggles of the people". (40) The priorities for theological
concern have been rapidly changing in the Third World, and key issues
such as violence, private property, human rights and social justice are
of far more importance today than the broadly intellectual pursuit of a
"theology of development" as such. Paulo Freire therefore states -

> "The theology of so-called development
> gives way to the theology of liberation -
> a prophetic, utopain theology, full of
> hope. Little does it matter that this
> theology is not yet well systematized. Its
> content arises from the hopeless situation
> of dependent, exploited, invaded societies.
> It is stimulated by the need to rise above
> the contradictions which explain and pro-
> duce that dependence". (41)

We therefore need to turn to the Third World, and to recognize that
there are vibrant theological concerns for social change.

Theological concerns for social change

The Conference of Third World theologians, to which we have already
referred, noted in their final statement that there was a substantial
measure of agreement between them in respect of the need to do
theology within the context of their respective socio-cultural milieu.
They agreed that theology had to be done in relation to the life and
work of the exploited and oppressed who were struggling for liberation.

They recognized that their countries had common problems, that experiences were similar in respect of the social, economic, political, cultural, racial and psychological situations in their countries; but that there were also differences in these situations which necessitated variations in theological reflection and praxis. While some felt that it was the need for political and economic liberation which offered the vital basis for theologizing in their areas, others preferred to regard the presence of other religions and cultures, the facts of racial discrimination and domination, and the challenges of Christian minorities in predominantly non-Christian societies as the basic situations to which their own work should pay primary attention. (42)

The concept of a comprehensive theology for the Third World was therefore ruled out; the realities of the need to take their respective sociocultural contexts seriously were respected, and the challenge of interpreting the will of God in Christ, as is made explicit in the Gospel, became an urgent task for each theologian as he returned to his respective country. They were agreed that the Gospel meant good news for the liberation of man, they were also agreed that theirs was the responsibility of contributing to the practical interpretation of what that good news meant for them and their own people in their own situation; in other words, theirs would need to be a search for orthopraxis rather than 'orthodoxy' in isolation from praxis. How all this was to be done would be determined by actual manifestations of the need for change and liberation in their own situations, and a clear identification of the point of engagement (Latin Americans prefer 'insertion') in the struggle for change and liberation. How then are these theological concerns for change to be interpreted in the Third World?

In a letter which he wrote to a friend, Paulo Freire commented that he had got the impression that the Third World could become a source of inspiration for theological renewal, because of its "utopian and prophetic character as an emergent world". He said that the developed countries could not exercise any prophetic role since they were societies whose future lay in maintaining their present affluence. (43) Such societies were denied hope, for they were menaced by their establishments which were afraid of any future that could shake their position. Thus their philosophical and theological tendency was pessimistic, "denying man as a being in the process of transformation". (44) If one was to think outside the normal channels in the developed countries, said Freire, one had to think oneself into the 'Third World' mentality. It is of interest to note that Freire had, on another occasion defined the concept of the Third World as ideological and political, and not geographical. It was "the world of silence, of oppression, of dependence, of exploitation, of the violence exercized by the ruling classes on the oppressed". (45) He therefore said to his friend that he thought the prime concern of Third World theologians was "to be men of the Third World", they had to steep themselves in it so that they could be men of the world - utopian, prophetic, hoping - renouncing power structures which represented oppression, taking sides

with the oppressed, "in a gesture of genuine love, which is not the
gesture of attempting an impossible conciliation between those who
opress, stifle, exploit and kill and those who are oppressed, stifled,
exploited and threatened with death". (46) This type of theological
action is being called for throughout the Third World.

Conclusion

Our discussion on the nature of theological method in this chapter has
pointed us to the close connection that there is between ideology and
theology, since both are related to structures of human thought as well
as human response to reality. We have seen that the locus for ideological activity in history and theological reflection on history are
identical, and that theology cannot exist without reference to the ideological milieu in which thinking man finds himself. A theological concern for development and social change, therefore, must be seen to
be basically an ideological concern that is enriched by the dimension
of faith. It is at the level of this faith-dimension that commitment of
life is possible for the Christian, within the context of community. Theology is a process of continuous critical reflection, and the consciousness
of the Christian as a being-on-the-way, a person in the fellowship of a
pilgrim community of faith, precludes any notion that theological reflection
should become fixed or static. At best, it serves as the dynamic motivation for doing what is right in obedience to the will of God in history -
orthopraxis is the primary theological objective. (47) Fresh historical
experiences will always require men of faith to re-evaluate their faith
if they are to hear the living call from the God who keeps on calling.
The writer of the Letter to the Hebrews reminds us that the Word of
God is "living and active" - our response to that Word must always
be living and active.

Christians throughout the Third World have been attempting to re-inter-
pret their theological modes of reflection in the light of their historical
situation. We need to focus on the Caribbean now in search of appropriate theological paths, arising out of the Caribbean experience, by
means of which we may interpret Christian social praxis as the sign of
God's creative, redemptive and sustaining love.

Chapter V

THEOLOGICAL PATHS FOR THE CARIBBEAN

"Men do not build themselves a
new world out of the fruits of the
earth, as vulgar superstition believes,
but out of the historical accomplishments of their declining civilization.
They must, in the course of their development, begin by themselves producing the
material conditions of a new society,
and no effort of mind or will can free
them from this destiny". (1)

These words of Karl Marx provide a useful indication of our main focus
in this chapter. The radical changes that are required for the determined
growth of a new Caribbean society must begin with 'historical accomplishments' rather than with untested theories. Every society is largely a
product of its own history and the development of new forms of social
interaction must be conditioned by those which have been experienced
already. The search for a new society is, for the Christian, a major
theological concern, and, within the context of the Caribbean socio-
historical experience, appropriate theological paths must be identified.

The use of the image of "paths" in this chapter is in keeping with the
discussion which is to follow, since we are to examine the elements of
the human experience in the Caribbean in our search for a new and more
appropriate way of doing theology. Paths are by their very nature guiding
routes through an un-defined area or environment, and they are usually
constructed by a series of clues and signals linked closely enough to
assure the traveller of the possibility of reaching the destination desired.
Further, paths generally result out of the human activity of travel, and
they provide assistance to humanity in the common pilgrimage and search
for new experiences and new places. The theological paths with which
we are concerned therefore must arise out of the experiences of the
people, the pilgrim people of the Caribbean who are engaged in a movement of change as well as a search for new ways of making a response
of faith to reality. We need to look further at the question of the need
for theological paths.

The need for theological paths

The following quotation from a group of Christians, although somewhat
lengthy, points to the need for theological paths which are suitable for
the experiences of specific people in specific circumstances -

102

> "The involvement of the Church and of churches
> in struggles for self-reliance, social justice
> and economic growth in the Third World must
> be based on critically examined motiva-
> tions and clear guiding principles. A vaque
> moralism that confuses assuaging guilt,
> with seeking justice or platitudinous
> preaching to others with solidarity is not
> merely not enough, it is not even a start.
> The value of simpler life-styles lies in
> escape from domination by material objects,
> not in any purely ritual imitation of poverty.
> It is necessary to seek a coherent integra-
> tion of Christian thought and theology with
> social action, not to treat the action as a
> vaguely meritorious or even obligatory but
> largely unrelated addition to thought and
> theology". (2)

The passage just quoted points to a serious gap in the theological traditions of the West, a gap which has often been the result of the way in
which theological reflection has been pursued. It has been caused by
the failure of preachers and teachers to seek for that dynamic interaction between human action in a given society and the totality of Christian thought. A theology which does not emanate from the actual situation
of a living community can hardly fulfill the requirements of that community for meaningful critical reflection, and for guides to action for
the response of faith. Theologies from some cultural situations, with
'historical accomplishments' peculiar to themselves, serve to provide
useful clues about how theology might profitably be done in other
situations, but they should not become unquestioningly the theologies
of the latter.

Several Third World theologians have outlined the need for appropriate
theological paths for their respective cultural areas, and they have
pointed to the fact that Western theology is not in all respects applicable
to non-Western areas. Koyama has called for a more appropriate
framework for doing theology in Asia; he calls for a "hot theology" for
Asia, since Western theology is a "cool theology" and does not really
fit the Asian cultural context. (3) Assmann makes similar claims for
Latin America. (4) Mbiti, writing from the African standpoint, insists
that theological sources must be drawn from the place and time in which
the Church lives. (5)

It is not only that Western theology is not totally qualified for meaningful
service in the Third World, but that within the Third World as well
systems of theology are not easily transferrable. The fact that there
are black Africans in southern Africa who derive religious meaning
and motivation from African Liberation Theology does not mean that

theirs is a suitable mode of critical reflection for Afro-Caribbeans or Afro-Americans, in spite of their identical ethnic roots. Similarly, the Liberation Theology of Latin America arises out of a historical and socio-economic situation that differs substantially from that of the people of the French Antilles - Martinique, Guadeloupe and Cayenne - in spite of the long dominance of Roman Catholicism in both regions. The search for theological paths has to be conducted within the socio-cultural context of the particular area, and as an exercise in which a broad spectrum of the community of faith is involved. It has to reflect the needs of the people for levels of interpretation in ordinary life which can underscore their basic needs for survival and development. Several writers in the Caribbean have suggested some directions for such a search in the region.

Survey of the search for Caribbean theological paths

There has been a general call for a new theological method in the Caribbean. Our discussion here can only point to a few of the more significant voices that have been raised in this connection. William Watty has called for the decolonization of theology in the Caribbean since, in his view, theology communicated in the colonial era was but a reflection of the colonial experience. Watty said, "What Christians thought about God could not be separated from what they thought about colonies". (6) He suggested that theology would be a superfluous element in human thought if it did not provide a people, in their actual situation, with an authentic and inspiring perspective and self-evaluation. Thus theology in the Caribbean needed to return to Caribbean history in order to "recover its vitality and relevance for ordinary people as well as for theologians". (7) Idris Hamid has also called for the decolonization of theology, and has suggested that it is not so much a metaphysical or reflective task as it is one about praxis - it is concerned with what the Church does and how it lives. Hamid refers to the decolonization process as something which God is doing, in his work of liberation, and of which he is calling on Caribbean people to take note. (8)

Robert Moore has shown that the Caribbean society has historically passed through two theological phases. The first was through the "theology of imposition", a process of remodelling men in accordance with the following re-working of a biblical passage: "Except he be born again he cannot enter into the Kingdom of God or the Kingdom of Europe". (9) The second phase was the "theology of imitation" which was the reaction of colonials to the "theology of imposition", and which was void of any creativity, historical sensitivity or relative assumptions. Moore has therefore called for a "theology of exploration" to be the main task of Caribbean theology - a process of interaction between God and Caribbean humanity and the Caribbean environment. Such exploration calls for a close acquaintance with the forces which have given, and continue to give, the Caribbean environment its peculiar structure. (10)

Horace Russell has briefly outlined some of the challenges which, in his view, are inescapable in any serious attempt at theological reflection in the Caribbean. (11) Among other things, he refers to Caribbean history, Caribbean anthropology and sociology, and the Caribbean 'calypso-mentality' as starting-points for appropriate theological reflection. Canon William Thompson has called on the Church in the Caribbean "to engage in the process of reconstructing its theology in a systematic and deliberate way". (12) He suggests that its new goal has to be the discovery of God as "relationship-in-community" in the actual Caribbean situation, that its content has to be "supplied by the Bible and existent societal conditions", and that its context must be found within the Church as the "Spirit-directed" community in the Caribbean. (13) Thompson is careful to point out that the Church is the context in which theological reconstruction begins, but he is not so careful to say where it leads, or if it does end up anywhere - for he speaks of the "provisional and transitory" nature of the theological enterprise that is limited to those who belong to the community of faith. He says that the three bases for reconstruction should be "the nature of God, the nature of man, and the nature of the World in the light of the Christ-event". (14)

Luis Rivera suggests a minimal framework within which a Caribbean theology of liberation might be constructed. He states that the basic goal should be to forge a "new perspective on the meaning of the whole biblical Gospel for the Caribbean peoples", and that a liberation theology is an appropriate theology for the Caribbean. He suggests that it should emerge out of the participation of Caribbean Christians in the struggle for human emancipation, and that such a liberation theology must have a witnessing character - it should witness "to the deep and profound sufferings which form part and parcel of" the struggle for human liberation, "and to the resistances offered by the oppressive forces to the emancipatory process". (15) Rivera goes on to point out that the proper methodological approach should be that of "the dialectical relationship between biblical exegesis, practico-political engagement and social analysis," and he discusses the relevance of the Marxist approach. (16)

Kenrick Khan, a Guyanese pastor and theologian now living in the United States of America, has suggested that a new Caribbean hermeneutic should pay close attention to the fundamentals of a theology of hope. He suggests that "a theology of promise in action" might be an appropriate way of relating the social and historical experience in the Caribbean to the basic christian faith in God's work of implementing what he has promised. (17)

The preceding discussion on what some Caribbean scholars have been advocating has consistently revealed a concern for methodology among their primary interests. This in itself must be considered as a necessary startingpoint. The question of how one does something is always crucial to the clearer perception of w h a t one wants to do. For the Caribbean theological scenario, the realization that it is possible to do theology in a new way is a significant historical break-through and should not be underestimated. It constitutes the beginning of the liberation of theology in the Caribbean.

The methodological quest among Caribbean scholars is therefore a significant wind of change, but it does not go far enough in the real search for theological paths and Christian praxis in the Caribbean experience. The search for theological praxis involves the clear identification of an implicit or tentatively theological inclination by the people; it involves in fact the search for a theology already engaged in by the people. The search is fundamentally conditioned by the type of questions which one asks. These questions must include the following: How did the people come to experience God in their lives? How did they know that it was God, when the oppressive and dehumanizing systems which they experienced also claimed divine support? What were the ways in which they chose to establish real and fulfilling relationships with God, if their institutionalized religious systems were so unfulfilling and restrictive? What was the connection between mass culture and mass theology in the daily experiences of the people? If these were integrated, how did they pass them on in an integrated fashion to their offspring? What are the marks of genuine theological praxis today in the light of what Caribbean people have already achieved, and in the light of what they are working towards? All of these questions open up a wide scope for enquiry.

Hamid complained that in the theological traditions in the Caribbean which were introduced and sustained by the missionaries, God was an alien. His famous words are -

> "God is really foreign to us. In the religious
> imagination of our people he is a benign
> white foreigner - 'an expatriate'. Even
> the categories of our religious experiences
> are imports which do not reflect our cul-
> tural and native experiences. We exper-
> ience God as an outsider in the bad sense
> of that encounter. He is not the God in
> our history and of our destiny. He
> has not been the God for us, but against us". (18)

This was Hamid's graphic way of articulating the historical fact that in the Caribbean the God who was presented to the people (and there-fore Christianity itself) was not identifiable with the living experiences of the people themselves. There was never any talk of the God of Israel, said Hamid, who when bargaining failed in Egypt "walked off the bargaining table and set his people free!"(19) He was hardly presented as the God who broke the yoke of oppression - "the God of the Bible has been hidden from our eyes". (20)

It is in the face of all this adverse history of theology in the Caribbean, said Hamid, that we must recognize that those who defied and cheated the systems that oppressed them were acting in real faith, even though "their authentic response to God was not recognized as obedience". Hamid therefore suggested that we need to look at, and examine, the many 'non-Church' ways through which the reality of God was "communicated, experienced and expressed among the people". (21) Hamid further commented, "It would seem that God had to do a lot of his work underground". (22) He said that God worked in and through the cultural fragments that were there among the oppressed, "he was present more in the canefields than in the cathedrals, more in the baracoons than in the basilicas". (23) So Hamid pointed to the need for an appropriate theological approach in the Caribbean that will "uncover the ways in which this God was understood and experienced", for it is in this way we could discover that an indigenous theology was at work in the Caribbean. The Caribbean people never believed all that the official Churches told them, Hamid claimed, "they used what they could, they fell back to what they had, and in many ways worked out their own salvation views". (24)

We have seen that all the Caribbean theologians to whom we referred tend to the view that theological paths for the Caribbean must be discovered out of the experiences of the people themselves. Their history, sociology and political life provide the broad framework out of which the need to do theology must be recognized. Caribbean theology must attempt to interpret clearly and positively the religious experience of Caribbean people - but it is not a task for so-called theologians alone. The "babes and sucklings" also express their religious encounters in mass movements. We need to pay some attention to these as well.

In some places there have arisen native responses in mass religious movements. Two such movements are Vodun in Haiti, and Rastafarianism in Jamaica. Although neither of these has been revolutionary enough to effectively confront and challenge the status quo, they both illustrate the possibilities for popular indigenous religious expression.

Popular Caribbean religious movements

The Vodun cult in Haiti dates back to the days of eighteenth century slavery, and was the result of a merger of African, Islamic and Catholic religions and cultural elements during the period 1750-1790. (25) It emerged as a powerful ceremony to weld the slaves together, in spite of the Code Noir which forbade the assembly of slaves. Most ceremonies therefore were at first held at nights. The ceremonies have basically remained the same since the early nineteenth century, consisting mainly of the invocation of deities, dancing, singing, fainting, and nervous excitement brought on by frenzied behaviour. The essential factor of the Vodun cult is the possession of the worshipper by the loas - the deity -

some of which are African tribal gods. In the Plaisance area of Haiti, George Simpson (whose research in this subject has been of an invaluable assistance to many students) collected a list of 152 loas, in which 57 were of Haitian origin, 16 were names of Catholic saints, and approximately 60 had African connections, the other 19 were of unknown origin. (26) The Vodunists believe that the loas have to be placated, since most loas are both good and bad, so that if one is punctillious about offerings and ceremonies the loas will be generous and lenient. Most of the worshippers think of their relationship with their loas as being contractual. Neglect of one's duty to one's loa is punished by sickness, crop failure, misfortune or even death. Most Vodunists are also Catholics, and although they acknowledge the omnipotence and supremacy of the Catholic God, they believe that God allows the practice of their cult if they are conscientious about their Catholicism. But they cannot afford to neglect their Vodun, since the penalties are very severe. The dead are second in rank to the loas, especially in Northern Haiti, they take a keen interest in the affairs of the world, and they either favour or destroy its inhabitants. Yet the belief in the reality and force (for good or ill) of 'zombies', 'diablesses' and 'lutins' - the spirits of dead human beings - is not peculiar either to Vodun or Haiti. It is common throughout the Caribbean.

There can be little doubt that the Vodun cult contributes substantially to the perpetuation of folk culture - its mores and taboos - among the poor and depressed peasants of rural Haiti. They exist on the bare fringes of life, and are constantly at the mercy of drought, disease and disaster - factors entirely beyond their control, factors which require them to honour, propitiate and thank those who live in the other world. As a social phenomenon, Vodun provides the main cultural device through which the poor peasant worshipper can release his/her agressive impulses, since socio-economic amelioration can hardly be expected. Simpson says, "Vodun ceremonies and magical acts perform, therefore, a mental hygiene function for the individual, and thereby contribute to preserving the status quo". (27) Vodun also provides a focus of recreation and social meeting, especially for hard-working peasants - opportunities for visiting, feasting, card-playing, story-telling, and dancing are provided. Further, Vodun helps to provide for its worshippers an explanation of the universe and their place in it, thus holding out to them some meaning and direction in life in an otherwise meaningless world. Finally, it must also be said that it is basically a cult for the poor working-class peasants who make up the overwhelming majority of Haitian society. The other classes embrace Catholicism and other status-giving sectors of Christianity. (28)

In Trinidad there is the Shango cult which represents a milder form of the Haitian Vodun. (29) Simpson suggests that participation in the Shango is not to be regarded as an escape from reality, since Shangoists regard their cult as one aspect of reality. There is no attempt to bring about social, economic and political changes. Simpson goes on to explain that "the emotional release from accumulated frustration obtained from Shango activity reduces the amount of fervor available for political activity". (30) The Shango cult therefore does nothing to challenge the perpetuation of the status quo.

The other important grouping is Rastafarianism in Jamaica. The phenomenon of millenarian movements requires some brief attention however, before we deal with the Rastafarian movement itself, for Rastafarianism is essentially a millenarian cult. Several scholars have investigated quite extensively the rise of millenarian (or messianic) movements throughout the course of history. (31) Norman Cohn, for example, made a study of millenarian movements in Europe during the Middle Ages. (32) He concluded that such movements always looked towards a moment of salvation, and that, for them, salvation would be collective, terrestrial (being realized on earth), imminent, total (utterly transforming life on earth to a perfect state), and miraculous. Cohn noted that such movements generally attracted unorganized people on the margin of society, unskilled workers, beggars and vagabonds - "the amorphous mass of people who were not simply poor but who could find no assured and recognized place in society at all". (33) Cohn says that such people were alienated from the Church, and suffered from their alienation, for "to be uncertain of the consolation and guidance and mediation of the Church aggravated their sense of helplessness and increased their desperation". (34) Cohn referred to such movements as "surrogates for the Church". (35)

Millenarian movements have sprung up all over the world - even Nazism and Communism have, in some instances, been interpreted as secular forms of millenary cult. The element of alienation is always present, but the "enemy" is differently pictured in different ages and in different countries. The common characteristic of such movements is usually a general resentment of an under-privileged class against those who hold power, status and authority. In many instances the latter are aliens in the society (or, at least, are regarded as such). The movements are generally concerned with questions of domination and dependence, and spring from sections of society where it is difficult to make their wishes felt, or their constitutional voices heard. In many cases they do not fully understand the processes of politics or of government, except that they know them to be working against their wishes and interests. Such people have no other means of communicating their feelings but in religious terms. They are therefore passionately in search of change, in search of a new redemptive process, a new socio-political framework, a new mode of integrity and social status - in fact, millenarian movements make the struggle for an entirely new community their basic objective. The ideals of this new community may not always be achievable within the socio-political circumstances with which they are most familiar, thus there is often an element of escape or separatism built into their language, behaviour, and socio-religious patterns. Some even attempt to escape from fighting to bring about change and improvement, since

109

they consider their new community to be beyond the boundaries of history and geography. Lanternari describes such movements as innovative, popular, and revolutionary, "new and able to renew, because they are spurred by the urgent and vital needs of oppressed people and societies caught in a dilemma, they look to the future and to the regeneration of the world". (36) Like the Cargo cults in the Pacific, and the Kimbanguist movement in the Congo, the Rastafarians are the Jamaican expression of millenary religion in the Caribbean.

The Rastafarian movement started in Jamaica in 1930, soon after the coronation of Ras Tafari - Haile Selassie - as Emperor of Ethiopia. Haile Selassie believed himself to be the only true lineal descendant of King David, and also the 225th of a line of Ethiopian kings stretching back to the Queen of Sheba. Jamaica was at that time in the throes of a severe economic depression, social conditions among the masses were miserable and the prospects for better days were nowhere in sight. Between 1930 and 1934 some Jamaicans who had returned from overseas - principally Leonard Howell and H.D. Dunkley from New York, and J.N. Hibbert from Costa Rica - began to preach that Haile Selassie was the returned Messiah, that there was Biblical support for this belief in Revelation 5: 2, 3, 5; and that the only hope of liberation for the black man in Jamaica was to return to Africa.

There had also sprung up in Jamaica about this time a secular group working for social improvement along the lines promulgated by Marcus Garvey. (37) The two groups combined their operations in 1934, and thus created a strong social movement among a substantial minority of the Jamaican working class - many of whom were out of work anyway. The early tenets of the movement included the belief in the superiority of the black race, the necessity to hate the white race because it was oppressive and evil, and the negation of the government and all other social and legal institutions. Over the past 40 years the Rastafarian movement has encountered many conflicts with the Establishment, and has undergone several changes as a socio-religious grouping because of its basic renunciation of Jamaican society as it is constituted (they call it 'Babylon'), and because of its predilection for various forms of a-typical social behaviour (including the use of marijuana). Barrett says, "their defiance of the society was admired by many who secretly felt the urge to do the same, but had not the boldness to exhibit their feelings". (38)

What do the Rastafarians believe today? A Jesuit priest, Fr. Joseph Owens, has conducted a very careful study of the Rastafarians in Jamaica (since it must be noted that there are now Rastafarian groupings in England, Canada, the United States and other Caribbean islands). His review of their beliefs is most helpful for our understanding of the movement. Owens is of the view that the Rastafarian movement challenges traditional Christianity in that it has already "decolonized much of the theology that they have received and have recast it into terms which reveal the

110

liberating and saving message of the gospel". (39) He notes that they
are preaching a message of hope and salvation "to people who are
estranged from or even antagonistic to the Churches. They are the
only ones making any sense to the thousands of young men who are
relatively uneducated, quite jobless, and completely left adrift in
society". (40) The principal Rastafarian doctrines are: -

(i)   God is man and man is God, though Haile Selassie is eminently
        divine.
(ii)   God is at work chiefly in the events of history.
(iii)   Life is a journey - a pilgrimage to the promised land, Ethiopia.
(iv)   Life is supreme and unending - the faithful man never dies.
(v)   The Word is the manifestation of divine presence and power.
(vi)   God's judgement on the wicked world is imminent.
(vii)   Sin has corporate dimensions - God's judgement is on nations,
        corporations, races.
(viii) Nature is sacred and sacramental.
(ix)   Rastafarians are God's chosen people, God's prophets who suffer
        for God's sake. (41)

Such a system of belief as has just been outlined is clearly reminiscent
of the Old Testament religion of the Jews, and of the earlier conceptions
of God (Yahweh). Rastafarians refer to God as JAH. It should not be
overlooked however, that in this system of belief no place is given to
the significance of the life and death of Jesus Christ. The absence of
this crucial factor makes it difficult for Christians to find a basic
working harmony with the tenets of the Rastafarian belief. Rastafarians
explain however that the Christ who is preached by the Establishment
has no liberating power for them - he is a white Christ, the incarnation
of the white man's God. Haile Selassie is the incarnation of divine
reality - but they do not go so far as to say that he assumes the place
of Christ.

The fact that their religious belief is interwoven with their cultural,
political and economic life-styles marks out the Rastafarians as a
significant religious movement in Jamaica. Their religious functions
answer the needs of many lower class Jamaicans "who would be completely out of place in the orthodox churches of the island". (42) Their
constant cry that the Jamaican situation is a hopeless hell, and that
Ethiopia is heaven, constitutes a prophetic stance which gives the
movement much vitality. In more recent times some Rastafarians
have modified their traditional position by establishing a branch of
the Ethiopian Orthodox Church in Jamaica, by becoming more closely
allied to the established Churches through the recent admission of
their Church into the Caribbean Conference of Churches, and by insisting
that Rastafarianism is more a religion of the heart - an inward treas-
uring of peace and love for all men. At the beginning of the 1970's
Rex Nettleford (whose acquaintance with Jamaican Rastafarians is not
inconsiderable) observed that -

> "the extreme claims by the Rastafari have
> been tempered with common sense and partly
> with the passage of time but largely on
> account of the practical measures that have
> been taken to meet some of their demands
> and by growing tolerance and greater under-
> standing in the society at large". (43)

Indeed Rastafarian songs and phrases now command popular usage in Caribbean society. Bob Marley blazed a new trail.

Within the broad spectrum of Caribbean religious expressions, Vodun and Rastafarianism represent two movements of the people which are significant for several reasons. First, they both constitute responses to reality as it is experienced by people in their daily lives. Secondly, they represent a re-interpretation of the role and function of Christianity in the lives of a people, as well as a cultural re-working of traditional Christian elements in the Caribbean. Thirdly, they both provide a system of meaning and a sense of direction in life for a people whose hope for better days shows no possibility of being immediately realized. Fourthly, both lay a strong emphasis on the centrality of liberation as the human need. Fifthly, both attract lower class and oppressed persons, in the main, and suggest that traditional Christianity is not considered adequate to express their needs for appropriate channels of religious response. Sixthly, both bring forward into the present the African roots of the people's past. This African connection can be of added significance when it is recognized that the Biblical record itself attests that Yahweh was first encountered by Moses in Midian, on African soil (Exodus 3).

There are, however, some considerations which would seem to indicate that these movements, although they represent the systematic expressions of the religious experience of some Caribbean people, do not provide us with an adequate framework for identifying appropriate theological paths in the Caribbean experience. First, they fail to place the emphasis on engagement in society, and rather encourage separation, withdrawal and escape. Secondly, they do not provide a comprehensive framework through which we might respond to the polyglot cultural mixture that is so real in Caribbean society. Thirdly, they do not provide a wide basis for the concrete interpretation of the Christian belief in God's revelation of himself through Christ and the world. Fourthly, the fundamental Christian concern for reconciliation in all its socio-historical dimensions poses great problems for these movements. Fifthly, they lack a basic religious element which enables man to acknowledge that hope and fulfillment must still be grounded in the complex realities of the total human experience.

Nevertheless, the existence of both religious movements in Caribbean society is a clear indication that there are many people in the region for whom Christianity, as it has been proclaimed and practised, has been less than meaningful, that the socio-cultural and economic connections of traditional Christianity in the Caribbean are in some instances quite alienating, and that the search for meaning and direction in life is just as real for the poor and the oppressed as it is for the rich and the rest. What then are the starting-points for a people's theology for the Caribbean? Where should we begin our search for theological paths? Several preliminary points must be taken into account.

First, the search for a theology of the people in the Caribbean involves an exploration into the identity of a largely ancestorless people. Caribbean people are essentially a New World people, cut off from their roots in Africa and India, ignorant of their line of ancestry, and partially void of their original and authentic heritage of oral and other cultural traditions usually handed down systematically from generation to generation. Caribbean people of today are more the ancestors of the future generations than they are the descendants of a line of ancestry. The systems of slavery and indentureship created such a discontinuity in the Caribbean human tradition, that it is possible to state that Caribbean people today are the foundation of a new ancestral tradition now that the threat to survival has virtually receded.

Secondly, the reality of the experience of human sub-ordination in slavery, indentureship and colonialism must inform such a search with insights of the dangers and disadvantages of certain personal relationships and social structures. It would be a grave mistake to assume that the historical traditions of Caribbean society did not significantly determine the human and social relationships in contemporary society. While these traditions should not be used as points of explanation or reference for every contemporary human situation, they should certainly form the starting-point for a better understanding of contemporary issues such as race, class, status, human initiative and family patterns. All these issues touch the human experience in the Caribbean in a way which theological reflection cannot afford to ignore.

Thirdly, the search for a people's theology has to be concerned with the dynamic tensions in the human experience between pain and possibility, integration and alienation, wholeness and breakdown, constant loss and survival, the continuing imminence of death and the capacity for regeneration. This point is of the utmost importance for it signifies what has been the underlying tension within the human experience in the Caribbean. They have had to do battle continually with the reality of frustration in all its dimensions, while holding on to any straw of hope that there might still be some truth in the saying that "out of evil comes good". To be continuously on the losing side in social, economic and political terms was bad enough, but to be also on the losing side in attempts to assert their very humanity evoked from Caribbean people a spirit of resilience and determination for survival that can only be explained in terms of that dynamic tension of which we are speaking.

Fourthly, the search must recognize the unmistakable and continuing acknowledgement of an assurance of the presence of God among Caribbean people. The question of the existence of God, or non-existence, is not an issue for Caribbean people, for it is that God who has been experienced as being on their side in all their situations. Such an acknowledged assurance arises out of the rigours of their oppression, depression and degradation, and their experience of a God who miraculously provides for, and protects, them is entirely beyond question. That such a God should demand continuous commitment and allegiance is never in doubt either, for at the deepest level of their response Caribbean people remain grateful to this God who is the main source of their hope, survival, and human strength. Religious experience and gratitude to God are basic to the understanding of the Caribbean human commitment.

Fifthly, a theology of the people in the Caribbean must motivate them towards engagement in creative action in community. It must inspire them to work relentlessly towards the emergence of such structures as would reflect in their historical existence their deepest commitment to God and to each other. This means that it must be a collective effort of critical reflection, devoid of individualistic piety that engenders spiritual competition and socio-religious stratifications. It must arise out of their actual historical experience in such a way that it motivates them to affect the course of history together, towards the greater realization of what the God of their experience wills for their social existence.

Finally, the search is for a narrative theology, a religious story that integrates their belief with their experiences for others to hear, and feel, and remember. Caribbean people often theologize in the spoken word, in movement, in communal relationships - their total engagement with the history and environment provides the main clues to what is basic for their belief and praxis. Religion and feeling go together. We turn therefore to an examination of the Caribbean human experience.

The Caribbean experience and the search for paths

In our survey of the social, political and economic realities in the first chapter, we saw that the Caribbean experience was characterized by structures of Poverty, Dependence and Alienation. We also indicated that in spite of the persistence of these structures Caribbean people had always exhibited a determined capacity to survive. Within those structures the business of living in the Caribbean has been a struggle of no mean proportions, and only those who have been born and reared in that situation, can testify to the dynamics of the inner realities of Caribbean existence. One of the sayings which Caribbean mothers pass on to their children goes like this: "Only those who feel it know it". Perhaps the saying itself is not original, or peculiar, to the Caribbean experience, but it has traditionally been used by parents and others to affirm that what they experience is not an illusion, it is real, and only they themselves can really tell what it is like. Thus the Caribbean realities we are about to discuss are the fragments of human experience which point beyond themselves to an inner world, a world that is the foundation of human response to social reality, and one that is unmoved even by the threatening structures to which we have referred. Its existence cannot be denied since the very nature of Caribbean existence, as experienced by Caribbean people themselves, is an indication of this inner vitality.

A group of Churchmen in the Caribbean, meeting in January 1975 to discuss the mission of the Church in the region, agreed that the basic mission of the Church was to proclaim the Good News of the Kingdom of God. The Churchmen went on to say that "in the Caribbean context this means the liberation of God's people to respond to Caribbean realities. In this confrontation a new Caribbean man will evolve and a new society and a new social life-style will develope.(44) Two points are worthy of note here. First, the Caribbean Churchmen recognized that actual response to Caribbean realities was essentially a 'confrontation' - the structures to be faced were basically dehumanizing, oppressive, and generally unacceptable to Caribbean people as they thought of themselves. Conflict was therefore inevitable since the human reality of the Caribbean experience was anti-thetical to the structural reality. Secondly, the Churchmen pointed to the possibility of the emergence of new realities, the annunciation of the 'new Caribbean man' as a result of the renunciation of inherited structures. The dialectical experience of the pain of the old and the possibility of the new is central to human reality in the Caribbean. What follows therefore is a description of some of the fragments of that human experience as an illustration of the extent to which Caribbean people are themselves engaged in this confrontation with poverty, dependence and alienation.

One of the constant sources of amusement for West Indians living in Britain is for them to encounter Britons who genuinely believe that all West Indians come from Jamaica. This is particularly striking to the West Indians in Britain when they witness the extent to which persons born on the same land mass are at pains to assert that they are Welsh and not English, Scottish and not Welsh. For the West Indian, England, Scotland and Wales are but sections of one large island, while Antigua is a whole island, different and distant from Carriacou, or Jamaica, or Trinidad, or Martinique. Thus the Caribbean is a group of islands and continental land masses, grouped by common interests and history, but including a varied mixture of cultures, races, and languages which are very distinct. The islandic mentality of the majority of Caribbean people gives them a particular orientation which sometimes proves to be advantageous, while at other times it works in the opposite direction. Accidents of places of birth have real effect on the Caribbean mind,

more especially in the aftermath of political sovereignty, but they do
not negate the basic sense of belonging to the region as a whole. Such
a sense, oddly enough, flourishes effectively in alien contexts like
Britain and North America, where West Indians from various islands
live together. The continuity of a s e n s e o f b e l o n g i n g in the face
of ethnic and geographical plurality and diversity is a basic factor of
the Caribbean human experience. The idea of going back to Africa is
sometimes used as an anti-thesis to this sense of belonging, but
Louise Bennett, in a poem "Back to Africa" written in Jamaican dialect
shows that the mixed ancestry of African, English, French and Jewish
makes Africa an oddity as a homeland as such. She ends her poem with
these lines -

> "Go a foreign, seek yuh fortune,
> But no tell nobody sey
> Yuh dah go fe seek yuh homelan
> For a right deh so yuh deh!"(45)

The depressing conditions under which most Caribbean people live cry
out continually for amelioration and change, and they are under no
illusions about the harsh and awful realities of hunger, deprivation and
limited possibilities for a better life. Nevertheless it is significant
that these conditions are not generally blamed on the historical past of
slavery and indentureship. Instead, slavery and indentureship are regarded as Red Sea experience (using the Exodus motif), and there is a
tremendous sense of p r i d e o f s u r v i v a l because of them. The
stories which grand-parents tell their off-spring about their experiences
on the plantations, and those of their own elders, are usually related
to the underlying theme: "we have past the worst, better days are
coming". The poem by E. M. Roach "March trades" speaks to this determination of the Caribbean person to turn the rigours of Caribbean
history into a certain future. Roach's poem issues this call -

> "Jagged lightnings dart/Thunders roll and roar
> Under close cloud ceilings/While barometers lower
> Let all be girt/In sinew, heart and spirit
> To take the buffet/And to prosper in it. "(46)

Thus actual poverty is not a curse for Caribbean people, nor even a
threat to life, but rather a motivation to survive and to work for change.

One of the consequences of the acknowledgement of their poverty by
Caribbean people is the general acceptance of a f u t u r e o f r e l a t i v e
p o v e r t y for the Caribbean. In this respect, they adopt a realistic
approach to the possibilities for economic development at home because of the severe limitations of resources and opportunities. They
also recognize the possibilities for greater material advancement
abroad in the metropolitan centres. Caribbean people therefore tend
to be migratory - in search of making a living - but the dream of
returning home is always real for most of them. In the Caribbean it-

self, the operative phrase is: "You can't make blood out of stone" -
this sums up the kernel of their own concept of development, in which
the ability to do better than before is the measure of growth, even if
that 'better' is still relatively far behind what is possible elsewhere.
The rigours of poverty must be fought in the Caribbean, and it would
be misleading to suggest that there is a pervasive attitude of complacency and tacit acceptance of their condition on the part of Caribbean people. The point is that they do not allow it to get the better of
them, hopelessness is hardly ever an element of their human condition,
however hopeless that condition might appear to be. The frequency
with which one hears the poor and unemployed exclaim: "God nuh going
mek me starve" is constant indication of living hope in the midst of
real poverty. (47)

Several Caribbean writers have suggested that there is a sense of void
and nothingness which characterizes the Caribbean person's self-under-
standing. Leading writers like V.S. Naipaul, Derek Walcott, Orlando
Patterson and John Hearne have described the rootless past of Caribbean personhood in very severe terms. (48) Take for example Orlando
Patterson's 'Blackman' in An Absence Of Ruins who, when
he is questioned about his identity and his destiny by a citizen in London
who challenges his 'savage' appearance although dressed up like the
English, replies -

> "I come from nowhere worth mentioning. I
> have no past except the haunting recollec-
> tion of each passing moment which comes to
> me always as something having lost. My
> ancestors, if they existed, left no record
> of themselves; I
> cannot say whether I am civilised or savage,
> standing as I do outside of race, outside
> of culture, outside of history, outside
> of any value that could make your question
> meaningful. I am busy going nowhere, but
> I must keep up the appearance of going
> in order to forget that I am not". (49)

Such a devastating and despairing caricature of the Caribbean personality
is not uncommon among writers who have had occasion to question their
own identity and pedigree in other societies that are alien, hostile, and
basically white. Unfortunately, most of the Caribbean novelists and
poets have had to earn their living abroad, principally in Britain. The
deep inner conflicts are always coming to the surface in their writings.
George Lamming points to -

> "Those who start life without a beginning
> Must always always recall their crumbling
> foundations. "(50)

Although no one could deny that slavery and indentureship were dehumanizing systems, nor could they deny that the humanity of Caribbean people was continuously in doubt, the crucial question is whether Caribbean people today deny their own humanity. The answer is a resounding NO. For Caribbean people their humanity has never been in doubt, even if their roots were shortened and tampered with by those who had the power and the will to do so. It is necessary to affirm therefore, that this sense of void and nothingness which comes through in the writings of several Caribbean artists is not the general experience of Caribbean people themselves. The present writer agrees with Dr. Gordon Rohlehr -

> "The greatest evidence of normalcy, and
> with it wholeness and capacity for depth
> in the Caribbean peoples, lies in the
> fact that the Oral Traditions have
> persisted in song, performance, preaching
> and rhetoric throughout the Archipelago". (51)

It is important to stress this point about the validity of the human consciousness in the Caribbean experience, since the search for a Caribbean theology is based upon the assumption that Caribbean personhood has never been questioned by God, and that this has been a fundamental feature of that abiding faith of Caribbean people themselves.

In contradistinction to this suggested sense of void in the Caribbean past, it is significant to note that one of the social sins in the Caribbean is the denial of one's past - particularly if one was born and brought up in poor, humble and rural/ghetto-like circumstances. A good example of the positive effects in professing humble origins with pride can usually be evidenced in the efforts of politicians to gain mass followings. It is generally the "man-from-among-the-people" in the Caribbean who is sure to get a hearing and a vote. Caribbean communities usually favour those who, having achieved wealth or fame, refuse to ignore their less-favoured elders and former companions.

Caribbean people have generally been resourceful in achieving what they have achieved with the limited means available to them. This resourcefulness has been in large measure due to the use of their wits in coping with difficulties of various kinds. There are those who would hold to the stereo-type Caribbean person as carefree, lazy, unproductive and unimaginative. For example, V.S. Naipaul (who was born and bred in the Caribbean) criticized his native region thus -

> "they will continue to be the half-made
> societies of a dependent people, the
> Third World's third world. They will
> forever consume; they will never create.
> They are without material resources;
> they will never develop the higher
> skills."(52)

118

Yet the tremendous capacity which Caribbean people generally have for making the little that they have go a long way is creativity in itself, and those who have known what it is to be constantly in want of the barest necessities of life also know the extent to which survival itself has been a creative struggle. The innate resourcefulness of Caribbean people gives them the strength to respond creatively to the limitations of Caribbean realities. Added to this is a pervasive spirit of sacrificial generosity and a willingness to share. Such virtues are generally known among poor and traditional societies, but the advance of modernization in the region has not significantly altered these human qualities. The logical corollary to such generosity is the desire to receive from others - this is often mistaken for a spirit of dependence; but when it is recognized that in many advanced countries the courage to receive is rapidly declining while the donor-mentality is fast becoming a symbol of superior status, it will be realized that gifts to those who are by nature cheerful givers are symbols of a caring humanity.

The distinct capacity of Caribbean people to adapt themselves to various cultural, socio-economic and ecological circumstances has sometimes been taken to mean that they lack a cultural identity of their own. The pluralistic nature of their society, and prevailing stratifications based on class and race, have rather created a cultural tendency for the Caribbean person. Adaptability therefore comes easier to him/her than to many other people from other cultures. The way in which Caribbean people have assimilated into North American, British, African and Latin American culture is strong proof of this capacity, and the fact that many of them have done well in terms of status - achievement (e.g. the late Lord Constantine in Britain) shows that they can achieve, if the opportunities are there. No one should underestimate the importance of cricket as the expression of the Caribbean potential - C.L.R. James has written extensively on this aspect of the Caribbean capacity. (53) Apart from sports and politics, the scope for achievement by the masses of Caribbean people is severely limited within the Caribbean itself, but the will to achieve is always present and it flourishes quite successfully in a wider context than the geographical entity of the Caribbean. This question of achievement is very significant and we shall return to it later in this discussion. (54)

Another important aspect of the Caribbean experience is the prevailing temperament of the people. They have an unmistakable love for simplicity and for that which is unambiguous. This is sometimes mistaken for a love of mediocrity and a preference for the lower levels of excellence. Their unsophisticated and simple life-styles render them uncomfortable with social pretence and the duplicities of more sophisticated social "graces". This love for the simple is coupled with a innate capacity to be frank, forthright and open in their social intercourse. Sometimes this frankness can be brutal, it often costs them something (if the person on the receiving end has the power to take reprisals and to victimize them), but they are generally quite unconvinced that life should be a choice of devious attitudes in which the verb "to have" is more valuable than the verb "to be". It is the courage to remain poor which releases in the Caribbean personality that determination to be straight-forward and frank. Because of this, they generally prefer to secure good and pleasant work situations with little remuneration, than to opt for a higher wage where strife and discontent are always in attendance. A favourite verse (from the Book of Proverbs) among Caribbean people is -

> "Better is a dry morsel with quiet
> than a house full of feasting with strife".

This is found in Proverbs 17:1, and there are similar themes in Proverbs 16:8 and 15:16.

In the Caribbean one often experiences the warmth of forgiveness and tolerance. This pervasive tendency to make allowances for human imperfections and weaknesses can only be explained by the existence of a strong sense of the nature and the value of humanity among the people. When it is realized that traditionally the whole social, economic and religious system was weighted heavily against the majority of the people because they were black, poor and 'illegitimate', the only explanation one can find for this strong sense of forgiveness comes out of the character of the people themselves.(55) Women are extremely tolerant and long-suffering with irresponsible and unfaithful male partners; the masses usually exhibit extreme tolerance even with obviously imperfect social leadership in the various institutions including the Church. Expressions of sympathy and concern are quite extensive among Caribbean communities, particularly in the rural areas. It is so easy to take such common-place gestures for granted, and to miss the importance of the fact that in such humane and gentle ways Caribbean people are really engaged in theological praxis. When the institutional Church excludes an unmarried mother from its fellowship, or refuses to hold a funeral service in its building for a man who in his life-time seldom went to Church, the community at large is often there to offer compensating warmth for the rejected mother and solidarity with the relatives of the deceased (who themselves might be regular church-goers) respectively. Which side God takes in such situations would be an interesting issue for debate.

Thus far, we have been illustrating fragments of Caribbean realities which have been evident from its geography and history, and from the manifestations of the typical personality. There is yet another dimension of the human experience which requires some inquiry - this has to do with human relationships and the manifestations of social interaction in the wider societies of the Caribbean: family, community living, Church relationships and general ideological tendencies.

The typical society in the Caribbean is matrifocal - the mother is the head of the family, and the children can often be fathered by one or more persons. The majority of the children in the Caribbean are born out of wedlock, and marriage (which was originally forbidden by law in Caribbean history, among the slaves) is generally acknowledged for its status-giving potential more than for its necessity for good family life. In the Caribbean human stability is still centred on the one-parent family, and the mother usually (sometimes the grand-mother) exercises authority in that family. The men tend to be more itinerant and irresponsible, and to seek for a multiplicity of ways in which to assert their virility and masculinity. Nevertheless such quests are always related to the basic underlying assumption that the females will be stable and less irresponsible. Within the family setting, how-ever, close, warm and affectionate relationships are generally ex-perienced, and the expressions of mutual care and responsibility be-tween elders and children (even in extended families) are the norm. It is within this very framework that Caribbean people exhibit a considerable amount of respect and care for their elders - chiefly in providing for their welfare and protecting their interests - and this aspect of life in the Caribbean underlines the deep consciousness of what it means to feel that one is really human.

There is also a very deep respect for community among Caribbean people, and this serves to regulate a good deal of their social behaviour. The power of gossip can always be felt, and choices of actions, re-lationships and life-styles are heavily determined by the force of what one can instinctively anticipate to hear by way of social comment. Some may regard this more as a fear of community than a respect, but when it is realized that most communities serve as protective environments for their members, the feeling of allegiance to that community hinges more on respect than on fear. In any case, the existence of certain social forces as deterrents against behaviour which the community, by consensus, would deem to be unwelcome is a very important factor in social life. For other factors are also important - dress, for ex-ample, is of valuable significance. Caribbean people love to wear fine and attractive clothes, as evidenced at weddings, funerals and Church-services. The importance of dress as one of the few avenues for self-expression and status in the society goes back to slave society, in which market-day (the one day-off for slaves) was the only occasion during the week when slaves could wear good clothes. The simplistic way of many clergymen in the Caribbean, who criticize their members for attending Church-services only to 'show off' their clothes, is to be strongly deplored. For if the Church provides an avenue through which poor, depressed and despised people can feel that they really are persons (distinguished by their attractive apparel), this should be regarded as a contribution to a process of humanization. The planters used the Church to subjugate the workers; if the workers use the Church to liberate themselves, what is wrong with that?

Caribbean life contains a substantial amount of movement and rhythm. Generally speaking, Caribbean people cannot stay quiet for long periods -

there is a spontaneity that marks them out as a distinctive people, and this is the measure of their gaiety, their constant wit and humour, their love for stories and story-telling, and their predilections for festivity. How such a temperament is nurtured and sustained within the structures of poverty, dependence and alienation is, in the final analysis, quite phenomenal. One of the historical "sins" of the Church in the Caribbean has been its refusal to give adequate recognition and acceptance to this basic fact of life in the Caribbean, which reaches its highest collective expression in celebrations at Carnival, and Christmas. It is the spirit of joy and the absence of bitterness which is carried over into their relationships with whites and other persons of different ethnic backgrounds. There are definite areas of suspicion and mistrust between Africans and Indians in Guyana and Trinidad, but these do not generally expose themselves in open rancour and bitterness. In spite of the terrors of the colonial rule, and all the debilitating relics which it has bequeathed to Caribbean society, Caribbean people as a whole display no bitterness or remorse even to the former overlords or to their heirs among the ruling classes. The proclamations of Black Power are peculiar to an articulate minority in the region, but even here the contradictions and ambiguities of those who take up its cause often overwhelm the consistency of their exercise. (56)

Like all other communities in the world, status is of considerable importance to Caribbean people, and this is usually accorded in relation to the types of occupation one pursues. What is more important however, is for Caribbean people to achieve a position of proximity to the status-holders, or even to claim affinity to them. Thus it is usual for a peasant family to discourage the children from pursuing a peasant career. The achievements of the children are usually appropriated to the self-consciousness of the parents and grand-parents. Status is important for the growing middle-class in the Caribbean. There can be little doubt that the whole Caribbean society aspires to be a middle-class society - and nothing should be said against such aspirations. Where the dilemma arises is in the search by the newly-arrived middle-class for new reference-points, in terms of their status, achievement goals and symbols and in despising "blue collar" work. It is here that imitative instincts are most powerfully to be seen, as the Caribbean middle-class appropriate to themselves mores and materials from metropolitan cultures, and question very seriously the value of those which are local. Tourism contributes to this process.

The majority of the Caribbean people generally pay more attention to the dictates of experience and natural wisdom than they do to theoretical formulations and book-knowledge. With the increase of educational opportunities it is reasonable to anticipate that in time the opposite will be the case. Nevertheless, a popular saying among Caribbean people - "Studiation beat Education" - gives a very precise indication of their preference for working out things for themselves rather than to submit to the guidance of those who would claim the authority of knowledge untested in their own peculiar circumstances.

Active Church-membership has traditionally played a very important part in the lives of Caribbean people. Children are baptized at a very early age, and Sunday Schools and other Church-related activities become an integral part of the process of growing up. The allegiance to the Church as an institution provides a means whereby the need to be known by the wider society can be met, the social benefits (quite considerable in most communities) can be guaranteed, and the status which it affords can be achieved. Their own religious perceptions are nurtured by their personal use fo the Bible - particularly such books as the Psalms, Proverbs, and the Gospels - and it is considered sacreligious to treat the physical Bible as any other book. For example, a tattered page which serves no more useful purpose is not usually discarded. The religious tendencies of the Caribbean people are carried forward into their ordinary daily lives as is evidenced for example by the frequency with which hymns and sacred songs are whistled and hummed, and by the use of scriptural quotations in conversations for guidance and references to life-principles. But in the midst of all this, it is important to point out that Caribbean people construct their own theological framework, interpret their own religious experiences in their own way, and carry on with the hard business of living according to that basis. The Church, as an institution, serves as a social manifestation to the fact that Caribbean people are by nature religious; but there is a large gap between official religion and actual religion as Caribbean people know it.

Finally, what about the ideological responses of the Caribbean people? How do they address themselves to the ideological superstructures which sustain the poverty, dependence and alienation of which we speak? The basic ideological response is that change is both possible and desirable. Like all other places in the world, the Caribbean has its conflicts and tensions - integrally related to a web of social problems - which sometimes erupt into violence. Nevertheless, it would be true to say that violence is not often used by Caribbean people as an instrument of social protest and change. While it might be possible to argue that they find other ways for releasing their tension and aggressive instincts - dance, quarrels, noise - it is also true to say that Caribbean people opt for a non-violent approach to change and revolution. There are more subtle forms of effective change which can be instituted, chief among which is the gradual penetration of the structures. Caribbean people therefore opt for a gradualistic type of ideological approach to social change, in which the realities of their physical and material condition force them into a pragmatism which seeks to derive the best out of every situation. This is not to suggest that the voices in favour of socialist revolution are not strong, (in the light of the historical fact of Cuba) but it suggests that, on the whole, the people of the Caribbean are as pragmatic in their response to the realities of their physical situation as they are in their response to the God of their religious experience. For them, their culture is the principal carrier of their religion.

What then are the imperatives which these fragments of the Caribbean experience suggest? What basic clues do they provide for the search for appropriate theological paths? In what ways can we begin to identify the signs that God is at work among these realities? Perhaps the most fundamental clue lies in what C. L. R. James has said about the people of the Caribbean, and it serves as a telling commentary on the experience we have been outlining above. James says that the Caribbean people were brought here, and thrown here (in the Caribbean) and told SURVIVE!! And they have survived.(57) God has been in the middle of that survival experience, bringing them through struggle, conflict and pain to a gradual, yet fuller, realization of who they really were - his people - and who they were still to become. The focus then is that of ACHIEVEMENT and FULFILLMENT, and perhaps the most appropriate theological paths might consist of reflections on the religious nature of human conflict and survival, human possibility and divine fulfillment.

The dialectical interaction between conflict and survival, between possibility and fulfillment, has profound significance for our theological analysis since it embraces so much of the reality of the Caribbean human experience, and relates to dimensions of the past, the present and the future. A continuing central element in the Caribbean historical experience from slavery through the colonial period was that of r e s i s t a n c e. Caribbean people have historically developed the human mechanisms which have enabled them to resist quite effectively the dehumanizing structures and systems with which they have been encumbered. Had there been no resistance, the Caribbean experience would have been radically different today. Caribbean people have been able to maintain a distinctive cultural substream in the face of the dominant Creolization process in their history, mainly because of the continuing resistance mechanism which shaped their response to reality.(58) To recognize the rigours of the system was the measure of their conflict; to resist them as best they could was the primary cause of their survival. This capacity to resist has therefore been brought forward from their historical past.

One of the cardinal themes which runs through many of the proverbs and sayings which Caribbean elders pass on to their offspring is the importance of c a u t i o n and s e l f - c o n t a i n m e n t as a strategy for s u r v i v a l. The present writer recalls some of these sayings which were handed down orally from his Grand-mother (whose Grand-mother was herself a slave). A few example should suffice:

"No put yourself in a barrel when match-box can hol' you."
"No hang your cottacou where you can' reach it."
"See de candle light before you blow out de match."
"Wha' sweet a' mout' sometime hot a' belly."

124

It was through such wisdom sayings that Caribbean people learned the art of survival within a generally hostile and oppressive environment. Again, the present writer recalls being instructed by his mother to be careful not to imitate his better-off contemporaries since "their bread is already buttered on both sides," and that "when a man is poor even his very words are poor". The main pre-occupation of Caribbean existence has therefore been that of survival; and it is because they have effectively resisted the system over the years that Caribbean people have endured the conflict and mastered the art of survival so far.

Political independence has not changed much of the effect of the system as it relates to the poor and oppressed. The realities of domination and dependence, poverty and alienation, are still structured within the society. The fundamental issue of human rights in the region poses serious 'problems' for many national governments. Thus the need for confrontation and resistance is still very real, and in this neo-colonial period of Caribbean history the object of resistance is the combination of institutions and forces which deny Caribbean people the right to participate freely in the social, political and economic process.

Thus the concept of achievement and fulfillment takes up survival as the human destiny in the midst of conflict with the social system, and endues it with a new meaning of human possibility for achieving greater and more liberating levels of survival and existence. The religious fact consists of God's continuing presence with Caribbean poeple as they struggle not only with their will to survive and to discover new possibilities, but also to achieve such social experiences as would signify that God is fulfilling his will for them through such achievement. Human achievement and divine fulfillment are therefore interrelated in our process of theological reflection. By 'fulfillment', as divine activity, we mean the work of God in bringing into reality the hopes and aspirations of religious people which they have acknowledged to be divine promises. God always keeps his Word. It is this assurance of Faith that motivates Caribbean survival and Caribbean achievement. Fulfillment thus means that God's word and God's will for the poor and the oppressed "comes to pass" - as the fruit of his promise. Fulfillment means the realization of a new process of human liberating experience.

There is another familiar proverb in the Caribbean which says: "What man has done man can do". This has often been coupled with another familiar saying: "God helps those who help themselves". These sayings contain much of the meaning of the achievement/fulfillment motif with which we are dealing, since they take up the past and the present and provide a religious motivation for praxis - for orthopraxis which is future-oriented. The achievement/fulfillment motif rests on the success of the past, the consciousness of real survival at the present moment in spite of all the human odds which continue to produce adverse pressures, and the motivation to engage in praxis for human response

to the divine will and promise for the future. Within the dynamic interactions of human resistance, survival and achievement, and the historical manifestations of divine fulfillment therefore, it is possible
for us to identify a theological framework for reflection on Christian
praxis in the Caribbean. In our next chapter, therefore, we shall
attempt to identify such a framework through an examination of the
Biblical witness in the light of the Caribbean experience.

Chapter VI

CARIBBEAN THEOLOGICAL EXPLORATIONS

"It must be borne in mind that the
tragedy in life doesn't lie in not
reaching your goal. The tragedy lies
in having no goal to reach. It isn't
a calamity to die with dreams unful-
filled, but it is a calamity not to
dream. It is not a disaster to be unable
to capture your ideal, but it is a disaster
to have no ideal to capture. It is not
a disgrace not to reach the stars, but it is
a disgrace to have no stars to reach for.
Not failure, but low aim is sin".

(Benjamin E. Mays) (1)

The foregoing words of the great Black American Churchman, Dr.
Benjamin Mays - who was President of Morehouse College from 1940
to 1967 - provide a very useful summary of our concerns for Christian
orthopraxis in the Caribbean. The central motivation of the achievement/
fulfillment theme is that there must always be on the part of Caribbean
people the determination to aim high, to reach out, to pursue the dreams
of the new Caribbean personhood - and never to give up. All of this
must have a strong theological foundation, as we are about to outline
in this chapter.

The Bible provides the main source for our identification of a method
of theological interpretation in the Caribbean - the search for a theology
which arises out of the living experiences of the people of the region
as they respond to realities as they perceive them. Such a method of
interpretation begins with a conscious recognition that official theology
(and some academic theology as well) has been inadequate as a tool for
critical reflection by the people. Indeed, as Taber has suggested, there
are generally found three levels of theological understanding in the
Churches - (a) that which is held by the hierarchy; (b) that which is
pursued by the theologians in the academic world; (c) that which is
maintained by the people in the pew. (2) Our main task here, however,
is not to opt for any of these levels - for it remains a grave cause for
concern that they do exist - but rather to understand Scripture itself
and to translate it into appropriate terms in the Caribbean culture, as
well as to understand that culture and translate it back into categories
which can be compared with Scripture. There has indeed been a theological gap in existence in the Caribbean which can only be filled by a

determined and systematic attempt to go back to the Bible, and to re-discover afresh the elements of that theological connection between the people's experience of God and their experience of Caribbean realities. It is in the light of such a re-discovery that a method of interpretation can be completed by a working out of the societal impli- cations - in the family, the Church, and the community - and thus lead to an interpretation of Christian orthopraxis in the Caribbean.

God, Christ and the World

If anything is certain in the Caribbean experience, it is that religion has played a vital role in the structures of human response in resistance, survival and achievement. The Bible gives clear and consistent evidence that religious man understood God, Crhist and the World in these terms. We shall look at each in turn.

The G o d of the Bible is one who reveals himself in concrete historical events. God is known to be who he is because of what he does. The supreme and central historical event of the Old Testament is the chain of experiences which a collection of slaves could recount - beginning from the rigours of slavery in Egypt, through their miraculous liberation by God, to the establishment of a national entity - and which culminated in the mutual ratification of a Covenant. The people of Israel interpreted their successful survival after escape from a situation of oppression and misery as the intervention of God in history on their behalf. God freed them from slavery (Exodus 13:3), from repression (Exodus 1:10-11), from humiliations (Exodus 1:13-14), and enforced birth control (Exodus 1:15-22). He had therefore sent Moses to lead them out of Egypt -

> "I have seen the oppression with which
> the Egyptians oppress them. Come, I
> will send you to Pharaoh that you may
> bring forth my people, the sons of
> Israel, out of Egypt". (3)

It was as a result of the successful mission of Moses that the Covenant was established between God and Israel - "I am the Lord your God who brought you out of the .... house of bondage. You shall have no other Gods before me". (Exodus 20:2,3). Thus it was in the Covenant that full meaning was given to the liberation from Egypt, and both must be seen as integral aspects of the historical encounter of Israel with God. What God has achieved must be remembered by Israel throughout its history within the terms of the Covenant-Relationship.

The whole of the Old Testament religion is based on this central fact of faith, that the God of the Covenant who has achieved success on behalf of his people in the past will continue to fulfil his promise of liberation in spite of the continuing structures of oppression and misery. On the part of the people there are ethical demands which are binding on them,

128

and the historical role of the prophets is to remind them of their response of obedience which the God of the Covenant (who always keeps his part of the bargain) requires. God is always the God who brought Israel out of bondage in Egypt (Nehemiah 9:18, Hosea 11:1). When they are in exile in Babylon, Second - Isaiah, the great prophet of liberation, awakens their memory of the Exodus event (Isaiah 52:1-10), and announces that God will set them free again. The worship of Israel is rooted in the Covenant-relationship between God and the worshipper, and the Psalms echo continuously the identification of God with his people. Psalm 78, for example, recounts in graphic style how God became the God of Israel through the Exodus-Covenant experience.

The theology of fulfillment is based on the Caribbean people's experience of God as the God of the Exodus-Covenant. It is of vital importance to establish the inseparability between Exodus and Covenant as a paradigm for theological interpretation today. It would be un-Scriptural to stress the political significance of the Exodus paradigm while ignoring the cruciality of the Covenant factor, for without it the paradigm loses its religious efficacy. God acts in history, resisting with his people the structures of oppression and alienation, but God also acts in a Covenant-relationship with his oppressed people. Just as the Exodus experience is manifested in a number of ways, the Covenant-relationship is understood to be in effect because of such experiences. God keeps on resisting oppression, delivering his people, and providing them with the need to achieve greater and more wholesome experiences of what freedom and humanity is all about. Thus, just as God has enabled Caribbean man to survive in the past, so will he enable him to achieve in the future; but this involves a conscious response of faith which issues into purposeful action. The God of the Covenant is therefore more familiar to Caribbean persons than the great Being who has traditionally been proclaimed as the One who enjoins strict obedience and observance of prescribed ritual on pain of punishment. The God of the Covenant is a liberating God, who provides a point of departure from, and relief to, the inhibiting structures of organized discipline, which is reflective of human order, but not always of divine grace.

There is a popular saying among Caribbean people - "nearer to Church farther from God". It grew out of a sense of alienation which developed among many persons who, because of poverty or the feeling of being rejected by the rigid disciplines against common-law unions, held fast to the belief that, although the established Church had despised them, they were still nearer to God than those who attended regularly. In more recent times it has been taken over as a defensive statement by those who were at one time active Church-members but are no longer so inclined. In its original usage however, the saying points to a deep sense of the nearness of a Covenant-God who does not behave like the Church which is called by his name. It was crucial for many oppressed people in the Caribbean that they should retain their abiding trust in a God who had done, and who should continue to do, great things for them, even if the fellowship of the Church was denied them. The following verse of a popular hymn is frequently sung in the Caribbean -

> "O God our help in ages past
> Our hope for years to come;
> Our shelter from the stormy blast,
> And our eternal home". (4)

It points unmistakably to the God of the Covenant who keeps his word.

What then are the ethical demands of such a Covenant-relationship, as far as the Caribbean religious response is concerned? The answer lies in the spirit of the Decalogue itself. Most Christians in the Caribbean, whether they can read or not, can recite the Ten Commandments. The Commandments have continued to form the basis of their social and religious conduct. The spirit of the Decalogue is comprised of three aspects - gratitude and loyalty to God, respect for elders, and discipline in community relationships. It is very significant that in Caribbean religious life these ethics of law are translated into ethics of principle, and form the basis for assessing right conduct and interpreting the social dimensions of sin. This calls for further discussion.

Just as the first four commandments explicate the duty of the worshipper to God, based on a spirit of gratitude and loyalty for what God has achieved for the worshipper, (or what he has enabled the worshipper to achieve) so Caribbean people perceive that the absence of a spirit of gratitude on the part of a person who has achieved some measure of social or economic success (manifested by neglect not only of the Church, but also of the parents and the parties who assisted, or of their less fortunate relatives or friends), is a grave sin. Hence there is the operative saying in the Caribbean: "Ingratitude is worse than Witchcraft". Caribbean people believe that ungrateful people, who fail to make a concrete recognition of the fact that they owe their success to God and to other people, are always likely to experience eventually the consequences of their sin. This is not to say that they emphasize a belief that God punishes ingratitude, but rather that the Sin of ingratitude carries its own inherent reward.

As we discussed earlier on, (5) the care of, and respect for, one's parents and elders is an important factor in Carribean society. The fifth Commandment is therefore of profound significance for ethical conduct. The failure to respect parents is usually regarded as an extreme form of ingratitude for all that they have done for their children, and this is all the more crucial when we consider the conditions of extreme poverty under which most parents are forced to bear, rear and care their children. The capacity which parents have traditionally displayed in denying themselves food and comfort for the sake of their children, in displaying that courage of deprivation "to suck salt and drink water" for their children's welfare, is only dampened by their children's failure to acknowledge the value of such sacrifice in later life.

The other five Commandments deal with the responsibility of the person in the community in respecting other people's personhood and property. Here again, the moral imperatives to share the responsibility for the better ordering of the community is very strong in the Caribbean experience. The people who are generally despised are those who are self-centred and withdrawn, those who over-reach themselves in asserting their right to property, and those who demonstrate by their life-style that they are in the community but not of it. In this context, it is important to point out that personhood is of much greater importance in the Caribbean perspective than property. For example, children and relations are much more the extension of one's person than are houses, or animals, or other possessions. This distinction has all kinds of implications for social mores and conduct, and makes life in poor societies far more human-oriented than it is in richer societies. Sin in this context, therefore, is the assault on the personhood of one's neighbour when one would hate to have to sustain such an assault on one's own personhood - it is the failure to "do unto others as you would like them to do unto you".

We may therefore conclude from the above discussion that sin is non-responsibility in the Caribbean experience. This is different from irresponsibility, in that it connotes the absence of a sense of appreciation of what God, one's elders and one's neighbours should mean to a person, and the refusal to acknowledge that certain responsibilities and types of responsive action should follow from such an appreciation. Personal achievement is thus devalued by manifestations of ingratitude, social neglect and attitudes of immaturity and selfishness.

When we turn to the Caribbean response to the Christ of the Gospel, we find a very close connection with the achievement/fulfillment motif which we are discussing. The Gospel tradition speaks of Jesus of Nazareth who was born in humble circumstances, and out of wedlock, and who from birth to death was hounded down by those who felt threatened by his person, his presence, and his power. The whole story is one of resistance in its most extreme forms - the Devil himself had to be resisted, as well as the Jewish authorities, the debilitating forces of hunger, poverty, disease, social rejection, hopelessness, and even death itself. Jesus was the one who not only went about doing good, but even brought good out of what was considered "good-for-nothing" (a typical Caribbean phrase which sometimes depicts alienation and anomie). Jesus was the champion of the poor, the outcasts, the weak and the helpless; he came into close contact with men and women in their broken state, and something always happened. Zacchaeus, Bartimaeus, the Syrophoenician woman and the 'adulterous woman' (6) are favourite characters who come alive, out of the Gospel story, in the Caribbean Christian experience. These were people who had felt the weight of the social and religious system of their day, and for whom Jesus had ushered in a new experience of liberation, survival, and change.

The Crucifixion itself does not become the symbol of defeat in the
Gospel story, but rather the supreme expression of what God - the
God of the Covenant - was continuing to do for his people. In the
Biblical witness Sinai and Calvary are the unmistakable signs of God's
liberating action in history. The Exodus-Covenant event is a foreshadowing of Good Friday-Easter Day. The Covenant-God raised up
Jesus Christ from the dead, just as he set Israel free. As the Covenant
results from the Exodus fact, so more supremely is the Resurrection
the epitome of the Crucifixion event. The Resurrection does not take
place after the crucifixion, it takes place in the heart of the
crucifixion. The collection of stories which speaks of appearances
of the risen Christ is a first attempt by the early Church to express
their firm belief in the continuity of the work of Christ at a level
where the structures of oppression and misery no longer have relevance. Thus if the work of God in the Exodus points to the creativtiy
of the human response having been made possible by him, in that he
made Israel a new people and gave them the power to become
who they were, so the work of Christ points to the continuity of
God's relationship with man in his historical situation, resisting the
structures of alienation and oppression, providing new possibilities
for survival, and bringing nearer to man the possibilites of achievement
and fulfillment. It must never be overlooked that just as in the Covenant
with Israel the nature of God's promise (to continue to be their God)
provided real hope, so too in the Caribbean experience the reality of
dependence on a God who promises, and who fulfills his promises, is the source of responsive hope in the face of poverty, dependence and alienation. The Crucifixion thus becomes the supreme demonstration of a God at work who keeps his promises to be with his people -
it is the historical ground for belief in the reality of divine fulfillment.

It is in the Fourth Gospel that we are afforded a systematic interpretation
of who the early Christians acknowledged Jesus to be. The writer of the
Gospel says that it was written for the purpose of evoking a response
of active faith to Jesus as the Christ (John 20:31). In that Gospel, however, there are not only the sayings of Jesus himself, in which he dis-
closes who he considers himself to be, there are also the descriptions
of 'signs' which point to a profound recognition of what God is achieving
through the work of Christ. The signs are powerful manifestations that
God is changing the terms of reference in the realities of human experience, so that water becomes wine, death becomes life, blindness is
changed to vision, and vision assumed is not necessaril real vision.
The continuing contrasts between light and darkness, death and life,
water and thirst, hunger and food are all powerfully interwoven into a
theological reflection on what the life and death of Jesus Christ was
meant to hold out to the man of faith, whose was the daily experience
of the rigours of the powers of the "prince of this world". Thus the
theology of fulfillment breaks through in the words of Jesus "In the world
you have tribulation; but be of good cheer, I have overcome the world"

132

(John 16:33). This is an oft-repeated verse among Caribbean people in the midst of their struggle for survival. It is the constant working out of the Christian assurance of survival and human liberation in the socio-historical milieu - in the face of overwhelming oppression, degradation and hopelessness - that constitutes the very cruciality of the Cross itself in a theology of achievement/fulfillment.

For the people of the Caribbean therefore, the story of the Gospel is the story of the achievement of Jesus, who although he was unique, was so much like them in many respects. His birth was just like theirs, in most cases - "illegitimate" and insignificant - yet he had a mother who cared for him right to his death. His encounters were similar to theirs - with the authorities, with oppressive structures and with situations that threatened loss of faith in God - but yet there was always an experience of triumph and victory in the end. His death was both the supreme act of human injustice as well as the supreme manifestation of God's love - their life continues to be at the receiving end of human injustice, and yet they are sustained by an active faith in the continuing love of God. Further, the work of Christ is accepted by Caribbean people as freeing man from sin in that they acknowledge Christ's death as the historical symbol of man's inhumanity to man. There is therefore a contradiction involved in being cruel and inhuman to each other while professing to be a follower, friend, or soldier of Christ. The thought of re-enacting the crucifixion by treating others unfairly and unjustly is always a powerful and liberating deterrent for the Caribbean religious person. Jesus is supremely the friend of the poor, down-trodden and oppressed, and his own co-identification with them in Matthew 25:40 is always used as a criterion for measuring the extent of human kindness and social justice. The theology of fulfillment thus finds firm expression in the life and death of Jesus Christ as portrayed in the Gospel and interpreted in the early Church. (7)

The significance of the World, within this theological framework follows from the reflections on God and Christ. The Bible makes it abundantly clear that the world is God's creation, that it is an extension of himself, that in it he reveals his love, his power, and his abiding presence, that everything is under his ultimate control, and that in the end everything returns to him. There is therefore to be no inversion between Creator and creature, between the God who continually creates and the created order which he sustains. God is known through his mighty acts in creation, his achievements, and God enables persons to achieve great things as pro-creators. A crucial issue in the Bible, therefore, is about the ownership and control of the good things (and of the power) in the world. Although human beings are created in the image of God, and stand at the summit of creation (Genesis 1:27), and although the person of faith has enough power to remove mountains (Matthew 17:21), yet human beings are still creatures and must relate to the world as stewards of its treasures. The world is the only context in which divine fulfillment is made manifest, and the fact that the

Word (God) becomes flesh places the highest possible value on human nature. Thus a person is to be at one with creation, as God has identified himself with humanity. This harmony between people and creation is broken when two things happen: when people worship creation and make it divine, and when they behave in a way which suggests that they themselves are ultimately responsible for creation.

The world then is a continuing sign of God's presence in the community of men. The world of persons and of things must become the symbol of God's creative work, of Christ's liberating work, and of the concrete manifestations of the Spirit in co-humanity - or community. It must signify G o d ' s c o m m u n i t y as the ideal experience of humanity, in which freedom, justice and love are consciously pursued as the highest levels of relationship between persons because they are in accordance with the will of God the Creator. All this the Bible makes clear in both the Old and New Testaments. The theology of fulfillment implies that the world belongs to God, that he continues to perform his work among persons, and that persons can only measure their achievements as being useful and valuable in so far as they reflect the purposes of God. One illustration from the Psalter should suffice. In Psalm 72, the implication is that the highest order of existence in human society is to be the king, to exercise power and authority over others. The psalmist says that the king exercises real power and authority when he is dispensing justice in the defence of the poor and oppressed, and when his administration reflects that righteousness, which is the very character of God himself. Other ilustrations may be drawn from Jesus' encounters with Pilate, (8) and the figure of Herod Agrippa in the Acts of the Apostles. (9)

Where then does the Caribbean religious experience place the world in its theology of fulfillment? Caribbean people hold to the belief that over everything else it is God's world, and that all power ultimately is derived from him. They acknowledge that although they are both poor and powerless, that although the distribution of the world's goods leaves them almost empty, they still have the capacity to affect that distribution while they have life. There is a very important saying among Caribbean people: "While there is life there is hope". The motivation to adapt to their environment is always very strong among Caribbean people, but they interpret 'environment' on a much wider scale than the actually defined boundaries of geography. The Caribbean world is a wide world, and the broad expanses of the sea around them help to undergird their understanding of themselves as belonging to a bigger world than that which they actually see. It is perhaps due to the fact that Caribbean people have had to be migratory to survive, and to be free, that their concept of the world has broadened so considerably. The close psychological connections which the "Caribbean Diaspora" have with the islands, although they live in Europe and North America, and which the people of the Caribbean have with Europe and North America, because their relations are sojourning in those places, are indicative of their deep feelings of belonging to a big wide world. Thus whatever they acquire is given to them by God to enjoy and to share, and the desire to have more is not always synonymous with the desire to be more. People who have been accustomed to having nothing know from living experience the validity of the dominical expression that "a man's life does not consist in the abundance of the things which he possesses". (10) The poor people of the Caribbean, though earnestly desiring a better share of the world's goods, cling faithfully to yet another saying from the Gospel tradition: "What does it profit a man, if he should gain the whole world and lose his own soul; what shall he give in exchange for his soul?"(11)

In summary then it can be seen that the theology of fulfillment which arises out of the realities of the Caribbean experience is integrally related to the Biblical tradition. God is the Covenant God who does great things for his people and who releases the possibility for his people to achieve great things. Jesus Christ is a historical event in the daily experiences of Caribbean people effecting the continuity of that creative relationship between God and man. The world is the community of God's continuing creative activity, in which his Spirit identifies himself with the man of faith as he attempts to live as a being-in-community, struggling relentlessly for the freedom, justice and love that are the concrete manifestations of the presence of God among men. It is impossible to ignore the Trinitarian formulation of the theology of fulfillment in all this, since we can recognize that the Triune God is at work - as Father in the creativity of new life, as Saviour in the continuity of freedom and survival, and as Spirit in the community of achievement and fulfillment. The implications of such a Trinitarian paradigm for a theological assessment of the development work of the Caribbean Conference of Churches will become clearer in our next chapter, suffice it to say that they constitute the key to the theological praxis against the triple structure of poverty, dependence and alienation. (12) We need to turn now to the implications of a theology of fulfillment for the family, the Church and the society.

Family, Church and Society in theological perspective

The Family is the theological workshop in the Caribbean, the place where theology is done, the place where theological praxis is caught rather than taught. This thesis is central to a theology of fulfillment since, as we have already indicated, a deeper experience of God and the warmth of Christian love and fellowship was more often to be found within the family than in the Church itself. It would be outside the scope of this study to engage in a lengthy discussion on the historical and sociological aspects of family life in the West Indies. The reader would be well advised to consult the works of Fernando Henriques, (13) Dom Basil Matthews, (14) M.G. Smith, (15) Raymond Smith (16)

Edith Clarke (17) among others. It is enough to state that the common-
law unions which predominate in the Caribbean owe their historical
origins to slavery and the plantation system. The system of marriage
which was sanctioned by the Church reflected Western European norms
of the nuclear family, and the Church held strongly to the practice
that such persons as lived in common-law unions were "living in sin".
It would be true to say that a combination of forces between Church
and society has historically placed the typical child and its parents
in the Caribbean under punitive circumstances; for the Church placed
a stigma on the unwed parents while the society, by its laws of inherit-
ance and customs of socialization, placed a stigma on the illegitimate
child. Although in recent times many of the legal disabilities have been
removed from statute-books in the Caribbean, Church discipline and
organizational life have not yet modified their basic attitudes to these
realities. So the family has had to turn in on its own human and
spiritual resources for warmth, affection and mutual acceptance.

The situation has been somewhat different among the growing middle-
class in the Caribbean, where the family has been based on the typical
European model - dominated by the father, but where in a good many
cases the father has established extra-marital relationships. The
middle-class family however is basically the same in its internal relationships as that of the common-law union, in terms of the cultivation
of spiritual resources and the promotion of warmth and affection, but
it differs in its heavier reliance on the institutional life of the Church.
The central thesis is not however affected - the family is the place
where most theology is done.

In the context of the theology of fulfillment therefore the family, as the
basic unit in the society, is the immediate environment in which the
realities of the struggle for survival are experienced, and the need
for achievement is cultivated. It is the social milieu in which Caribbean people work out their daily skills of responding to the challenges
of poverty, dependence and alienation, and in which the art of resistance
is developed. It is also here that they have their daily experiences of
God, as he reveals to them the mysterious ways of being set free for
greater possibilities of achievement. The importance of the family as
the unit for theological praxis cannot be over-stressed, therefore,
since it constitutes the most guaranteed form of social existence for
man's response to the realities of his religious experience. Further,
because we recognize that the theology of fulfillment is essentially
an oral theology, in which the categories for critical reflection are
transmitted and exchanged through sayings, proverbs and passages
of scripture, the family is the ready-made training ground for the
transmission of such theology. Family life is therefore of profound
significance not only for social stability and growth, not only for personal and social fulfillment and satisfaction, but also for the theological praxis which seeks to pursue relentlessly the need for survival
with dignity and justice which lies at the heart of the Caribbean human
existence.

Something needs to be said therefore about the essential nature of Christian family life if it is to be a liberating experience for Caribbean people, and if it is to constitute a major source of spiritual strength in the pursuit of human development in the region. No amount of theological argument can dispense with the fact that the Gospel tradition states unequivocally that Jesus was born out-of-wedlock. He grew up in an ordinary carpenter's home under Mary his mother and Joseph his step-father. Their care and concern for him at the age of twelve, when he stayed behind in Jerusalem, displayed the normal pattern of family relationships. Jesus, Mary and Joseph have always been held out to the world as the 'Holy Family'. Why does the Church persist in not acknowledging the modern versions of that family that are based on stability, love, and mutual caring and sharing even where there has been no social or legal contract?

Is it not true that the essence of Christian family life consists in the maintenance of an environment in which the love of God and his liberating work among men can be powerfully felt and concretely responded to? Does not the Covenant God enable men, women and children to respond to him freely through each other's love and mutual support? The way ahead for the Church in the region would seem to lie in the deliberate proclamation of love and stability as the central ingredients of Christian family life, coupled with the existence of commitment and mutual responsibility; while at the same time retaining the functional importance of marriage as that which can socially guarantee the persistence of these ingredients. Children and parents of common-law unions need to experience the pastoral care and outreach of the Church of Christ who himself was engaged in resisting structures of despoliation and misery, but who triumphed over them all. Caribbean family life needs to be a happy experience b e c a u s e o f the ministry of the Church, rather than in s p i t e o f that ministry today.

The Church might therefore begin to recognize that there is already in West Indian family life the foundations for the praxis of a theology of fulfillment. The family, as a unit in society, can in many cases become the main environment within which the need to achieve is not only cultivated but actually fulfilled. This requires the promotion of an ethic of responsible love and stability through which the Church, while holding to marriage as the ideal, could embrace in penitence and genuine service the realities of the human conditions under which God's people actually live. The continuing ministry of condemnation by the Church inhibits the possibilities for real achievement and spiritual maturity within the family. We shall be discussing several aspects of Christian maturity in the final chapter. (18)

When we attempt to work out the implications of what the C h u r c h means within the framework of the theology of fulfillment, we find that Karl Barth's definition of the Church still provides a good starting-point. Barth wrote –

"The true Church is the multitude of
those who are called, called out,
called together and called up by the
revelation of God in Jesus Christ, as
the Word, to which the Bible testifies". (19)

Barth's comprehensive definition involves several useful aspects for our
purposes. It means that the Church as a people of God, a Covenant
community, has a special character which cannot be ignored. It is a
responsive community which has heard the Word - the Call - of God.
It's proto-type is still to be the QAHAL of the Old Testament, the community of those who have been called together by God to be his people.
Secondly, the definition implies that the Church must possess, and be
guided by, a distinctive view of the world and the world's structures.
The fact that it is set apart because of the Word - the Call, the great
"Thus saith the Lord" - does not remove it from the world but rather
gives it a distinctive faith, an attitude of response to the reality it
experiences. Thirdly, such a community that is called together is
guided by the Promises of the Word; the confidence that God is able
to accomplish all that he promises sets them free to engage in the
eschatological struggle of bringing into reality the Kingdom of God on
earth, for the Word is the Word of the Kingdom. This means that in a
very real sense the Church is a community of change-agents, agents of
liberation, agents of achievement, living signs of divine fulfillment in
the face of strong pressures to the contrary. Fourthly, the Church is
by definition a community of the Word, and the Word is Love. Any
attempt to reflect the love of God in concrete terms which ignores the
human demands for justice, freedom and self-fulfillment is by nature
doomed to failure. The community of the Word must essentially be a
community of achievement as well with all the moves towards survival,
justice and dignity which human achievement and divine fulfillment
essentially demand.

The Caribbean experience of the Church has been one of painful ambiva-
lence, and this point has been made quite explicitly already in preceding
discussions in this study. (20) Yet the Caribbean people have largely
been successful in maintaining their allegiance to the Church as a
social institution, while at the same time sustaining their own consciousness of being called out by God in accordance with our Barthian
definition. In other words, the deeply spiritual experience of most
Caribbean people has been the fact that they have been called by God
out of the Church itself and its institutional framework. It is this, and
this alone, that accounts for the proliferation of hundreds of small
Christian groups away from the established Churches. Thus the paradox
has been that God has called Caribbean men and women out of, and away
from, "the Church" in order to be the Church - the community of
those set free. To the extent that the life of the Church is an inhibiting
and enslaving experience, it is to that same extent that one may safely
assume that the glory of the Lord has departed from it.

The essential task of the theology of fulfillment, as indeed of any other type of theology (be it oral or otherwise), is to affirm that truth is not contained in words, structures or institutions. It must affirm that truth is rather to be found in the dynamic encounter between God and man in his social existence, as he recognizes the integral connections between his historical struggle for survival with dignity and ultimate reality. The material reality of poverty, dependence and alienation must be met by the spiritual reality of a God-of-the-Covenant engaging man in the struggle to achieve. Man is not alone, he struggles along-side those who take as their point of departure the call of God to achieve through struggle. So the experience of being the Church is at the same time the common experience of being engaged in a struggle to be set free from poverty, dependence and alienation, a struggle to achieve a measure of human existence in which the call of God to be free is not qualified by a co-erced acceptance of enslaving human structures. The Church in the Caribbean is alive and faithful to the good news of liberation and fulfillment in so far as it allocates and exploits all its resources - human, spiritual and material - towards the resistance of oppressive structures, the survival of all men, and the successful achievement of better forms of human existence in accordance with the will of God.

The question may still be asked: what is the means of determining when human existence is in accordance with the will of God? The possibilities for a satisfactory answer lie in the Biblical concept of the "image of God". Barth was keen to emphasize this concept, but he failed to work out its relational implications for social existence, especially in situations dominated by oppressive structures. It cannot be justifiably argued that man, as the image of God, should be forced to live under conditions of poverty, deprivation, dependence and alienation all the days of his life. If such be the case, what kind of a God does this image reflect? Man, in his social and historical existence, is called to become who he is, the image of God; God is a God who acts in history; it is absolutely correct to affirm that man is enabled by God to engage in that struggle to realize in his own time, place and space the possibilities of that image. Divine fulfillment is manifested through incarnate situations.

Certain implications follow from what we have just been discussing. The Church must be the community where solidarity with the struggling people - and not sympathy - becomes the central fact of its existence. Sympathy against injustice does not necessarily induce change. The call of God-in-Christ, from the Exodus to Easter, is that oppression and alienation must be shattered, and the will to do something about it must be collectivized and concretized. There is no logical reason for the Christian community to constitute an interruption (or interlude) in that process of survival and fulfillment which is uppermost in the lives of most of its people.

The need for p r o p h e t i c p r a x i s is also essential in the life of
the Church in the resistance and denunciation of structures which
inhibit the growth of the image of God. This involves an activation
of the sense of being called out by the Word to announce the immediate possibilities of new ways of being human. Finally, the Church in
the Caribbean must be the agency through which the proclamation of
the urgency for m e t a n o i a n a c t i v i t y is kept alive. Any Church
which loses that sense of urgency to shatter the structures which inhibit change towards God has lost its sense of being called. "Metanoia"
is traditionally the Greek word for "repentance" or "change of mind".
Our use of the term "metanoian" here however, is meant to convey
that totality of resistance to oppression and alienation that issues into
survival and achievement. It is not just a new look or another view
that we seek, with our whole selves and our resources we move forward
to break down, under God's liberating grace and guidance, all that
signifies the distortion of the image of God in man. This is therefore
a continuing activity, for new structures themselves become old and
inhibiting, but a theology of fulfillment is a theology of the people -
people who are yet alive - and while there is life there is change. The
job of such a theology is to work for change-for-the-better all the
time; this is the essential meaning of development itself. The spirit
of urgency which characterized the witness of Jesus Christ in the
Gospel is also that which should characterize the theological response
of Caribbean Christians to social praxis. The combined pressures of
poverty, dependence and alienation, the realities of social injustice,
the crying need for human liberation in the region, all suggest an urgency for purposeful and positive action that is unmistakable. At best,
Christians can attempt to be prophetic by renouncing the existing ways
of life and by announcing in practical ways what is their response to
the mission of God which they consider to be urgent. God works principally in the NOW.

The theological implications of what the achievement/fulfillment motif
entails for praxis in the s o c i e t y will be our chief focus in the earlier
section of the next chapter. Nevertheless, it is necessary to complete
the discussion about the theological paths of human experience at the
three levels of Caribbean existence - the family, then the wider constituency of the Church as the community of faith, and then the society
as the context in which the struggle for survival and achievement is
a daily concern. Perhaps more than any other people in the world,
Caribbean people have had to develop their own art of social analysis
and praxis for survival and achievement. It is because their art of
analysis has had to be so practical and realistic that they have had to
master the art of interpreting their religion as an important instrument
of social resistance and human survival. Along with both Marxian and
Christian thought, Caribbean analysis has always been based on the
recognition that man is a social being, that history is the important
vehicle of revelation, conflict and achievement, and that man's thinking

and praxis must be oriented towards the future. They have recognized the importance of the need to struggle against persistent poverty, dependence and alienation. They have lived close to the possibilities of a new society in which oppression is no longer a daily experience - a utopian consciousness of social life. They have constantly rejected both by implication and social behaviour the ideological superstructures by which their overlords have presided over social systems. They have been conscious of the realities of power, especially economic power, but have been able to exert a substantial amount of collective pressure in resisting many of the attempts at manipulation which their overlords have made.

Reinhold Niebuhr said: "Society needs greater equality, not only to advance but to survive; and the basis of inequality is the disproportion of power in society". (21) Niebuhr went on to point out that it was in the recognition of the goal of equal justice "and in the analysis of the roots of present injustice the proletarian sees truly". (22) The challenges to the Caribbean man which emerge out of the daily experiences of plantation society - where the ownership of the means of production is still concentrated quite heavily in the hands of the few, and where the benefits of production are still so unfairly distributed - all point in the direction of a praxis of resistance, survival and achievement. Consequently the society is the place where the achievement of justice is possible, and where the power to achieve must be strenuously acquired. To that extent therefore, society is always the context of achievement and fulfillment in which proper analysis is made of the existing constraints, and of the strategy best suited for the situation.

In its social dimensions therefore, fulfillment theology as it is perceived by Caribbean people takes as its theme the firm belief that it is not God's will that people should be as poor and depressed as they are. It motivates them to engage with others under similar social conditions to fight for amelioration and change while avoiding the likely possibility of losing what has been achieved so far. There is always a continuous dynamic interaction between consolidation and initiative, between taking full account of what has been gained and moving forward to break new ground. To quote Niebuhr again -

> "The question which confronts society is,
> how it can eliminate social injustice by
> methods which offer some fair opportunity
> of abolishing what is evil in our present
> society, without destroying what is worth
> preserving in it, and without running the
> risk of substituting new abuses and in-
> justices in the place of those abolished. "(23)

There is sufficient evidence in Caribbean social existence to support the view that Caribbean people are guided by the principle outlined in Niebuhr's comment. Their political and socio-economic praxis is

conditioned by the need to achieve higher and better alternatives rather
than to replace one inimical and oppressive system by another. Thus
fulfillment theology stresses the gradual unfolding of the society of the
future as Caribbean people struggle to achieve greater levels of freedom, justice and dignity, and as they consciously acknowledge the
present structures of society as relative and subject to change. What
it must go on to stress, however, is that the future itself is relative,
and that it derives its efficacy from its relationship to God. In Caribbean religious experience, the future belongs to the God-of-the-Covenant
without whose providential care and liberating grace they could not
have survived. The phrase: "God will provide" is not therefore
a sign of resignation among our people, it is rather the basic affirmation
of their deepest response to the realities of social existence.

Conclusion

It is important to recognize that Caribbean people have always been
accustomed to doing theology for themselves. They have had to work
out for themselves a method of critical reflection and religious praxis
that constituted their own authentic response to their daily experiences
of reality. Sometimes they derived spiritual benefit from the religious
institutions, but very seldom; for most of the time they were on their
own with God working out the best methods of resistance and survival
in the midst of dehumanizing and alienating social structures. It was
in verses like the following -

> "What a friend we have in Jesus,
> All our sins and griefs to bear;
> What a privilege to carry
> Everything to God in prayer"(24)

that underprivileged people came to a working understanding of who they
really were, and who they really could become. Their family life, as
the main workshop for their theology, provided the principal haven for
their need to achieve some measure of human fulfillment, and their
concepts of God, Christ and the World urged them on to struggle for
better living, for they believed that God had promised to be on their
side. Thus the Church could only be true to its Lord if it reflected in
its witness and service the call of God to challenge the structures which
prevented men from achieving the full realization of what is meant by
the 'image of God'.

The theology of fulfillment therefore provides an appropriate framework
for the interpretation of the development programme of the CCC between
1971 and 1977, and in a plantation society where structures of poverty,
dependence and alienation remain endemic, the objectives of economic
growth, self-reliance and social justice must have theological significance.
It is to this area of analysis that we shall now turn in the next chapter.

142

Chapter VII

THE CARIBBEAN CONFERENCE OF CHURCHES
AND THEOLOGICAL PRAXIS

"We are trying to achieve a measure of
self-sufficiency. We are not building
a society that can be flush; not to
every man a car nor to every young lady
a transistor. We are not aiming at that.
We are aiming to produce food for the population so they can be relieved from their
pre-occupation with survival and concern
themselves with the pre-occupation of
creativity". (1)

With these words Dr. Robert Moore summed up in 1975 Guyana's official
policy objectives in their praxis for structural change and human development. The passage reflects the essential meaning of development for
the Caribbean - a movement of the people from the level of survival to
the level of creativity. This was pursued by the CCC through its
CADEC programme between 1971 and 1977. Our concern in this chapter
will be to attempt to interpret this programme in the light of the theological framework we outlined in the preceding chapter, and by the use
of a paradigm of the experience of the Triune God at work in the Caribbean. Before we do this however, we need to examine the theological
perspectives which have been in evidence in the CADEC programme
itself, and also to discuss some of the theological imperatives involved
if the Church is to function as an instrument for social change.

Theological perspectives within the C.C.C.

Throughout the period under review, 1971 to 1977, one of the main
problems for the Churches was the difficulty in arriving at a working
consensus of how the original vision of change and development in the
region should be pursued. The General Secretary of the CCC, in his
Report to the Second Assembly, referred to the prophetic vision which
motivated the formation of the CCC, and said it was associated with a
common conviction among the Churches that the Church had to be on
the side of the poor, underprivileged and oppressed. He referred to
the many criticisms of the CCC by the Churches themselves about the
way in which the CCC was pursuing that vision. He also acknowledged
that there were those who believed that -

"the Churches are expressing an authentic
dimension of their mission and bringing
hope into situations of utter hopelessness. The evidence of this belief is
building up steadily. Inevitably it
leads to the expectation that the CCC
will take sides in struggles for justice and in so doing will have to oppose
political, economic and social forces". (2)

The General Secretary was articulating a fundamental problem of what
happens when the Church engages in certain types of social activity
without a clearly defined, and generally agreed, theological framework.
The question of h o w the Church engages in social praxis is bound up
with the theological question of w h y it should engage itself - and that
'why' should find its answer within the daily experiences of the people.
Much of the 'prophetic vision' of which Neehall spoke had already been
the daily experience of Caribbean people in general, it had been the
crux of their struggle to resist and to survive. What was new in 1971,
for the Churches in particular, was the courage and collective conviction
of certain churchmen - whose commitment to Caribbean development
could no longer be held in doubt - so vividly expressed in practical
terms and a relevant vocabulary.

The year of 1971 ushered in a significant discontinuity of religious
language and hermeneutic in the ecclesial tradition of the Caribbean.
Churchmen acknowledged the possibilities of interpreting the mission
of the Church by the use of new linguistic symbols and concrete objectives. What they did not institute was the framework for doing theology
in a new way - new, that is, to the received ecclesial traditions, but
not so new to the authentic human experiences in the Caribbean itself.
No regional conference or consultation had been convened by the
CCC to identify an appropriate framework for theological reflection on
the goals which were set for it in 1971. (3) A small team of evaluators
which looked at the structures and operations of the CCC early in 1975
made the following recommendation among others -

"That a clearly enunciated Policy
Declaration be provided in which
the vision and thrust of the CCC's
theological and practical commitment
be expounded. This would imply that
beyond C a l l e d T o b e a statement be
made, integrating the theological
and biblical basis on which the CCC's
efforts, in all aspects of human
development, can be seen as an
essential dimension of Christian
mission for the Caribbean". (4)

No known attempt was made by the CCC to implement this recommendation. The regional Conference on Evangelism which was sponsored
by ARC in Trinidad, in September 1975, did not address itself to this
task. A small seminar was held in Barbados in December of that same
year, sponsored by CADEC's Education for Development Programme,
and attended by participants from Barbados and the Windward Islands.
This seminar had as its theme: "Development as a Form of Ministry"
and its report suggests that the participants re-affirmed what was
already a basic assumption of the CCC, namely that to engage in
developmental activity for social change was a legitimate part of the
Church's business. (5)

In September 1976 another small team which had been appointed to
evaluate the possibilities of integrating the programmes of the CCC
submitted its report. The team comprised of the Director of CADEC,
a Projects Analyst of CADEC, an Anglican priest partly employed by
the CCC, and a Sociologist. It is useful to note that its first of ten recommendations called on the CCC to define, not a theological framework
but, its "ideological framework within which it intends to approach
development and renewal in the Caribbean community". (6) The report
suggested that a proper organizational structure and programme methodology would depend on an ideological perspective and the objectives which
the organization hoped to achieve. It went on, "in particular the CCC
must define the specific christian dimension which it aims to bring to
community development in the Caribbean". (7) Without suggesting what
might be an appropriate ideological framework and the 'specific christian dimension', however, the report went on to its second recommendation, namely that of the re-arrangement of the CCC's organizational
structure.

Thus by the end of 1976 no attempt had been made by the CCC to tackle
the basic work of identifying the essential tools required for theological
critical reflection on its praxis and programmic objectives. When
therefore the General Secretary uttered the following call -

> "There must be greater theological
> clarity within the CCC so that the
> solidarity which ecumenical action
> for justice presupposes will be seen
> to be rooted in our Christian faith". (8)

he was manifestly under-stating what was a crucial need in the CCC,
since there was an absence of a clear theological basis itself. The
General Secretary suggested however that the absence of ideological
clarity in the CCC was perhaps due to the fact that its theological position
was still not clear.

If in general terms the development programme of the CCC was implemented without a clearly defined theological framework, there was one eminent
exception in the Human Rights programme during 1977. In his report to

the General Secretary in November 1977, the Co-ordinator of the
Programme, James Tucker, outlined at the beginning some guidelines
for reflection on what he called a "Theology of Rights". It was the
only Programme Report to the Second Assembly which was placed in
a theological framework. Tucker suggested that Caribbean people had
been called into a covenant relationship with God, and that their rights
had their foundation in God and his faithfulness. Caribbean people's
rights were therefore God's rights and this fact was strong motivation
"to the resolution that the rights of the weak are not for long going
to be dependent on the patronage of the strong".(9) God therefore called
for the reconciliation of social structures with human needs and human
rights, he demanded that men should engage in a struggle for an alternative community based on human dignity and justice. Tucker suggested
that if the Church remained fixed in an animated suspension, pleading
neutrality, and failed to resist "the perpetuation of unjust structures
which have equity for the few, a measure for the worker and none at
all for the structurally unemployed" it was serving the danger of "making
mockery of God's rights in the region".(10) Tucker went on to state that
work was not the punishment for disobedience (as suggested in Genesis 3)
but an indication of man's status as co-creator with God. The right to
work was made legitimate by the commandment not to steal, and by the
various injunctions of Paul to his early Christian colleagues. There
was therefore a "fundamental importance given to work as it relates
to the dignity of man in the Christian community".(11) Finally, Tucker
insisted that all rights were to be seen as a whole -

> "The unity of rights, as it seeks
> expression in social organization,
> with its foundation in God's rights
> and faithfulness to his people, is,
> therefore characterised by a struggle
> to create an alternative community".(12)

The contribution of James Tucker to our theological debate is important
for at least four reasons. First, it signifies that there has been an
individual attempt to identify a theological framework for at least one
segment of the development activity of the CCC. Secondly, it illustrates
the type of integrative perceptions which existed among some of the CCC's
personnel in terms of focussing a specific programme on the over-all
objective of structural transformation through faith-in-action. Thirdly,
it emphasizes the experience of God as a covenant relationship, thus
identifying God's action and man's response as being inseparable.
Fourthly, it underlines the fundamental theme of the theology of fulfillment by calling for the active engagement of the Church on the side
of the poor and oppressed towards the achievement of alternative structures through which the image of God in man might be more concretely
realized. If man has the right to be human, man also has the right to
achieve such conditions through which God's liberating will for him

might be fulfilled in his social existence, and through which God will continue to make possible his very humanity.

The basic theological perspectives of the CCC are perhaps best intimated by the three major ecumenical gatherings which were held during our period. These were: The Ecumenical Consultation on Development at Chaguaramas, Trinidad, in 1971; The Inaugural Assembly at Kingston, Jamaica, in 1973; The Second Assembly at Georgetown, Guyana, in 1977. We shall deal with the Reports of each gathering in turn.

Glimpses of theological concerns are evident in the three main sections of the Chaguaramas Report. First, there is a confession of sin against God and the Caribbean people for the Church's "neglect, silence and complicity in the process of oppression on the plantations", and an affirmation to resolve to do penance by becoming "instruments in the service of the Gospel and its liberating power". (13) Secondly, disquiet about the curricula in theological education in the region is expressed, since they often contribute to the "dehumanization of theological students by its failure to deal with their own problems and with the issues of society". (14) The Consultation felt that such a situation often led to the "alienation of a significant number of persons from the ministry of the Church". (15) It therefore called on theological colleges to reflect in their syllabuses "the effort to incorporate courses which will relate theology to the human situations as to develop a true Caribbean identity". (16) Thirdly, there was a resolution submitted by the women participants at the Consultation which called for equal sharing of rights and privileges between men and women in the Church. The pre-amble read as follows -

> "An integral part of our Christian
> faith is that God's love for all his
> children makes no distinction of work
> between male and female. They are
> equal in value in God's sight;
> therefore, distinctions which assume an
> inferior-superior relationship are
> contrary to the will of God. The
> right of each person to achieve his
> or her maximum potential as a child of
> God is basic to any understanding of
> the gospel of Jesus Christ". (17)

The fundamental theme of that pre-amble serves to underline our own perspectives in this study that the right of persons to achieve their maximum potential as being made in the image of God is the essential criterion for theological praxis in the Caribbean. The fact that it was only cited as a principle for equal rights for women in the Church hierarchy is disappointing, for it was the most important premise from which to work out so much of the other concerns which surfaced at the Consultation.

Two years later, when the Inaugural Assembly of the CCC was held in
Kingston, the theological foundations for development praxis were
more in evidence, but there was still a basic lack of clarity, consistency and contact with the Caribbean situation as it then stood. The
theme, "The Right Hand of God", had been recommended by the present
writer and adopted by the Steering Committee planning the Assembly.
It was designed to incorporate the continuity between the experience
of Israel in the Old Testament, the liberating work of Christ and his
ascendancy over temporal structures of oppression (he is seated at the
right hand of God - Hebrews 10:12), and the struggles for survival and
self-fulfillment as the daily experiences of Caribbean people. The
Hymn which was composed for the theme (given in the Appendix) (18)
is a graphic description of what God is believed to be doing in the Caribbean, but it does not work out clearly the inescapability of theological
praxis on the part of Caribbean Christians. The final verse of that
Hymn stops short at the need for Joint action -

> "The right hand of God is planting in our land,
> Planting seeds of freedom, hope and love.
> In these Caribbean lands
> Let His people all join hands,
> And be one with the right hand of God". (19)

The call which the Assembly issued to the churches of the region merely
attested to the power of the "right hand of God" in the conduct of the
business of the Assembly and in the possibilities for working out common
commitment and common witness to Jesus Christ. (20) It did not enunciate
that which was basic to the understanding of the realities of that power,
namely that Christians in the Caribbean had the covenant-responsibility
and the liberating privilege of working together for the creation of the
"right hand of God" on earth - the place of God's favour. To miss the
Biblical message that God's power and God's favour (Grace) are inseparable is to miss an essential part of the Good News - the Gospel. The
symbol of "the right hand of God", as the instrument through which
God achieves his purposes for man and fulfills his promises in the historical situations of man's existence is an important theme in the Biblical
revelation.

It was in the "Call to Work" and the "Call to Reconciliation"
that the Assembly outlined some theological concerns as a basis for some
of their recommandations. With respect to Work, the Assembly
asserted that God was continually at work in his creation, and that the
Bible enjoined that it was the duty of man to work. For if man was to
consider himself an instrument of God for the improvement of himself
and his community, "then work must be seen as a necessity and a
responsibility". (21) The refusal to work, or the denial of the opportunity
to work, was for man a dehumanizing experience. Although there were
several factors which helped to generate in Caribbean people what the
Assembly called "a negative attitude towards work", they still contended

that the Church should adopt a number of measures to counter the effects of the present structures which militated against work and the opportunities for work. (22) There was a significant comment which cast serious doubt on the capacity of the Church in the Caribbean to motivate change without first changing itself -

"It was noted that the institutional
Church in many instances is least
qualified to inspire the change required,
because it is built on the oppressive
value system and seeks to maintain
itself by supporting such a system". (23)

"Reconciliation" in the Caribbean was explored from a number of angles at the Inaugural Assembly, and it was directly related to the realities of alienation and separation as continuing experiences in the region. They therefore affirmed that the many structures of alienation in the Caribbean and the world at large, with which man was presently encumbered, needed to be overcome. They expressed the belief that "it is God in Christ who takes the initiative in overcoming all forms of alienation and separation", and that -

"God has charged his Church with the
specific ministry of reconciliation
which entails the radical assertion
that both man and structures need to be
changed if man is to realize his true
humanity in liberation.
We urge this Assembly to recognize the
areas in which God's work of reconciliation is being manifested in our area and
respond by active participation in His
ongoing work". (24)

The Assembly agreed that the cries of the oppressed people of the Caribbean for economic and social justice were evidence of God's initiative in reconciliation. The Assembly expressed the belief that God was fulfilling his purpose of reconciliation through secular agencies and movements - such as those in pursuit of national sovereignty, cultural identity, and more power for oppressed groups. Nevertheless, there was a strong call to the Caribbean Churches to demonstrate their mission of liberation in -

"a) Sensitizing the oppressed and the oppressor
b) Becoming catalytic agents in the change of structures, and;
c) In initiating creative conflict that will lead into reconciliation". (25)

The Churches were therefore being called upon to eliminate all forms of discrimination and alienation within their structures, and to work for the realization of an "authentic Caribbean existence". This would only emerge as the reconciling work of God in Jesus Christ was brought to bear upon the following areas of social existence: Management and Labour; Race relations; Class distinctions; the Generation gap; Language barriers; Relationships between persons of different faiths or Christian denominations; Political rivalries; Urban and rural tensions; Relationships between expatriates and natives; Educational systems; and Family life.

The question of power had also received considerable attention at the Assembly, but the Report did not indicate what were the theological bases for the directions which were being suggested. The Report charged that both the ecclesiastical and the secular powers were responsible for perpetuating a system in which "poverty, unemployment, illiteracy, and non-participation in decision-making processes are the lot of the masses everywhere". (26) Such a system did "violence to the human spirit", the Report claimed. The Church was called upon to set its own house in order by engaging itself in the life of the masses -

> "to liberate and advance all the people
> together in order to avoid a situation
> whereby bloody revolution is forced upon
> the under-privileged as their only means
> of liberation". (27)

Thus the Inaugural Assembly had made significant theological advances on the positions taken at the Chaguaramas Consultation.

The Second Assembly which took place in Georgetown in November 1977 had as its theme: "Working Together With Christ". This was undoubtedly designed to bring the CCC to a much clearer understanding of what it had been attempting to initiate since 1971, and what was the Christocentric basis for its entire operation both in the field of Renewal and in the field of Development. The preacher at the Opening Celebration of the Assembly, Archbishop Pantin of Port-of-Spain, had suggested that the theme should emphasize that men, as Christians, were entering into the work of Christ rather than believing that it was Christ who was entering in man's work. Christ's work, he said, was one of liberation and that all the work of the Conference should be seen in that light. The preacher urged -

> "So let us indeed be liberators, but let
> us be the kind of liberators that Jesus
> wants us to be: full of strength and
> courage and determination, but also full
> of forgiveness and patience and humility.
> Without these we cannot really enter into
> Christ's work, we will not be working to-
> gether with Him". (28)

There is enough evidence to suggest that the participants at the Assembly did in fact address themselves to what was involved in entering into Christ's work of liberation in practical and concrete ways. The reports of the Working Groups disclosed that there were not merely searchings for theological foundations for action (praxis) but also for the implications of such theological praxis in the Caribbean context. The Group which was naturally most theological in orientation was that which considered the Sub-theme: "Working Together With Christ In Proclaiming the Gospel". Its report is quite illuminating.

The report indicates that the Assembly saw the meaning of the Gospel as having an inescapable connection with men in their varying needs, as it spoke to them of God's love in word and action. It stated that "the rich have to be challenged to share and the poor have to be assured of their worth and human dignity". (29) It therefore suggested that such programmes of the Church, like Christian Education, should involve the whole Christian community rather than the youth, and that they should be developed into forces of liberation within the life of the Church, rather than of domestication. The quality of congregational life and relationships needed to be such that it provided the right environment for proper Christian growth and development.

The concerns for Theological Education echoed those which had been expressed at Chaguaramas and Kingston, but the Assembly went further this time to spell out what was needed. It said that the process of developing a "Caribbean Theology needed to be stepped up since there was still a great need to "deepen the 'Caribbean experience' and articulate this in relation to the great Christian truths". (30) It also called for the creation of symbols and the use of language which spoke "more specifically to our Caribbean situation if our theology is to contribute meaningfully to the process of liberation". (31) There was a call for the deepening of the experience of community that is shared between Christians and persons of other faiths and ideologies by dialogue and joint social action against poverty, hunger, social injustice and the denial of human rights. The Assembly urged that the need for further indigenization of the Gospel among Caribbean people should be given attention, though it cautioned that sensitivities should be respected in relation to what new forms were appropriate and acceptable. In speaking of the mission of the Church, the Assembly suggested that the Churches were -

> "called to be not only institutions
> rooted in society but as a witnessing
> People of God working as leaven for
> fundamental social change while wit-
> nessing to the love of God in Jesus
> Christ". (32)

Thus the Church had to be sensitive to all people, especially the poor and oppressed and it had continually recognize that "solidarity with

Christ and with all peoples for full human development must be part
of the liberating process to which God is calling us". (33) It was important that Christians should be seen to work together in
unity 'that the world might believe' (John 17:21).

The resolutions which were passed by the Assembly clearly showed
that there had been a substantial amount of theological reflection on
the total Caribbean experience, and that concerns for basic human
rights, and for the family, were of top priority. The CCC had moved
on from a position of generalization on theological issues and had now
reached a point where specific areas called for concentrated reflection
and action. Thus, while reaffirming the basic need for the Church to
engage in Gospel proclamation and praxis, the Assembly indicated
exactly where that praxis should urgently address itself - human rights,
and the human family.

The rights of workers in Guyana were affirmed by the Assembly, as
well as well as solidarity with those in Latin America, Southern Africa
and Grenada whose basic human rights were allegedly being violated.
The most significant of the resolutions on human rights, however, contained these words in its pre-amble -

> "Whereas our biblio-theological stance is
> that man was created in the image of God,
> that his 'guarantee of certain rights are
> based on God's right to his claim on
> human beings' that man through Jesus Christ
> is expected to live the abundant life -
> that he has the right to self-determination
> in economics as well as in politics". (34)

It went on to call on the Church to support any action which guaranteed
the rights of freedom of worship, assurance of work opportunity and
adequate standards of living, education for all, health care for all,
creative use of leisure and culture, security for the aged, and the
productive use of unutilized land. Such a resolution clearly demonstrated
the will of the CCC to become engaged in theological praxis at a point
of contradiction in Caribbean society. The point of contradiction would
be indicated by the structures of oppression - poverty, dependence and
alienation - which inhibited the growth of Caribbean personhood into full
accord with what the image of God should be seen to be. It was in
this regard that another resolution expressed the mind of the Assembly -

> "Whereas it is our biblio-theological
> conviction that through Jesus Christ we
> are called upon 'to set at liberty those
> who are oppressed'.
> Be it resolved that the Church affirm
> its solidarity with those persons who
> are not guaranteed the aforementioned

actions that lead to full human development, within the society of which they are
a part". (35)

The "aforementioned actions" refers to the basic rights outlined in the
former resolution to which we have just referred. Thus the direction
of the Assembly was clear, the achievement of basic human rights
was the primary objective of theological praxis in the society, for without such conditions the Caribbean experience would not reflect the
liberating process which the Gospel enjoined.

The family was also considered to be of great importance. The Assembly
regarded it as the nucleus for education, better nutrition, and the promotion of higher levels of social and human values. The primacy of the
family in the process of the realization of the image of God could not
readily be disputed, since it was in that context that man worked out
daily what it meant to be a "being-in-community". The Assembly
therefore adopted a comprehensive resolution on a number of aspects
of the need for the improvement of family life in the Caribbean, on the
establishment of Family Courts in the region, and on the need to increase public awareness about the undesirable rise in the rate of male
and female prostitution. (36)

Our survey of the progression of theological reflection from Chaguaramas
to Georgetown has served to indicate that where in 1971 the Churches
had acknowledged the need for radical change in the Caribbean experience, but had not articulated what the theological dimensions of that
change involved, by 1977 a process of prolonged dialogue and reflection
had resulted in a specific analysis of what shape and function the appropriate theological praxis should take. The seeds of that Chaguaramas
dream were sown in the hope that the "concept of the New Caribbean Man"
should be realized. (37) The necessity for the power (right hand) of God
to initiate the process was acknowledged at the Inaugural Assembly.
The continuity of the work of God in Christ was the central affirmation
of the Second Assembly. The need for the renewal of community as
the condition most appropriate for the birth of the New Caribbean Man
remains inescapable. It is therefore in the theological interrelationship of God's action and man's response that we might best examine
the significane of Creativity, Continuity and Community as an appropriate
approach to the theological interpretation of the Development Programme
of the CCC from 1971 to 1977. We need to look first at the Church in the
Caribbean as an agent of change.

Some theological reflections on the church as an instrument of Caribbean development

There are a number of preliminary considerations which must be mentioned in connection with our attempt to reflect theologically on the Church as an instrument of Caribbean development. First, we should take note of the fact that the term "Caribbean" denotes more than a mere geographical entity. It is meant to include all those who share in, and are genuinely affected by, the realities of the Caribbean experience whether they actually live in the Caribbean or not. Migration has been such an important element in Caribbean patterns of resistance, survival and achievement, that the members of the Caribbean Diaspora whose physical environment consists of the First World habitat, are still nevertheless to be regarded as that which they deeply consider themselves to be - an extension of the Caribbean. The second consideration follows from the first; there are those who live in the Caribbean who are hardly touched by the Caribbean experience we have been describing. Tourists and expatriate residents within the region may well remain untouched by that experience.

Thirdly, the Church cannot be considered in isolation from its historical connections with the global christian community - many of the assumptions that are made within the Church in the Caribbean are identical with its counter-part communities in other parts of the world. The Church must therefore be understood to be a part of a world-wide fellowship of believers, while it remains in the Caribbean a particular manifestation of a universal (catholic) movement. Fourthly, as a movement existing within a particular socio-historical framework, its essential nature as a community of those who have been called is to be demonstrated chiefly by the unique way in which it motivates its members to respond to socio-historical realities. This means that the Church's greatest social challenge lies in its ability to affect the structures of human response in a way which no other social movement can. Fifthly, the notion of 'Church' must not be constrained by the scandal of denominational division. It would be disastrous to confine God's liberating work of fulfillment and the Christian response of faith-in-action to prescribed boundaries which result from man's alienation from man.

With these preliminary considerations then, it is useful to explore the Biblical tradition again, and identify such insights as may assist us in our theological reflections on the nature of the Church as an instrument for social change and human development in the Caribbean. We will not exhaust all the possibilities of the Biblical tradition obviously, as such an attempt would certainly be impossible, and would in any event constitute a major study of its own. Our purpose here will be to identify the main biblical insights which point to the Church as a living expression in the society of God's continuing work for human salvation.

154

The Old Testament saw Israel as the People of God - the covenant community within which, and through which, God's continuing work of creation and redemption was to be proclaimed in word and deed. The New Testament speaks of the Kingdom of God as that which incorporates and transcends the Old Testament concept of the Covenant community. It calls into being a new community of all those for whom the life, death and resurrection of Christ initiates a new and living way of proclaiming God's continuing work of creation and redemption. The Old Testament community was essentially comprised of poor, oppressed and "grass-roots" members. The Israel of the Old Testament is a nation of poor people, whose relationships with God are distorted and disturbed when wealth and prosperity blur their vision of what their Covenant responsibility demands. (38) The Kingdom of God, as it is proclaimed by Jesus in the Gospel, is essentially comprised of those who acknowledge their need of God. Human nature is such that it is usually the poor and underprivileged, and those who do not revere wealth, power and status, who are most likely to be members of the Kingdom of God. The Beatitudes (Luke 6:20-23), the Woes (Luke 6:24-26), the story of the rich young ruler (Luke 18:18-30), and the parable of the rich man and Lazarus (Luke 16:19-31) are all irreversible signs of the relatedness of the poor and oppressed to God's kingdom. (39)

Development by, and in solidarity with, the poor and oppressed, therefore, is the concrete and historical focus of social praxis for the Christian Church in the Caribbean, particularly as it is the principal (but not the only) instrument for the realization of the Kingdom of God on earth. Development can be a sign of the breaking in of the Day of the Lord - for which the Covenant community must always be at work. Because the Church happens to be a social institution in which both poor and rich, oppressed and oppressor, rulers and ruled, profess equality of membership (although it is often difficult to ignore the fact that some are "more equal than others"), it is blessed with a strategic opportunity and challenge to work from within its own structures for social reconciliation and human justice in all its dimensions. Through its liturgy and its work the Church is understood to be the extension of that divine work of reconciliation of which Paul speaks in 2 Corinthians 5:19 - "God was in Christ reconciling the world to himself". Max Weber points to the significance of the Lord's Supper as that which ushers in Christian freedom through its commensalism. Weber shows that it was commensalism that destroyed the ritual barriers in the world of the early Church, and which made possible an oathbound fraternity and medieval urban citizenry. He speaks of the early Church as "the community of the eucharists". (40) This principle of commensalism as the sign of community is of significance to the Church today, if it is to understand the meaning of its liturgy and its work as concrete signs of social reconciliation and human liberation. The ritual barriers which are done away in the liturgy are signs that the social barriers can also be removed.

The Church then is not simply a community of eucharistic believers, it must in all respects become a community of faith-in-action, through which might be realized the meaning of that which God-in-Christ continues to do. The belief that God emptied himself and became human must constantly be accompanied by a demonstration in practical and concrete terms of what that emptying (kenosis) means in socio-historical existence. Belief in the emptying of God's self is indicated in concrete terms by a level of human obedience "even unto death"; there is continuity in the kenotic process which results in a confrontation with every structure that dehumanizes mankind. The New Testament therefore focuses on this confrontation through the Cross, the place of crucifixion. Crucifixion, or confrontation, is an experience that is both ancient and modern in the Christian's response to God's self-emptying love. The poor of the Caribbean have come to know the love of God in a way which has sustained them in their darkest hour. It is mainly through the Christian Church, as the social institution through which the poor can find meaning for life, and to which they totally align themselves, that the fruits of that love can come to mean "abundant life". The summary of that love-in-action reads like this: "I came that they may have life, and have it abundantly" (Jesus). (41)

The images of the Church in the New Testament convey an underlying sense of vitality, liveliness, movement, change, praxis. Paul Minear has produced a very important work on the study of these images. (42) Yet there is an important passage in the Fourth Gospel which has a profound meaning for the Church's understanding of itself if it is to respond to the realities of the Caribbean experience, and to re-orient its efforts and resources towards Christian praxis for Caribbean development. The Fourth Gospel says that during the Last Supper Jesus got up and undressed, wrapped a towel around his waist and began to wash the feet of his twelve associates gathered at the meal. Judas was among them. The action was reminiscent of the saying in Mark 10:45 "the Son of Man came not to be served but to serve". Jesus explained his actions by saying that his point was to demonstrate the full extent of what commitment to faith-in-action involved - it meant humility, it meant humiliation, it meant service - and the example of the washing of other people's feet would be an important guide for Christian discipleship.

No Christian in the Caribbean should fail to recognize the image of the human experience which this episode conveys. Jesus was a Jew, and Jewish slaves were normally exempt from the humiliating act of washing other people's feet. (43) Yet here Jesus assumes the deportment of a slave and applies himself to the most humiliating service. Caribbean ancestors - the slaves - were normally dressed like Jesus was for this event, and their only way of putting meaning into life was to work for the benefit of all, including those (like Judas) who appeared to be their support in life but were actually their source of oppression. The washing of Judas' feet could be taken to mean that he too had need for such cleansing, and that those who today sustain for their own ends the enslaving and dehumanizing structures which oppress others, can still be touched at some point of their existence. Caribbean realities still cause many people to function as if they were slaves, yet such 'slaves' can be enabled by God to make contact with oppressors at points in their lives where change might be possible - for oppressors too are still human beings. Although there can be no guarantee of what the results will be (Judas, though washed, still remained unclean) Christian service to all is an essential part of obedience to God's call to witness to the presence of the Kingdom of God.

If the washing of the feet in the Upper Room was meant to demonstrate proleptically the meaning of the Cross, the Cross itself demonstrated proleptically the nature of the mission of the Church in society. The Church as the community-of-faith-in-the-Crucified must continually be prepared to undress - to change its appearance, its image and its structures - and to work like a slave at the points of human contact where cleansing, renewal and reconciliation (development) is possible in the social order. But it can best do this together - as a community - and the need for unified action in society can only be met by the coming together of the various strands of that movement of Christians in the Caribbean. The attempts at joint co-operation and action by the Churches, through the CCC, which focus attention on social reconciliation and human development through structural change, are an important step forward in the search for more appropriate forms of Christian praxis and service. The more the Churches can adopt a common agenda for such praxis in the society, so much the more they will be likely to reduce the areas of contradiction within and among themselves, and strengthen their common resolve to confront the areas of human contradiction in the wider society.

The wise use of its resources in the service of the Kingdom of God is an inescapable task of the agency of the Kingdom. Jesus provides clues in the Gospel about the importance of vigilance and prudence ("phronēsis") in the identification, allocation and exploitation of available resources. (44) The fact that the CCC has been able to mobilize a substantial amount of resources - both financial and otherwise - is a cause for great awareness of the possibilities for sharing. The Great Parable of Sharing (Feeding of the Five Thousand - John 6) indicates that much can be accomplished with little, provided that the praxis is initiated as an act of interpreting the will of God. It announces that the Covenant God is at work in specific projects and circumstances directed towards meeting human need for fulfillment and liberation, and also enabling men and women to work for that change in social existence which might signify more clearly what is meant by the love of God. Yet the mere allocation of resources to points of need cannot announce the concrete enactment of the parable of the Kingdom of God in the Caribbean, about the mustard seed growing into the big tree. (45)

It is the complementary educational role of the community of faith, which seeks to use its projects and programmes as 'signs' of something deeper and more illuminating that can help to proclaim the good news of God's liberation in Caribbean society. Word and deed go together, and the paths of evangelization which only pass through neutral action - however successful social projects might be - must always fail to re-echo that gospel truth that man does not live by bread alone. Thus the Church is faithful to its Lord when it uses its resources in the service of the poor and the oppressed in a pattern of joint co-operation and co-ordinated action, and when that process of resource utilization announces through praxis and preaching that God's self-emptying love bears fruit in the midst of human struggle for survival and self-fulfillment. The Church as an instrument for Caribbean development is essentially that community for the realization of the image of God in its socio-historical dimensions, and performs its evangelical task through a relentless struggle for human reconciliation with divine fulfillment. In practical terms this means justice, freedom, equality and solidary love, and by the grace of God, the Church in the Caribbean must announce through its very social existence that Jesus Christ restores in all men, while he himself continues to be, the real image of God.

Finally, there is the question of genuine discipleship, and it becomes an issue because of what Jesus once said: "For what will it profit a man, if he gains the whole world and forfeits his life? Or what shall a man give in return for his life?" (Matthew 16:26). This question follows on from a discussion on the grave cost of discipleship. Jesus says that to be his disciple one must deny oneself and take up one's cross and follow him. There does not appear to be an easy way out. There is no call for a tactical compromise with the forces opposed to discipleship, or for retreat, or even for revolution. No substitute for crucifixion/confrontation is suggested, no substitute for radical change (a change at the root of the matter). All too often in the missionary tradition of the Caribbean, the question which Jesus raised has been offered to the poor and oppressed and hungry people as a salve, a palliative, a compensatory thought for their deprivation. They have been made to believe that God prefers their poor condition since that is a sure sign that they have not forfeited their life, their "soul". The Church as an instrument of human development in the Caribbean must cause the question to be put again, but with a radically different agenda. It must ignore the alternative emphasis of "either-the-whole-world-with-forfeiture-of-life" and make a radical choice for "neither-the-whole-world-nor-forfeiture-of-life". This second alternative places the emphasis on the "both/and", and involves a strategy of theological praxis which passes inevitably through confrontation and disruption. It is God's will that the "whole world" should be available to all men, and that involves liberation and salvation. In view of present circumstances in the social order, to pursue such a theological objective necessitates certain conflict. The image of God in the crucified Christ signals the Church to engage in that conflict.

To sum up then, we can say that the engagement of the Church in the social process must necessarily be at the point of contradiction-confrontation-crucifixion, the point where the historical moment presents the challenge for the cross. This point is today denoted by the search for self-development in the Caribbean, the struggle to effectively resist the prevailing structures of poverty, dependence and alienation, and to achieve a higher degree of survival with dignity and greater self-sufficiency and self-fulfillment. The Church as the community of faith is also the poor Church, and it must attempt to work out its faith in the Crucified Christ in terms of social reconciliation and service, however humiliating and self-effacing. It must mobilize its human, spiritual and material resources co-operatively towards the development of people (whether they are its members or not, for the Church has no choice but to remain an institution which functions for the benefit of those who are not even its members) towards higher goals in their social experience. It can only work for radical change without if it is prepared to undergo radical change within. Radical change will always have to include a re-appraisal of the goals of the world and a re-interpretation of social values - the servant becomes the greatest, the poorest are really the richest, and the last become the first. The true Kingdom of God resembles no social order on earth, and Christian faith in praxis becomes a distinctly historical paradox.

The work of the CCC in the area of development between 1971 and 1977 is perhaps one of the signs we have that the Covenant God is at work in helping the covenant community - the Church - to change itself. The Christian denominations in the Caribbean have been working more closely together than at any other time in their history, and at an agenda for development which has no denominational hue. Indeed development concerns have pointed to that unity in the Church of the crucified Christ which has otherwise been blurred by concerns for religious diversity. There is unity in diversity in the Caribbean, and this has been demonstrated through the work of the CCC. There is plurality in the unity of the Godhead, and this is the experience of the community of faith in the Caribbean. Our main concern for the rest of this chapter therefore, will be to illustrate how an interpretation of the experience of the Triune God at work in the Caribbean is signified by the development programme of the CCC. The Churches, under God, have been working together for the promotion of creativity, continuity, and community in Caribbean social existence.

Creativity and theological praxis

We pointed out at the beginning of our study that poverty was a continuing experience in the Caribbean - it is an economic reality. Percy Selwyn has shown that countries which are small, poor and remote, like most of the islands in the Caribbean, stand little chance of doing anything very significant to radically change these economic realities. (46) Natural resources are severely limited, and patterns of consumption grossly overwhelm the capacity for production. The plantation society continues in the Caribbean, and the only realistic prospect for the rest of this century at least, is for a future of relative poverty. Yet the way in which the economic system works can still be modified to provide a better chance for change for the poorest people of the Caribbean. The essential challenge of the structures of poverty is to stimulate economic growth towards a better standard of living for all the people in the society. Sustained economic growth among the poor is effectively attempted, not so much by providing help for the poor, but rather by the transfer of the power necessary for them to begin to help themselves. It is precisely at this point in the socio-economic system of the Caribbean that the structures have been heavily weighted against the poor. Not only have they generally had no one to intercede for them within the systems and institutions which could provide resources for self-help, but they have generally fallen far below the minimum qualifications required for access to such resources. The effects of the saying already quoted are severely felt: "when a man is poor even his very words are poor". (47)

The criteria which are used by the CCC's Development Fund Committee for its support of project activity in the region have already been outlined in Chapter 2. (48) These criteria clearly indicate that CADEC was determined to provide assistance for the poor and underprivileged who would not normally qualify for financial or other forms of material assistance from any other group or institution. Project support in Agriculture, agro-related industries, training in arts and crafts, and such project ventures have all been designed to achieve even a modest measure of sustained economic growth among small groups of poor people. The intentions declared by CADEC were that these groups would in turn serve as catalysts in their own areas for stimulating similar, or related, types of economic activity. Yet the important thing about the project assistance cannot merely lie in the measure of relief which it brings to a small group of people at a time. Some words of Richard Dickinson are relevant here -

> "It is not the task of the Churches to
> enable a few of the poor to become
> affluent, in a kind of tokenism of
> success; it is the churches' task to
> help the masses of the voiceless and
> exploited to be heard, the masses of

the estranged to be reconciled, the
masses of the alienated to discover
common aspirations and affirmations -
to discover a unity within diversity". (49)

The work of CADEC in the field of project assistance goes beyond the
material aspect to the basic social dynamics involved in bringing dispossessed groups not only into creative interaction with each other,
but also into creative tension with the structures which have made them
dispossessed. The emphasis on project activity has not been on attainment so much as on interaction - the interaction of the poor with the
social, cultural and economic processes, thus releasing the power of
the poor for greater creativity, and also broadening and deepening the
total concept of development. Thus CADEC explains the purpose of its
Development Fund in these words -

> "The Fund is not an end in itself. It is
> merely a tool in a programme of education
> for development. This programme seeks to
> uncover Caribbean man's opportunity and
> potential for his complete liberation". (50)

The significance of the relational component of the work of CADEC is
therefore to be seen in its determination to stimulate creativity for the
people's self-development and humanization. The work of the Education
for Development programme in promoting catalysts for awareness-
building, the instrumentality of the Communications programmes in
providing and inculcating new skills for sharing indigenous ideas and
values, the incisive policies of the CCC newspaper "Caribbean
CONTACT" in reflecting critically on social and political issues
in the region, are all part of this over-all thrust for bringing to the
surface the creative instincts of the "New Caribbean Man". Sustained
economic growth is not possible unless the people use their own creative
energies and skills to survive against the pressures of structured
poverty. Their capacity to achieve greater self-sufficiency would
inevitably have to be determined by their collective resistance to
the systems which rendered self-sufficiency so difficult. No survival
with dignity could be possible without creativity.

What then is the theological meaning of such creativity in the Caribbean
religious experience? How can the struggle against structured poverty,
as demonstrated in the development programme of the CCC, be understood as Christian praxis? It is precisely in this very search for creativity that the best clues are to be perceived. The essential nature of the
Covenant-God is that he is a God of love, and that love is disclosed as
love-in-action. There is nothing static or void of dynamism in it. The
traditional doctrine of the Trinity has always maintained that all the
operations of the Trinity demonstrate the true meaning of love-in-
action, and that all the operations are inter-related and "consubstantial".
The Fatherhood of God is revealed in divine love as creative activity,

not only in bringing the world into being - and thus being ultimately responsible for it - but also in sustaining the world. Man, as made in the image of God is responsible for working out the meaning of that faith in God's creative love by his own creative response to that love. This involves undoubtedly a creative struggle to achieve that harmony between himself and the social environment which best reflects the demands of that image. It is mainly in work - working for himself, working with others, and working for his family - that man responds creatively to that love-in-action which is the revelation of God as Father. Jesus reminded his hearers with these words: "My Father is working still, and I am working" (John 5:17).

It must not be denied that work will always involve failure and loss, much suffering and pain. Yet work opens up the possibilities for self-fulfillment which creative action affords. It is mainly in the taking of initiatives towards their own self-fulfillment that Caribbean people can make a radical break with much of their past, since initiatives were traditionally taken for them rather than by them. The meaning of creative work as a divine possibility for achievement and fulfillment, and as a mode of theological praxis, cannot be over-emphasized. Creativity is both the sign of God's action and man's responsive action. To the extent that the CCC in its development programme attempts to generate the possibilities for greater creativity and creative interaction, the engagement of the Church in theological praxis is in evidence. For the underlying struggle for survival is assumed, and the release of the creative energies of Caribbean people is taken to be the basic and concrete commitment of Christianity to responsive love. This has to be a social reality. Creativity thus becomes the dynamic motivation for making a qualitative improvement to the nature of survival in the Caribbean experience. When the pre-occupation with survival is superceded by the pre-occupation with creativity, survival itself becomes the framework within which qualitative changes are likely to lead to more liberating experiences. Creativity always involves risk, but where that risk is directly related to one's determination to improve the quality of one's survival, even failure and suffering can become liberative.

Christian action for development is creative action, and the assault on poverty in the Caribbean can best be assisted by the Church through its insistence on the need for the achievement of goals that are realistic, but also goals that are attainable through the dynamic creativity of people struggling for their liberation. "God helps those who help themselves"; and the CCC can proclaim in word and deed the meaning of God's energizing and creative love by engaging with the people, through its constituent member-Churches, in a process of critical reflection on the action which it helps to initiate. Theological praxis demands that reflection on action points to an understanding of God's love-in-action in a given historical situation. The struggle for economic growth through the promotion of creative action and productive work can indeed signify that God has not turned his back on his people. The Covenant-God is at work in a most distinctive way, and it requires that the people of the Covenant should perceive themselves as being creatively responsive by working out in their own situation what is the meaning of all that God has promised to fulfill in them.

The theological significance of Continuity for social praxis

The political patterns in Caribbean society have been shown to be directly related to the economic patterns. We saw in our opening chapter that the realities of dependence were particularly obvious in the political sphere of Caribbean society, even if these were overlaid by patterns of formal independence in some territories. Dependence continues to be a daily experience of Caribbean life at most levels, and the poor and underprivileged are those who would know the harshest realities of that experience. We have said that development must not be seen in terms of economic growth alone, since man does not only consist in the abundance of the things which he has. Development also means self-reliance, and in the Caribbean situation this must be perceived principally as the continued determination of Caribbean people to make their own decisions. Self-reliance then would not so much imply the cessation of assistance from others - whether internally or externally - but moreso the capacity of Caribbean people to assert their own integrity and to determine the structures and objectives of their own social and political destiny based on an enlarged self-confidence and the fuller attainment of their human potential.

The Caribbean experience has been that most of the people have been forced by economic pressures to be dependent on the powerful and privileged few. The first of the four main programme objectives outlined by CADEC emphasized the need to promote self-dependence among the people of the region by enlarging their capacity to generate and sustain indigenous development efforts. CADEC's priorities for action and the patterns of its programmes therefore placed the highest premium on the needs and priorities as expressed by the people themselves. In this respect it was guided by the results of a very important Consultation on Rural Development, held in 1972.

The Consultation had recognized that the Caribbean people were facing a serious challenge in attempting to forge for themselves a type of political activity which would "encourage rather than undermine their capacity to develop their community in accordance with their own priorities and life styles". (51) It had stated that people were processes in themselves, and that it was crucial for Caribbean people to realize that "the sources of power lie within themselves functioning as communities". (52) It was therefore essential that groups should be motivated to analyse their own situation and needs -

163

"with a view to determining what kind
of development they want for their
communities and what action to take.
This process should take place essentially within the groups. Outside
organizations or individuals which
have opportunity to encourage it, should
be careful not to impose their own views
and interpretations". (53)

The emphasis should therefore be placed on the process of capacitation
which was defined by the Consultation as that by which "people who have
identified their needs find ways to utilize their potential and secure the
resources they need in addition to their own potential". (54) It was also
seen as that process by which "a community moves from where it is
to where it wants to be. It involves resistance to all forms of exploitation
of the resources of the community for purposes other than such as will
benefit that community". (55) The Consultation felt that the educational
systems in the Caribbean militated against the achievement of goals
which a community set for itself, and also against the process of capacitation.

CADEC's work over the period in assisting with the formation of community groups, in sponsoring a variety of small seminars and training
courses in leadership capacitation, and in appointing a number of persons from local communities to its committees and sponsored groups,
was all in pursuit of these goals for self-reliance. Further, CADEC
successfully managed to reduce the bilateral contacts between funding
agencies and metropolitan organizations and local community groups.
This was to have the desired effect of enabling groups to determine
their own priorities and programme plans, rather than to accommodate
themselves to what they knew such bodies would expect to hear, or be
more readily disposed to approving. CADEC itself had to reinforce
its own structures of self-reliance in the establishment of programme
priorities and in regional decision-making. The emergence of the
Consortium arrangement as the mechanism for accepting financial
support from external agencies was a sign of this determination. Its
major programmes have been drawn up without reference to external
sources, and have represented a concerted attempt by the Churches in
the region to respond to the demands of their own situation rather than
to instructions and persuasions from abroad.

Self-reliance when seen as self-determination follows naturally along
the theological course we were pursuing in the previous discussion about
economic growth and creativity. If we continue with the use of the
Trinitarian disclosure of divine love-in-action as our focus, we can
interpret the meaning of the divine self-disclosure in Jesus Christ as
continuing love - love as divine continuity. The cardinal religious truth
about Jesus is that he is the representative, par excellence, of God's

reliability, God's continuing expression of concern and liberation for his people, God's power to fulfill all that he promises. The same Covenant-God who made himself known in mighty acts to Moses and his people continued to manifest himself - only now most supremely - in the life, death and resurrection of Jesus Christ. Thus divine love is not only creativity, divine love is also continuity - it never fails, it accomplishes all that it sets out to do, it places religious man in the realm of confidence where no other force on earth can reach. Jesus preached of that continuity in the divine love, which demanded the response of faith from religious man - the man of faith. He called on his disciples to be continually on the alert - to watch;(56) no one who put his hand to the plough and then gave up was fit for the Kingdom of God; Peter began to submerge while walking on the water because his faith failed; the Centurion's faith in God's power received high praise.(57) Jesus said, "he who endures to the end will be saved", (58) and that the true disciple had to take up his cross daily and follow him. His agony in Gethsemane is the epitome of that human response to divine continuity - "yet not what I will, but what thou wilt".(59) When he is about to die, the cry from the Cross (in the Fourth Gospel) is "It is finished".(60) The theology of fulfillment takes its supreme expression in this factor - fulfillment and continuity go together in the Cross, for the demonstration of human love at its greatest meets with the demonstration of divine love at that point - "Greater love has no man than this, that a man lays down his life for his friends".(61) Divine continuity makes possible man's liberating growth.

Self-determination is an essential quality in the continuing struggle for human liberation and self-fulfillment; it is indispensable for the proper flowering of the human personality. Human continuity for the Christian means the continuing determination to fulfill one's role as pro-creator with God, becoming what one really is. Creative action which lacks a sustained continuity is virtually self-defeating, just as economic growth without an appropriate measure of self-reliance is counter-developmental. Theological praxis for self-reliance is therefore an inescapable commitment of the Christian Church in the Caribbean, since the realization of the image of God in its social and historical dimensions depends on the attitude of continuity and determination, of constant obedience to divine will and purposeful Christian commitment, as were so powerfully demonstrated in the Christ event. The determination to pursue relentlessly the goal of our high calling in Christ is repeatedly stressed in the New Testament - this must certainly have its social and historical implications. The writer of the letter to the Hebrews is grounded in the realities of social praxis when he makes the exhortation to "lay aside every weight, and sin which clings so closely, and let us run with perseverance the race that is set before us, looking to Jesus the pioneer and perfecter of our faith".(62)

Self-reliance as an essential objective of theological praxis does not in any way detract from the reality of the Christian's dependence on God.

It rather entails the active and concrete pursuit of our common calling in Christ, and the support of such social structures in human history which would clearly distinguish our dependence on God from what it means to be dependent on others. The crux of the Christian faith is that the only reality we have as human beings, as living creatures, is our complete and absolute dependence on God as Creator, Liberator and Sustainer. "Absolute" here refers to ultimacy, not such as denotes distance and lack of concern, but rather that basic and unconditional experience of the Triune God of love as the essential quality of our lives. In a very real sense, therefore, it is the daily working out of what it means to believe that God-in-Christ is the very source of our historical existence that constitutes the main agenda for the Christian pursuit of self-reliance in our social existence. This calls for the constant awareness that we are beings-in-community, and that self-reliance is a communal objective, a societal ideal rather than an individualistic ambition. Self-reliance thus involves collectivity, and mutual responsibility, and a quality of inter-dependence that liberates rather than domesticates persons.

Finally, there is the basic issue of survival as a primary concern in the Caribbean religious experience. The connection between self-determination and the need to survive is obvious. The theological dimension of the survival concerns in the Caribbean experience relates chiefly to the underlying belief that the Covenant-God has made it possible in the past for Caribbean people to survive the conflicts and pain of slavery, indentureship, hunger and oppression, and that that same God will continue to make it possible for them to continue to survive. The element of trust and confidence in the divine promise therefore has its social manifestations among Caribbean people, in that they can interpret the fact that they have survived so far as a sure indication that greater possibilities lie open towards the future. Self-determination therefore is essential to the business of survival, and human continuity is the fulfillment of the promise of divine continuity. The theological significance of continuity therefore, lies principally in the Christian response of liberating growth to the liberating love of god which was revealed in Jesus Christ. It points to a relentless experience of being set free and of praxis for the freedom of others. Caribbean people are encouraged not to give up, but to press forward towards greater and better forms of social existence, because they can depend on the Covenant-God who never gives them up. This is the Christian quality of self-reliance in Caribbean development.

Community as the goal of Christian praxis

The structures of poverty and dependence which are in evidence in the economic and political spheres in the Caribbean are made worse by the structures of alienation which dominate the lives of so many Caribbean people. Alienation must be seen as that experience of marginalization and meaninglessness which comes frequently to most people in the region, by reason of their inability to participate effectively in the social process. The Caribbean experience of alienation is no projection or abstraction, it is an existential fact that marks out in no uncertain terms what are the limitations, or boundaries, of social life where there is neither justice nor meaning.

Within the development process it is reasonable to suggest that the assault on alienation should be denoted by a struggle for social justice, just as dependence was to be counter-acted by more self-reliance, and poverty by economic growth. At no stage should these be perceived as three separate and distinct operations or concerns. It is the totality of the human experience that cries out for liberation and development, and the process of development must not only be conceived as an integrated whole consisting of different aspects, but it must also be pursued with equal vigour and sincerity in all its dimensions. A concern for bread and for charity which overlooks a concern for self-determination and justice robs itself of any real and lasting concern for humanity. For it is not enough to ask of the poor and the oppressed what is the measure or extent of their oppression. It is vitally important to search for the real answers to the question: WHY? When we begin to look for the real causes of alienation in Caribbean social existence, we are already on the path to discerning the real structures of social injustice and to opening up the possibilities for radical social change.

The development programmes of the CCC have made their most distinctive contribution to the total development process in the Caribbean through the persistent determination to look at causes of alienation, to ask radical questions which governments and other bodies have either been reluctant or afraid to ask, and to suggest by word and action ways in which these causes might be attacked. It was one of the significant objectives of the CADEC programme that it should promote the greater participation of a greater number of people in the decision-making process of society. This objective was to be seen more in its qualitative dimension than in its quantitative dimension, that is, the aim was not to engage more "cooks to make the soup" (for too many cooks would spoil it!) but to promote a deeper awareness of the social process among a greater number of people, and of their potential participation in it, so that they themselves would determine what should be the optimum level of popular participation. There is a tremendous difference between being kept out of a particular process by those who wish to maintain control of it for themselves, and being able to decide freely whether one wishes to be more or less active within that process.

Thus the important criterion was to emphasize the fact of community and the essential part which each person had to play in the realization of common goals and objectives.

Between 1971 and 1977 the CADEC programmes did indeed make a determined effort to emphasize the development of community as an inescapable objective of the process of full human development. CADEC recognized that there was still evidence of "the authoritarian pattern of society fostered by colonial institutions and the plantation economy", but that it was possible to "demonstrate in action that the range of things which people acting as communities can control is wider than they now realize". (63) It also determined that political manipulation, which was a serious cause of divisiveness and alienation in the Caribbean, should be exposed and discouraged, and that as far as possible the political will of the people should be stimulated towards becoming more aware of their total situation and determining by consensus what should be done about it. CADEC was however fully conscious of the predominance of individualism in communities, and began to work for the general reduction of individualism in the interest of the total community. It agreed in one of its earlier Consultations that -

> "To encourage the voluntary denial of individualistic tendencies must be the basic responsibility of the total community, since benefit for the community must be seen to be benefit for its individual members". (64)

The projects which CADEC supported therefore tended to have a very strong community basis, and only in very exceptional circumstances did individuals, whose projects had clear community-oriented potential, receive financial or other assistance. The promotion of co-operatives as a working base for economic growth and self-reliance among marginal groups was in evidence in many of the projects assisted, and the establishment of training facilities pointed directly to the benefits to be derived by communities, rather than individuals. The material assistance programme, DERAW, has focussed attention on groups and communities where there are most needy cases of poverty and deprivation, and although direct assistance is made to individual families or persons, the programme still operates within the context of a community-based exercise in so far as a local group determines where the neediest cases really exist. It is the community which receives assistance on behalf of one or more of its members. The community decides on the pattern of sharing, and how that sharing of material can generate a wider sharing of concern, of opportunity, and of resources, for its own advancement and welfare.

The more recent efforts by CADEC to promote more appropriate methods of technology in the Caribbean must be seen in the context of the struggle against alienation. For just as CADEC has supported a number of CCC-related programmes in the field of cultural expression and cultural identity, and also served groups whose aims were to discover the cultural roots of Caribbean people, so the search for an appropriate technology for Caribbean people is an attempt to give full recognition to their own potential and to exploit the resources and the skills more familiar and more readily available to them. Programmes of cultural identity and appropriate technology help to point to the possibility of an authentic Caribbean way of doing things, and to attack the experience of alienation. The need to achieve can always be stimulated when people are made to realize that what they have - talents and resources - are good enough to do great things. The search for creativity is always a struggle against alienation, and the capacity to reach out to higher levels of achievement by one's own creative energies can never fail to be a potential for increasing human dignity.

The communication programmes which CADEC has initiated and sponsored over the years 1971 to 1977 have also been directed against the structures of alienation. The issues which are raised monthly in the only regional newspaper in the Caribbean - "Caribbean CONTACT" - usually provoke a response of participation from the alienated people, and those who recognize the pressures under which such people have to survive. The facts that in some countries the official policy is to keep a very strict control on the entry of the newspaper into those countries, and that the Editor, Rickey Singh, was refused permission to continue his work in Trinidad (presumbly because of the types of socio-political analysis in which the newspaper engages) are both strong indications of the significance of CADEC's communication programmes.(65) The training of professional communicators in Caribbean perspectives and sensitivities goes a long way towards reducing the dominance of the foreign media on the Caribbean psyche, and the production of Caribbean-oriented radio and television programmes ensures that Caribbean people get an opportunity to share their lives and concerns with a wider community. For, after all, that is what 'communication' really means - the Latin word "communicare" means "to share" - and the process of communication in the Caribbean must more and more become the medium of sharing between indigenous communities, and less and less the domination of local communities by external values and social forces. It is in this light also that the value of the many regional meetings which CADEC has sponsored must be seen. They are opportunities for sharing and meeting, between peoples who hitherto had little opportunity to do so, and who were therefore alienated from each other by forces of suspicion, insularity and lack of information. To become more informed about each other in the Caribbean will not only counteract the basic islandic mentality of the region, but also attack the experience of alienation at one of its most important points of influence. Here again, it is the emergence of the new Caribbean Spirit - by communication and integration - that will help to bring into being the realization of the new Caribbean Man.

CADEC launched the Caribbean Community Appeal in 1973 as an educational programme as well as a fund-raising campaign. It was designed to challenge the Church constituency primarily about the need to become more actively involved in the development programmes, which it was implementing, by making financial contributions for its support, and by becoming more aware of how the development process was directly related to the life and work of the Church. One of the earliest advertisements of the Appeal said this in part -

> "Development is biblical - and now!
> In the Old Testament, freedom for the
> people of Israel in the Jubilee year in-
> cluded: Liberation from slavery/
> Freeing from debt/ An opportunity to
> share the resources of the promised land
> It involved: Political freedom/ The
> sharing of material goods/ Human dignity/
> Freedom of the spirit
> This kind of freedom God has promised
> all his people through Jesus Christ Our Lord.
> So we have got to learn about world
> development so that when we talk about
> it we shall talk sense about it. But
> we have to do more than talk.
> We have got to work. We have got to
> give our hard-earned money so that
> people will take world development seriously.
> . . . .
> Development is for everyone, equally.
> But at present, some are much more equal
> than others.
> SUPPORT THE 2 % APPEAL". (66)

This was clearly an attempt to encourage the Caribbean community in general, and the Christian community in particular, to share some of their scarce resources with others as a part of the development process. It is significant that the freedom motif was employed as the reason for participation in the development exercise; it was to demonstrate that people could do much more to rid the region of the pressures of human alienation by working for greater equality among Caribbean people. Thus the Caribbean Community Appeal was to become the major programmic instrument through which the ordinary members of the Churches could actively participate in, and be identified with, the new developmental thrusts which CADEC had initiated on the part of the Churches. The fact that the amounts raised over the years have been minimal, when compared with the overall CADEC Budget, does not detract from the sacrificial nature of the gifts from the generally poor Church-members, nor does it signify the extent to which the man in the pew understands and supports what CADEC is attempting. The indications

are that the man in the pulpit is often the stumbling-block to more
regular and effective contact between the ordinary Church-member
and the CADEC programmes. The community of sharing is a necessary
environment for the growth and development of the new Caribbean
Man.

> "As thou in bond of love dost join
> The Father and the Son;
> So fill us all with mutual love
> And knit our hearts in one". (67)

That verse of a popular hymn to the Holy Spirit expresses quite faithfully what is the theological link between the struggle against alienation
and the growth of the new Caribbean Man. For if the Godhead is
known as love-in-action made manifest in the world, and that love
spells creativity and continuity, it also spells out in concrete terms
what is the real meaning of c o m m u n i t y . God is revealed to us as
Spirit in the fact of community. The community of the Godhead calls
for the mutuality of love among men of faith, and the undying propensity
to share with others that which God has so freely allowed. Furthermore,
it is only by living in community that the man of faith can hope to
achieve any concrete realization of the meaning of the image of God.

In this respect, the Gospel speaks of the essential character of the Kingdom of God as the community of sharing, to the point where God himself gave his only Son - the highest and most perfect expression of
himself - to achieve the liberation of all humanity. The Acts of the
Apostles and the letters of Paul all point to the sociality of the Holy
Spirit. The Spirit is experienced, not in terms of magical or super-
human power and vitality, but in the realization of the common bond
of the community of faith through which the diversity of spiritual gifts
proclaims the unity of divine love and human liberation. Theological
praxis therefore consists of the working together of the community of
faith towards greater community, for it is in that way, and in that
way alone, that human alienation can gradually be overcome, and the
historical dimensions of social justice can reflect the real meaning
of the image of God in society. The emphasis of the Caribbean Conference of Churches in working together across denominational lines,
and also across lines of faith and non-faith, is in keeping with the
demands of the Gospel to build up community by breaking down barriers
of alienation and subjugation.

Hans Kung says that the Spirit is no other than God himself -

> "God close to man and the world, as
> comprehending but not comprehensible,
> self-bestowing but not controllable,
> life-giving but also directive power
> and force. He is then not a third
> party, not a thing between God and men,
> but God's personal closeness to men". (68)

Such a statement includes a great deal of what is involved in the theological meaning of community as the demonstration of the Spirit. For as man strives for a community of freedom, love, justice and humanity, man is enabled by the nearness of God which is his Spirit. Paul speaks of the Spirit himself bearing witness with our spirit - they are never identical, but in faith they are closely related in the praxis of solidary love and social justice. Social justice means sharing and caring, and the New Testament abounds with examples of such sharing and caring as concrete demonstrations of what Christian orthopraxis entails.

Thus Christian praxis for the development of the Caribbean is basically action for community at its deepest and most human level of realized existence; and an important sign of theological praxis is to be seen in the Churches' co-operative and ecumenical attempts to fight against human alienation in the region. The promotion of social justice must be a major concern of a people's theology of achievement and fulfillment, since it denotes a determination to resist collectively the structures of alienation, and also to survive with human dignity in the face of threatening and dehumanizing forces. The struggle for human community therefore, and belief in the historical praxis of the Spirit are inter-related. The development programme of the CCC between 1971 and 1977 represents an unmistakable sign of the Church's prophetic action against human alienation in society. It indicates that the Church in the Caribbean is prepared to become deeply involved with the restlessness, despair, aspirations and struggles of the people in the region, because the Church remains a provisional and pilgrim community. It responds to God's historic call out of the historical moment. It announces through this development programme a profound understanding of itself as a human community that is still the people of God. It seeks to realize what is the meaning of man not only as a being-in-community, but also of man as made in the image of God. Through the realities of the Caribbean experience, it loses itself -

> "in binding up wounds, caused by
> aggression, hate, prejudice and greed,
> by 'sticking out its neck' in the battle
> for more just and socio-economic structures,
> and by serving whole-heartedly the provisional
> goal of greater humanization". (69)

The concrete working out of what is meant by belief in the Holy Spirit, and in the need for active response to that belief in the Caribbean therefore demands a close relationship between the will of God to fulfill his promise and the Caribbean human endeavour. The Spirit of God is also the Spirit of Christ. He is creative, liberating, and also just. Creative action towards greater self-reliance and social justice must therefore be the hall-mark of Christian social praxis in the Caribbean, informed continuously by the need to respond through love and obedience to all that God wills for man through Christ. Caribbean Christian endeavour

172

must spell community and common action, just as the early Church understood action for community to be a demonstration of the working of the Spirit through the lives of men. In the final analysis, the only social programme for the Church in any and every age is J e s u s Christ himself - a theological interpretation of the CCC's development programme between 1971 and 1977 provides us with just one example of what such a social programme can mean in Caribbean terms.

Economic and cultural liberation

True human development entails the active engagement of people in their own self-development. Even if catalysts and incentives originate from without, the actual praxis for development requires that people become the principal agents of their own process of change, of their own social destiny. This is a fundamental factor in the search for humanization, the struggle for liberation. The following quotation is particularly relevant -

> "Attempting to liberate the oppressed
> without their reflective participation
> in the act of liberation is to treat
> them as objects which must be saved from
> a burning building; it is to lead them
> into the populist pitfall and transform
> them into masses which can be manipulated.
>   At all stages of their liberation,
> the oppressed must see themselves as men
> engaged in the ontological and historical
> vocation of becoming more fully human.
> Reflection and action become imperative
> when one does not erroneously attempt to
> create a dichotomy, between the content
> of humanity and its historical forms". (70)

With these words, Paulo Freire sums up very succinctly the essential characteristics of the liberation process - that people must be subjects rather than objects, and that action and reflection must go together. Any analysis of action for development in the Caribbean must include a search for these characteristics.

We suggested in our first chapter that Caribbean society was characterized by structured poverty, dependence and alienation. The common experience was one of domination - economic and cultural domination. Development in the Caribbean therefore had to be seen as the struggle for economic and cultural liberation. To confront the structures of domination by engaging in the struggle for liberation would indeed be revolutionary action in the Caribbean, as in any other region of the world. However, revolutionary action could not be undertaken f o r the people, it had to be taken by the people themselves. Furthermore, no single movement, or popular institution could bring about the transformation of the Caribbean. Nevertheless, such movements could w i t n e s s - by conscientization and praxis - to the need of, and the possibilities for, such a transformation. Witness is of cardinal importance to liberating praxis.

It is in the light of the foregoing reflections that the work of the CCC, in its attempt to engage in the development process, must be seen. With its meagre resources (human and material) it was impossible to do much that would make a radical difference (quantitatively) to the conditions existing in Caribbean society. It could not succeed in breaking down all the structures of dependence, nor in providing material assistance to all the poorest of the poor in the region, nor even in effecting significantly higher levels of popular participation. Yet insofar as it has promoted and extolled the need for creativity, continuity and community as essential ingredients for the authentic development - humanization - of society in the Caribbean, it can be said to have borne witness to the possibility of liberation in the future. It is the relentless challenging of the structures of economic and cultural domination with the means at its disposal, and the consistency of courage to risk confrontation with the status quo - both ecclesastical and national - that constitutes the primary theological significance of the development programmes of the CCC between 1971 and 1977. It has engaged in the theological praxis by bearing witness to the need for liberation in the Caribbean, and has initiated action on several fronts to move Caribbean people onwards and upwards from a pre-occupation with survival to a pre-occupation with creativity. The essential mission of the Church in the world is to bear witness to the liberating work of Jesus Christ, who was himself a man - a sharer in common humanity. Paulo Freire is absolutely right when he affirms -

> "If we have faith in men, we cannot
> be content with saying that they are
> human persons while doing nothing
> concrete to enable them to exist as
> such". (71)

To have engaged in action for the pursuit of economic and cultural liberation in the Caribbean was to have demonstrated a concrete dimension of faith in Jesus Christ, as well as in Caribbean humanity. Not only is it too early to measure the results of such engagement, but it is also impossible to do so theologically. The engagement is the crux of the matter - for with St. Paul it is important to say - "neither he who plants nor he who waters in anything, but only God who gives the growth". (72) In a very real and concrete sense, for the man of faith, the future belongs to God. To witness to the transformation of social, economic, and political structures towards the greater humanization and liberation of Caribbean personhood is to share in God's creativity, continuity and liberating community.

Conclusions

Our discussion in this chapter has shown that between 1971 and 1977 the development work of the CCC has been in pursuit of a vision for greater self-sufficiency in the Caribbean. The participation of the Churches in the development process in the Caribbean has not however been generally informed by a commonly agreed theological perspective. The General Secretary himself complained about the need for theological clarity at the Second Assembly in 1977. The major pre-occupation of the ecumenical gatherings, during our period of review, has been with the emergence of the "new Caribbean man", and between 1971 and 1977 there has been a general development of thought about what this should mean in social, political and economic terms. We have seen that the vision of the "new Caribbean man" can also become a theological perspective if Caribbean man is seen as being made in the image of God, and that to pursue this vision in social and historical terms can become the main agenda of Caribbean Christian praxis.

The Church as the community of believers in the Caribbean, is also a principal agency of the Kingdom of God. By its very nature it must remain the poor Church, ministering and witnessing in concrete terms on behalf of justice, freedom and love for the people of the region - particularly the poor and the oppressed. Through witness and service, through the use of its common resources and opportunities, it is to become an important instrument for human development in the Caribbean. The development work of the CCC indicates that the Churches have already been engaged in this process together. Their assistance to people in struggling for economic growth, through encouraging greater creativity, is in faithful response to God's creative love in the world. Their promotion of self-reliance among dependent peoples points to God's call through Christ for continuity and trusting endurance. Their promotion of, and search for, community among men signals not only a struggle for social justice but also the nearness of the Spirit of God whose power is particularly experienced in a community of sharing, caring and loving. Christian social praxis is the response of the community of faith to the revealed solidary love - creative, continuing and societal - of the Triune God. The pursuit of economic and cultural liberation is thus the concrete demonstration of theological praxis.

The theological paths which we identified in the previous chapter have provided for us a useful framework in which to interpret the development work of the CCC. We have been able to provide a perspective through which that specific activity might be seen to be Christian orthopraxis - the response of faith to the experience of the Covenant-God in the Caribbean. The theology of fulfillment has pointed to God's continuing role in working on the side of the poor and the oppressed, and also to the continuing struggle of Caribbean people to achieve such a measure of survival out of their conflicts with social systems that possibilities for greater humanity may emerge as well - possibilities for dignity, freedom, equality, justice and self-fulfillment. All of this is the proper business of theological praxis, and the Churches have initiated a significant process of social change and human renewal by their consolidated and singular efforts in the CCC. What then of the Caribbean Church in general, and its own need for renewal?

The importance of improving the quality of human survival in the Caribbean and responding to the need for human fulfillment will continue to be a major concern for the Caribbean Church. The way in which it seeks to reinterpret its mission, to re-deploy its resources and exercise its power, and to minister to the expressed needs of the society as a whole will be measured against this objective. For survival and preservation must be replaced by survival and fulfillment; the former spells complacency and accommodation while the latter spells struggle and change, growth and maturity; but none of this will be possible unless the Church is willing to confess to its own need for change and renewal, for liberation and maturity.

The need for greater self-reliance is matched only by the need for greater social justice and material well-being. None can question the validity of the secularization process in the Caribbean Church today. The Church has indeed come of age, but it needs to become the Church of the age. The community of faith is comprised of growing "new Caribbean men", and the structure of their response to the call of the Covenant-God to be his people in a particular socio-historical milieu must be characterized by a deeper awareness of what the Gospel of liberation and fulfillment has to do if it is to take root in that milieu. To fail to make ourselves aware of what this means in our social existence is to be non-responsible, and for the Caribbean theological experience non-responsibility is what we call Sin. There is an urgent need for a greater sense of Christian maturity in the Caribbean. Our final chapter will therefore deal with this important issue.

Chapter VIII

TOWARDS GREATER CHRISTIAN MATURITY

> "You need milk, not solid food;
> for every one who lives on milk
> is unskilled in the word of righteous-
> ness, for he is a child. But solid
> food is for the mature, for those
> who have their faculties trained
> by practice to distinguish good from evil". (1)

The meaning of maturity

The words quoted above from the "Letter to the Hebrews" provide the main focus for our discussion in this final chapter. The writer of that Letter clearly perceived that maturity consisted in having one's faculties trained "by practice", or in the 'school of daily living', so that one could continually meet face-to-face with reality and so make clear distinctions about pros and cons - "good and evil". Maturity itself involves the growing capacity to respond to the challenges of life which generally present themselves in ways which tend to induce confusion and indecision. Edward Carr once suggested that immature thought was often predominantly "purposive and utopian", but he went on to warn that thought which rejected purpose altogether was the "thought of old age". For Carr therefore, mature thought was that which combined "purpose with observation and analysis". (2) It is this combination of the three dimensions of mature thought which must also characterize the real meaning of Christian maturity. The sense of Christian purpose - or the continuing consciousness of being a Christian - together with the aptitude to see things as they really are, and to analyse them according-ly, these constitute the basic attitudes for mature Christians in their actual historical context. But just as utopia and reality are interdependent, so too are theory and practice, and Christian maturity necessarily involves the growth of the Christian in the active pursuit of all that he believes that Christ means to the world of humanity.

The writer of the "Letter to the Ephesians" is very clear on this point of Christian maturity as the integral relationship between faith and praxis. He says that within the framework of the "body of Christ" - and this is taken to mean a dynamic and functional interrelationship of those who have accepted Christ and all that he means for the world - the 'saints' are equipped for the work of the ministry. It is important to remember that 'ministry' means s e r v i c e and n o t s t a t u s. The writer goes on to explain why the 'saints' are equipped - if is for the building up of the body of Christ. This building up of the 'body of Christ' has a specific goal; it reaches out to a particular objective that is defined in this way -

> "until we all attain to the unity of
> the faith and of the knowledge of the Son
> of God, to mature manhood, to the measure
> of the stature of the fulness of Christ". (3)

The implication is clear: Christian maturity has its intrinsic criterion as well as its expressed purpose. Manhood has to be increasingly humanized, people must become more and more human. Further, this process must take place within the unity of the faith and keep as its goal "the measure of the stature of the fulness of Christ". Christian maturity cannot subsist individually therefore, it draws its meaning and its relevance from the community of faith, and the community of faith draws its own meaning and relevance from its particular focus - Jesus Christ.

There are some basic qualities which follow from all of this if Christian maturity is to have effective meaning for the process of human salvation (or liberation). First, humanity itself is understood to be co-humanity, persons share in a wider fellowship of human existence, and our reality consists both of our dependence on God, through Christ, and our inter-relatedness with one another. Secondly, there is a mutual responsibility which is inherent in this inter-relatedness, and no amount of argument can cause this quality to become dispensable. Personal relationships carry mutual responsibility and we cannot exist without them. Thirdly, there is required of us an ever growing level of generosity of spirit and magnanimity as would more accurately reflect growth into the "fulness of Christ". The Gospel makes it abundantly clear that the historical Jesus, whom we acknowledge today as the Christ of our faith (God's anointed one), was in every respect anxious to demonstrate a quality of generosity and magnanimity which unmistakably pointed to the power of the love of God over the forces of evil. Evil thrives where generosity of mind and spirit is excluded. Finally, Christian maturity is liberative, and liberation has an essentially communal nature. Further, when a community experiences true liberation there is real joy. We can therefore say that there can be no true liberation where there is neither community nor joy, and Christian maturity demands that such human temptations which proffer 'happiness' and 'comfort' at the expense of other people should be resolutely resisted in the name of Christ. We agree with Daniel Jenkins when he writes thus -

> "the Christian community is meant to be
> the place where, above all others, fellow-
> members of Christ neither keep each other
> down nor do each other down but build
> each other up, as the necessary condition
> of growth toward a common maturity". (4)

Because development also aims at maturity, and because, with St. Paul, we can say that "we know that in everything God works for good with those who love him" (Romans 8:28), we come to understand action for development as an active concern for Christian maturity. Christian maturity must encompass that active desire for service that would denote purposeful and positive change in the society, together with growth in effective vitality, resulting in more wholesome levels of existence. Christian maturity involves a creative and self-liberating involvement in change.

It is within the context of the foregoing discussion that we are to understand the significance of what we have been attempting to examine in this study. The fact that the Church in the Caribbean has begun to make a systematic attempt to participate in the process of development is a historical sign of Christian maturity. The rest of this chapter will therefore be concerned with summing up the main issues that have emerged during the current study with reference to the implications for the growth of Christian maturity, and also to examining some of the broader implications for the future mission of the Church in the Caribbean if this process of growth is to make any qualitative difference to its programmes. For as Jenkins rightly suggests -

> "A Church is at its most mature when it is
> forgetting itself in helping the other parts of
> the life of the community reach their own
> maturity, as that in its turn is to be under-
> stood in a Christian context". (5)

The CCC and the promotion of Christian maturity

Our study has indicated that the Caribbean as a whole is characterized by poverty, dependence and alienation. These are the current realities of the human experience in a society which has had to pass through the rigours of slavery and indenture, plantation and colonialism, neo-colonialism and underdevelopment. We have seen that the human condition has been directly affected by the socio-economic and political condition, and that the dialectic of domination and dependence continues to be at the centre of the stage of Caribbean existence. The way forward requires radical changes that will confront the existing structures of the economic system in such a way as would enable all of the people in the region to participate more effectively and with greater self-confidence and deeper meaning in the total process. We have seen that the demand for economic liberation rests very heavily on the need for a radical change in the political will of the region, such as would enable the poor majority to share in the public apparatus of decision-making. Economic liberation would need to be accompanied by cultural liberation, thus motivating the people to identify and confront the structures of alienation within their very responses to reality. Cultural alienation can mainly be countered by the collective affirmation of all that is common, familiar and most authentic, and by the subsuming of the imitative instincts under the creative energies of the human spirit in the region. The Caribbean experience thus called for radical efforts for development - structural and human - and all the institutions which controlled the allegiance of the people were naturally expected to become engaged in the process of transformation. Structural transformation and changing consciousness must always coinhere for human liberation to be authentic. The way Jesus puts it goes like this: new wine and new bottles are appropriate for each other.

We were particularly concerned to focus attention on the efforts which were initiated by the Caribbean Conference of Churches to engage in this process of development in the region, as a prophetic and pioneering ministry on behalf of the Churches. We saw that the Consultation at Chaguaramas in 1971 had provided the major signal for the involvement of the Churches on an ecumenical basis, and that by the Second Assembly in 1977 a series of initiatives in the fields of renewal and development was already being recorded by the CCC. These initiatives were in pursuit of four main objectives -

(a) to generate self-dependence;
(b) to provide catalysts for development;
(c) to provide material assistance for those willing to help themselves out of their depressed condition;
(d) to promote wider participation in the socio-political process, and also to encourage reconciliation among estranged social groupings.

These objectives were to give systematic expression to the understanding of development as a process of human liberation and the struggle for social justice accompanied by growth in self reliance and economic welfare. The CCC interpreted its programme of development as a direct imperative of the Gospel of Jesus Christ, and sought to encourage its member Churches to incorporate such programmes within the mainstream of their agenda. But there was an absence of theological consensus on how such innovative praxis was to become a concrete expression of the mission and ministry of the Church in the Caribbean. Indeed, theological concerns for social change had already been widely debated and pursued in several parts of the Christian world. The ecumenical debate on theology and development had gathered considerable momentum at the global level. In specific areas of the Third World, notably in Latin America and Africa, indigenous methodologies were already being established for interpreting their respective socio-historical situations theologically, and for engaging in liberating social praxis in accordance with their own response of faith. Faith and praxis were, for them, inseparable, as they analyzed and responded to the realities of their respective situations. No such methodology has as yet emerged in the Caribbean, and our concern has therefore been to identify some signposts by which we might discover a theologically illuminating way of interpreting the involvement of the Churches in the process of Caribbean development. The specific development programmes of the CCC between 1971 and 1977 provide a suitable story through which we might suggest an appropriate framework for such a theological interpretation.

Historical consciousness in the Caribbean experience has been largely dominated by the will to survive. The business of survival in the face of continuing pressures of poverty, dependence and alienation, has provided the basic concept for doing theology in the Caribbean. If it is true to say that the Covenant-God has been mainly responsible for the survival of Caribbean people in the face of their oppressive structures, it is right to believe that it is the will of the same God that the same people should struggle creatively for the improvement of their condition, and for the transformation of social structures which deny them the possibility of achieving a quality of existence consistent with the belief that man is made in the image of God. If it is true to say that Jesus Christ, as the supreme revelation of God in history, has proclaimed by word and deed that God's love is essentially love-in-action, solidary love, it is right to believe that this love is to be understood today as the existence of God's work of fulfilling and accomplishing with the man of faith whatever he attempts to achieve in the struggle for freedom and self-fulfillment. Human achievement and divine fulfillment of the promises of liberation are therefore inseparable and indispensable for Christian theological reflection in the Caribbean. The struggle to achieve a greater measure of social justice, self-reliance and economic welfare signifies the theological meaning of community, continuity and creativity. For God's solidary love sustains human existence most powerfully in community, it affirms the value of continuity by resisting the spiritual forces of death and domination, and it makes the man of faith a pro-creator with God in purposeful creative activity for the advancement of his welfare. It is within that framework of creativity, continuity and community as theologically illuminating aspects of God's action and man's response that the Church in the Caribbean might profitably interpret the development programme of the CCC, and its contribution to economic and cultural liberation in the Caribbean.

Thus far we have been summarizing the main issues in our study, leading up to a suggested framework for the interpretation of the Churches' engagement in development praxis, mainly through the agency of the CCC. Such an engagement signifies in historical terms that the Church in the Caribbean (now no longer the mission field of metropolitan Christianity) has indeed come of age. Further, it signifies also that the Church in the region has begun the process of becoming the Church of the age responding strategically and systematically to the historical realities and challenges of the day. It is within this context that the continuing work of the CCC is of profound importance, if it is to continue to be an important ecumenical instrument for the promotion of Christian maturity among the Churches. We therefore need to look at five areas of concern to which the CCC will be expected to pay further attention if its catalytic role is to be enhanced in the future.

First, the overwhelming dependence of the CCC on funding from outside the Caribbean should not be rationalized away or taken too lightly; it is a factor that must be seriously confronted. All of the programmes which are implemented by the CCC, in both their sectors of Renewal and Development, are dependent on the funding available for their support. In almost every instance such funding is dependent on the endorsement and approval which the programme receives from external decision-makers and on the eventual transfer of financial resources into the region. The basic spectacle in this scenario consists of programmes determined in the Caribbean but enabled through external resources. Thus there is a close relationship between local ideas and foreign capacitation for such ideas. (The reader might be tempted to respond that this is an improvement on the days when both the ideas and the capacitation originated outside.) What this in fact means is that there are likely to be some programme areas, locally conceived, which may never be implemented because they fail to be endorsed and approved by foreign agencies. This places certain constraints on the process of planning priorities within the CCC itself, since programme possibilities will be weighted not so much in terms of their urgency and their capacity to respond effectively to locally expressed needs, but rather in terms of the availability of funds from abroad. The principal partner agencies in metropolitan countries which support the work of the CCC are generally presided over by decision-makers whose attitudes differ sharply from those of the personnel employed to carry out their decisions. The latter are often progressive and reasonably sensitive to actual needs and priorities in the Caribbean. It is chiefly the gap existing between the paternalistic perspectives of metropolitan decision-makers and the felt needs of the Caribbean poor that requires serious attention. To what extent can such a gap be effectively narrowed, and whose responsibility is it to see that something is done about it? It is difficult to conceive that the poor could re-orient (-educate) the rich away from their paternalism and insensitivity to the poor, especially where geographical distance between them is so extensive. Christian maturity would therefore seem to demand that the CCC assume a greater responsibility for determining and pursuing local priority programme needs even at the cost of reducing their dependence on external decision-making and financial support.

The second consideration follows on from the first. If most of the funding that is used by the CCC originates outside the region, to what extent can the Churches genuinely consider the CCC to be their Conference? What does 'accountability' mean in such a situation, and to whom is the CCC chiefly accountable? A review of the operation of the CADEC Programme for 1976 shows that the Development Fund Committee approved an amount of (US) $ 339, 850 in loans and grants for projects in the region, (6) while the total amount raised in the Caribbean for the support of the CCC (from both Church and non-Church sources) was (US) $ 37, 628. (7) The local funds are raised annually through the Caribbean Community Appeal. In 1977 there was a significant decrease in the sum raised through that Appeal, for only (US) $ 29, 899 was realized. (8) It is true that there are other significant local resources which the Churches make available to the work of the CCC, such as specialist expertise, the use of buildings and other facilities, together with other gestures of good-will and co-operation which are really non-quantifiable. But the situation still does not inspire confidence in the belief that the member-Churches are demonstrating a large measure of Christian maturity. This should manifest itself in their concrete and active commitment to an organization which they have established, and which purports to function on their behalf. Christian maturity necessarily involves growth towards higher levels of stewardship, responsibility and accountability, and it would seem legitimate to expect the member-Churches to re-double their efforts in raising the level of mutual accountability between the CCC and themselves. As long as the CCC remains for the Churches a type of 'optional extra' the real quality of their avowed commitment to praxis for social change is likely to be called into question.

Thirdly, there is need for a careful re-appraisal of the scope of the CCC's development programmes and programme priorities to determine the extent to which they enhance to process of Christian maturity, or else dissipate its thrusts. There is no doubt that the motivating factor for the establishment of some programmes was the availability of funds from abroad. Some programmes have actually ceased to function when funding sources have failed.

Perhaps the top priority needs to be given to the question of communications, and the need to share ideas, insights and information between persons and groups across the region. The role of C a r i b b e a n C O N T A C T in this regard can hardly be over-stated, but that newspaper, as an instrument of analysis and education in the region, will need to develop a simple and more attractive style and format in order to reach simpler and ordinarily educated minds. There are indications that the future of the newspaper is in doubt because of the cessation of financial support from some external sources. (9) The importance of sustaining the newspaper as a viable tool for regional integration needs to be fully appreciated by the Churches, and only time will tell whether or not they have actually done so. It will be a mark of Christian maturity and responsibility that the Churches, through the CCC, focus specific attention on conspicuous areas of social need, and also provide support for the maintenance of an effective channel of communication for the region which is not constrained by the predilections of the power-groups in the Caribbean.

Greater attention should also be paid to the interrelationship of health care and family life education within the Caribbean development process. Between 1971 and 1977 the CCC does not appear to have placed much priority on this area of human concern. It is undeniable that this area has a direct bearing on the welfare of Caribbean society, and is of particular importance to the whole process of human development. The ministry of Jesus Christ was a liberating one, and this was repeatedly evidenced by his efforts to heal those who were sick, and to restore broken families to their proper state of wholeness. It must surely be in such an area that the CCC might be able to discover yet more fertile ground for signifying its activity as theological praxis, and for convincing the doubtful Christians that development action and theological praxis converge at the points of human need and suffering. Indeed, in its widest sense, the healing ministry of the Church encompasses action for development and human liberation, and Christian maturity demands that special regard should be paid to the ministry to broken persons, broken relationships, as well as to the social structures which thrive on keeping people in a broken state (economically, culturally and otherwise).

Fourthly, enough has already been said to indicate that the Churches have not yet begun to make efficient (or effective) use of the CCC facility. The historic importance of such a movement in the region lies in the fact that the Churches now have available to them a regional network - flexible and creative - which other institutions in the region do not have. The possibilities for ecumenical sharing of ideas and personnel, for integrated planning and action, for joint ecclesial reforms and dialogue, are all there to be exploited. The Churches have the opportunity to pioneer a greater and more effective thrust at regional unity and co-operation at a time when other such efforts are flagging, notably among the political leaders. Christian maturity requires of Caribbean Churches that they become alert to "redeem the time", and to work out in bold historic terms what are the similarities and points of convergence between Caribbean unity and Christian unity. The fervent pursuit of regional integration by the Churches can indeed become a dynamic sign of human reconciliation in accordance with the will of God.

Fifthly, the bold objectives which are outlined in the CCC Constitution demonstrate a new perspective of mission, witness and service, which is generally absent from the life of the Churches in their denominational activities. Ecumenism often appears to be an 'optional extra', if we are to judge by the lack of attention that is paid to it in the official counsels of the Churches. The process of incorporating the stated objectives of the CCC into the official priorities and programmes of its member-Churches has been extremely slow. The Churches have preached at "Capernaum" what they have not preached in "their own country". (10) There is clearly a point of contradiction here which requires urgent attention and honest action on the part of the Churches. Christian maturity also entails that the Churches face up to the contradictions which their sponsorship of the CCC forces on them, and that they incorporate into their systems the same changes and objectives which they have endorsed at the regional ecumenical level.

This leads us on to look at some of the broader implications for the future of the Churches themselves, if the meaning of the CCC is to be concretely reflected in the wider fellowship of the Churches.

Christian maturity and the Church for the future

The essence of human growth lies in the fact that one is always open towards the future. Growth in Christian maturity entails that response of faith which always acknowledges present positions or attitudes to be provisional and subject to change. It is the continuing sense of being in a position that can only imperfectly represent man's right response to God's call that underlines the provisionality of all Church praxis. Thus Wolfhart Pannenberg describes the Church as a "symbol of the coming kingdom", (11) it is a foreshadowing of the kingdom of God which is yet to come. It must therefore hold itself open to the future, growing gracefully in the capacity to manage and cope with change, and resisting the human temptations of "confusing human achievements with the absolute, the penultimate with the ultimate". (12) With respect to the Caribbean Church therefore, James Tucker writes thus -

> "A young Church is emerging, a Church that
> has abandoned the theology of fatalism and
> tragedy. It is a Church which believes that
> the things that have been placed here were
> placed for our use and enjoyment; that God
> intended us to survive and to survive with
> dignity. It tells us that we must forsake
> consumerism, wear what we can produce, eat
> what we cultivate and that which is natural
> to us. Most importantly, it tells us to be
> human". (13)

Tucker's reference to a "theology of fatalism and tragedy" relates to the traditional missionary approach to theological interpretation of suffering and deprivation in the Caribbean. Most of the Christians were made to believe that God had "ordered their estate", and that they had no alternative but to bear it bravely and to "take it to the Lord in prayer". Tucker also stresses the importance of survival, and of survival with dignity. He suggests that this is the main Gospel of a young and growing Church in the Caribbean. Wherever there is youth there are possibilities for marked growth, possibilities for fulfillment, possibilities for maturity. Tucker also insists that the young Caribbean Church is announcing the importance of being human. It is on this point that Hans Kung also draws the connection between being Christian and being human -

"Being Christian cannot mean ceasing to be human.
But neither can being human mean ceasing to be
Christian. Being Christian is not an addition
to being human: there is not a Christian level
above or below the human. The true Christian
is not a split personality". (14)

The Caribbean Church for the future will therefore need to work out very
concretely what is the call of God to be fully human, and to continue the
process of discovering and re-discovering the full implications of its
belief that the Word became flesh. Structures of social existence will
be of great significance for this process of theological reflection and
praxis, but it will also need to pay particular attention to some aspects
of its own internal styles and polity which call into question its genuine
growth in Christian maturity. We can point to only four aspects here. (15)
These aspects include: the Liturgy, Evangelism, the participation of
Women in the life and mission of the Church, and the interaction between the historic and the newer Churches in the process of ecclesial
renewal and Caribbean development.

Liturgy

The activity which is common to all Christian Churches is that of worship.
It is the most visible sign of their existence, and (sometimes) of their
vitality. Not only is it the most common and visible among them, it is
also the most important aspect of their existence as community. J.G.
Davies (whose work and scholarship on the liturgical aspects of the life
of the Church has been of invaluable help to contemporary theological
debate) describes worship in this way -

"Worship is a social rite which symbolizes
the totality of what is meaningful to the
people involved. It provides for encounter
with socially shared symbols that unify
human experience in the world, invest it with
meaning and relate it to ultimate concern". (16)

For Davies, liturgy and life are inseparable, for it is the human encounter
with the "Everyday God". Yet worship is more than that - it "becomes
a celebrating of hope and a centre of stimulation for the active reshaping
of the world". (17) Davies therefore warns against Christianity becoming
a ghetto if its liturgical activity does not bear any direct relationship to
changing the world. This is the same point which is made very strongly
by Cunningham, Eagleton, Wicker, Redfern and Bright. They describe
the liturgy as a political force - "a force constantly working to transform
human society into its own, communal image". (18)

It is important for the Churches in the Caribbean that they resist the
temptation of taking the liturgy for granted, of sharing in it in a mech-
anistic fashion, or of treating it as the least challenging part of their

ministry. To ignore, or to be unmindful of, the political dimension of worship, and to refuse to connect the values of Christianity to the values of the world beyond through effective liturgical action, would be a gross departure from the paths of Christian maturity. The liturgy must be seen to have a specific political function of achieving the communication of Christ to the world, towards the establishment of a radically just and humane society. The levels of human experience at the socio-economic and political levels must be connected to the liturgical functioning of the Christian community - the former must be affected by the latter. All this raises a further point about the liturgy and its relationship to social needs.

Davies says that "worship should be a source of creative and inventive imagination in the service of love". He goes on to speak of it as the "liturgical expression of the love of neighbour, and its point of reference is always beyond itself in the world of human need". (19) This is in agreement with Brian Wicker's statement that in the liturgy, a community of people who are "radically equal before God and each other" are to be also "wholly committed to serving each other, and finding their own life in that dedication to common needs". (20) The Churches of the Caribbean must recognize in their liturgical activity the developmental thrust of service to social needs, and the evangelistic imperatives for demonstrating human compassion; for it is not by accident that the four Gospels include the Feeding of the Five Thousand as a liturgical, political, eschatological and developmental sign of the efficacy of the ministry of Jesus. (21)

The liturgical life of the Church thus provides ample opportunity for creativity, for continuity, and for community, among the people of God. It constitutes the principal connecting link between what the Church does within itself and how if functions in the world around it. It provides for the celebration of the hope for liberation in all its forms, and makes possible the human symbols of achievement and divine promise as liberative signs of man being made in the image of God. It can motivate the people of God - in their state of powerlessness - to engage in the struggle for working out in their socio-historical existence what such an image should mean. The liturgy is a fundamental instrument of liberation in the hands of the people of God - Christian maturity demands that it should be used effectively.

Evangelism

The importance of evangelism as a central function of the Church cannot be over-stressed. It is beyond question that the ministry of evangelism, the preaching of the Gospel, must be performed by word as well as by action. Evangelism, as a direct fulfillment of the Gospel must perform a liberating rather than a domesticating function. It must ground itself in the meaning of the Gospel for today, and prepare the community of faith for the unfolding of new possibilities in the future. By the effective process of learning what today is all about and what is the word of the Lord for today - however imperfectly that word is received - the evangelistic process will have accomplished most of its task of pointing towards tomorrow. The use of appropriate images and symbols, the application of familiar experiences, and the confession of an imperfect understanding of religious mystery, are all important components of effective and honest proclamation.

Much depends however on the basic theological approach to proclamation in the Caribbean, and on the capacity of the preacher to guide the people in their own use of these components through the "wilderness experience" of their social existence. Theology as critical reflection must be a people's tool, and it is by the patient and imaginative role which the preacher can perform in helping the people to theologize - both in word and deed - that the Church can break new ground for evangelism in the future. There can be no authentic evangelism without authentic divine self-disclosure, and the more the Church can prepare the community of faith to be open to God's continuing evangelism of disclosing himself in concrete and historical situations, so much the more the meaning of the Gospel can become the spring-board for faith as social praxis. A very small percentage of the community's time is spent "in Church", or in organized encounters; the power of the Gospel to affect what happens to the rest of their time must be an important consideration of the Church for the future.

Women

The Caribbean Church for the future will need to pay particular regard to the major sector of its membership - the women. The promotion of human dignity in the Church has been seriously undermined by the way in which the role of the women has been limited. There can be no doubt that women constitute the main-stream of the Church's life and witness. Yet, in the Caribbean in particular, women in the Church have been made to suffer innumerable indignities - because they are women. In a male-dominated Church they have been subjected to a role of 'faithful servant' without any serious recognition of their true status or function. The issue lies much deeper than the ordination of women, for in fact, the historic subjugation of women in the Church has tended to render the contemporary debate on women's ordination a non-issue for most Caribbean Christians. For most of them, it does not matter.

The Gospel proclaims that in Christ all are set free, and that the distinctions of rank between male and female are eliminated. The frequent mention of the presence of women at several episode points in the Gospel story would seem to suggest that Jesus had already begun to demonstrate that liberating process for the women of faith, in spite of the fact that there were none among the Twelve originally chosen as disciples. More important however in the ministry of Jesus, was the fact that he provided for women a p o i n t   o f   s o c i a l   r e f e r e n c e   which was liberatingly responsive to their various needs. This is indicated, for example, by the Syrophoenician woman, Mary Magdalene, the Mother of Jesus, and the Woman with the haemorrhage. The Church in the Caribbean will need to interpret very concretely what this means for today and tomorrow. In a male-dominated society, women have social and human needs that should be appropriately met and with liberating effect. The challenge to the Church is not only to open up the traditionally male sanctuaries to the women, but also to ensure that the community of faith expresses such a concern for caring and sharing that would incarnate what Love means. There can be no true community without free and authentic participation.

The newer Churches

The fourth aspect relates to the relationship between the historic Churches and the newer Churches. Most of the membership of the latter group is comprised of the poorer classes in the Caribbean, while there is a more varied cross-section in the former group. To put it another way, it is very difficult to find the rich and the middle-class among the Pentecostal groups. They therefore consist of a significant body of Caribbean people who have attempted to connect their socio-economic experience with their religious experience. Walter Hollenweger, who has done extensive research on the Pentecostal Movement, has shown that one of the functions of Pentecostal sects is to overcome the feeling of deprivation be it "status contradiction, loneliness, poverty, sickness, racial discrimination, speech and language difficulties, handicaps of character, etc."[22] He has suggested that the central point of the group therapeutic process which helps in overcoming this feeling of deprivation can be found in the Pentecostal service, and he contends that it is in the sphere of liturgy and preaching that the Pentecostal movement has made its most important contribution.[23] Hollenweger admits that in some societies the Pentecostal movement is "a necessary island of humanity. For the poor it provides a home, relative economic security, care when they are sick and basic educational opportunities".[24] Hollenweger's comments are appropriate to the Caribbean experience as well.

The Caribbean reality goes further than this however; and the following quotation from a Pentecostal pastor illustrates the problem -

> "Board members had decided not to join the CCC
> since it would have been confusing to members
> who had fled from the established Church in
> search of Christian conversion and experience".[25]

There is a socio-historical reality that most Pentecostalists today are either past-members of the historic Churches, or children of past-members. The "adversary complex" is therefore quite acute in the newer groupings, and sometimes finds expression in the historic Churches as well. Furthermore, the new developments in the CCC have not helped to lessen the traditional tensions between both groupings, since in Pentecostalist circles it is said -

> "The 'Church' is left out in the doings of
> CADEC. There is no attempt to bring people
> closer to God". (26)

Thus the whole nature of theological praxis, and the basis of the Church's engagement in human development is an area of great dispute.

The question of ecumenism is therefore much more urgent for the Church that is concerned for the future. It will involve a deep and painful assessment of the meaning of the phrase "Christ is divided", as it describes the Christian presence in the Caribbean. The coming together of compatible groupings at the expense of genuine dialogue between the apparently incompatible will bring the real meaning of ecumenism into question. There can be no doubt that all sectors of the Caribbean community of faith will have much to learn from each other. Theological praxis involves a learning to learn, and if this first learning can point to possibilities for dialogue and mutual interaction, then learning at the second stage will undoubtedly provide new possibilities for even more radical theological reflection.

The fact of the matter is that in today's world both sides need each other much more than they are prepared to admit. The historic Churches have traditionally emphasized that which is given and unalterable in the Christian tradition, while the newer Churches have tended to emphasize that which is known and recognized in the present experience. Both emphases are important if the Caribbean Churches are to take seriously the theological meaning of creativity, continuity and community, and if they are to remain in full communion with the Holy Spirit who is the Lord of Life. The search for Christian unity is not identical with a search for uniformity, for there is a unity in diversity which the Spirit gives. But this unity in diversity passes through the route of dialogue and mutual recognition that there is but One Lord. The following question by Bishop Newbigin speaks very strongly to all the Caribbean Churches as they would adopt a mature approach to their future existence -

> "If in the experience of a local Christian
> fellowship we have known that there is in
> Christ a freedom which is not lost but
> gained by the willingness of each both to
> contribute his insight to the common seek-
> ing for the Spirit's guidance, and also to
> defer to the corporate insight of the whole
> body as to what that guidance is, on what
> principle do we deny that the same process
> can operate and ought to operate over a
> wider sphere?"(27)

Continuing challenges for mature Christians

In concluding this study, we need to identify, very briefly, some of
the challenges which seem to the writer to be indispensable for mature
Christians if they are to be seriously involved in effective and dynamic
theological praxis. These challenges arise out of the need for Christians to be in the world, to be of the world, but not for the world.
The traditional distinction in Christian preaching between being in the
world but not of the world appears to the present writer to be at
variance with the person and proclamation of Jesus Christ. He was
certainly in the world, and was also of the world - in the very real
sense of co-identification with humanity and all that it entailed. But he
was not for the world, since by his life and death he witnessed to
the belief that the world itself was for God, and thus ushered in the
process of reconciling the world to itself, and the world itself to God
its Creator, Liberator, and Sustainer. Christian preaching therefore
needs to guard against the prohibition of being not of the world,
since this so readily spells withdrawal, resignation and disengagement
at the very point where the Gospel clearly enjoins the exact opposite.
Christians cannot be for the world, because they are, by their re-
deemed nature, already engaged in witnessing for God in their worldly
existence, against the historical domination by the "Prince of this
World" (see St. John 17: 14-19). Christian maturity demands fervent
and intelligent Christian witness in such a situation, and there are at
least four continuing challenges to be identified within the context of
liberating praxis for social change in the Caribbean.

First, there is the challenge of searching unceasingly for an inter-
cultural theology. One of the most effective ways of controlling
others is to maintain control over what they believe. Consequently,
liberative praxis is partly characterized by one's assuming control
over what one believes, and over the process by which one arrives
at what is to be believed. Theology, as a process of critical reflection,
should therefore be seen as a servant, rather than as a master. Bishop
Desmond Tutu, General Secretary of the South African Council of
Churches, rightly speaks of theology as a risky but "exhilarating
business of reflecting on the experience of a particular Christian community in relation to what God has done, is doing and will do". Tutu
goes on to say -

> "Thus theology must necessarily be limited
> by the limitations of those who are theolo-
> gizing - ethnic, temporal, cultural and
> personality limitations. This means that
> theology must of necessity be particularis-
> tic, existential and provisional. It must
> glory in its in-built obsolescence because
> it must be ready to change if it will
> speak meaningfully to the situation which
> it addresses". (28)

191

Not only will mature Christians therefore need to acknowledge that
there is a plurality of theologies, but they will also need to search
for a mode of theological communication and dialogue which affirms
rather than denies this plurality. Such a mode of theological dialogue
is only possible if Christians of different cultural, ethnic, and ideological circumstances firmly recognize that they have something good
(in terms of the Word from the Lord) to share with each other. It is
in this way that the reality of interdependence within the functioning of
the 'body of Christ' can be reinforced. The search is thus for an
inter-cultural theology, and Hollenweger asserts that the task of such
a theology is indeed the search for a "'body of Christ' - theology",
for unless theology is not just to rationalize our own cultural biases
("a theologically defended cultural imperialism") it should seek to "be
open to this universal and sacramental dimension of the Christian
faith". (29) Such a search must not be for the academics alone, or the
academics in particular, for indeed, God has a way of concealing things
from the "wise and prudent" and revealing them to "babes". (This is
not so much because God makes such a distinction between persons,
but because the "wise and prudent" refuse to qualify for entry into the
'Kingdom' by not becoming "as little children".) Inter-cultural theology
is therefore a people's theology which does not absolutize a people's
culture, but uses that culture towards the construction of a people-to-
people theology.

The second challenge relates to the political options which are
open to mature Christians in their praxis for liberation and fulfillment.
This is an issue that is likely to cause division among Christians for
the rest of time. Positions have been, and will continue to be, polarized
about the way in which Christians should witness to their Lord in the
political sphere. Pope John Paul II warned his fellow Catholics in
Mexico - in January 1979 - about their involvement in politics. He reminded the Bishops, Priests and Religious attending the Conference
of Latin American Bishops at Puebla that they were not social or
political leaders, and that their religious motivation could be weakened
by a secularizing mentality. The Pope further stated his position in
the face of the growing appeal of the Latin American theology of liberation.
He said -

> "Some people claim to show Jesus as
> politically committed, as one who fought
> against Roman oppression and the authori-
> ties and also as one involved in the class
> struggle. This idea of Christ as a political
> figure, a revolutionary, as the subversive
> man from Nazareth, does not tally with the
> church's catechism". (30)

However, the Pope later came out in open support of equity, equality,
and justice for the poor of Latin America before he left Mexico.

Another illustration of the range of the debate on political options can
be found among Christians in Tanzania. Bishop Yohana Jumaa of
Tanzania received a Christmas (1977) present from President Julius
Nyerere of the same country - it was an ebony chalice and ciborium
embellished with ivory. The Bishop re-acted this way -

> "I am taking it with me on Sundays to use
> in the parishes I visit, to show our people
> and let them know that the Church and Govern-
> ment are working hand in hand to help people
> to a fuller life, and care for them in
> spiritual and material matters". (31)

Such apparently harmonious relationships between the leaders of Church
and State in Tanzania suggest a level of mutual support which some
Christians would consider somewhat risky to the freedom of witness
which the Gospel of Jesus Christ enjoins. The reflections of another
Tanzanian churchman, Laurenti Magesa, are also interesting -

> "the most immediate task for theology to
> act as a liberating force in Tanzania is
> to show to the church in this country the
> importance and primacy of involvement in
> all sectors of national life. Ultimately,
> this means involvement in TANU and politics". (32)

Politics is about power. It deals with the struggle for power among
persons in society. It is therefore full of contortions and false claims.
Andre Dumas, (whose reflections on this issue are most illuminating)
reminds us that politics is a "matter of adding up the forces at one's
disposal". (33) For the Christian, in the search for a political theology,
it is important that the Gospel is not devalued or watered down, or that
politics is idealized - for the Gospel has to be incarnated, and politics
has to be demystified. The essential dimension in all this is that of
faith. It is that faith which will distinguish itself from pluralism, for
pluralism "tends to relativize choices to such a degree that it dissipates
them in scepticism". (34) Dumas rightly says that faith acts neither
with "fascination" nor terrorism, that faith will recognize the inherent
contradictions in political theories, and will therefore not be surprised
at setbacks. For Dumas, then, "the task of faith is to achieve the freedom to eat meat without swallowing idols". (35) Jesus had taken part
in political life "without swallowing the idol of political success offered
to him in his temptation by the devil". (36) Dumas further insists however, that at the centre of faith is a Cross which rules out "self-love
by making place for others", and also a resurrection which sets people
free to use political systems without having to idolize them. (37) He
therefore concludes that, for the Christian, faith is "the salt of political
life, which should be free from fear, educated by reverence, sustained
in an incarnate freedom". (38)

The mature Christian in the Caribbean will therefore be challenged in the way in which political systems are supported or condemned. The political climate in the region is becoming more complex with the proliferation of political parties and the growing polarization of political positions among Caribbean people. These are to be seen as significant developments which demand positive and effective Christian response. It is only by an unswerving determination to rise above the claims of political positions to having divine sanction, and to interpret the meaning of the Cross and Resurrection as signs of human achievement and self-fulfillment, that the Christian will be able to use his faith for a healthier involvement in politics. No political system will be perfect, or fully reflect the mind of Christ, but the man of faith, acting in faith in taking his political options, will perhaps become "leaven, hidden and at work in the dough of human history".(39)

A third challenge for mature Christians lies in the nature, meaning and goal of d e v e l o p m e n t itself. Our whole study has been mainly concerned with the Christian involvement in Caribbean development. It is crucial to point out that the Christian concern for full human development is not only a matter for the CCC and the Churches (as social movements) - it is inherently a human concern that lies appropriately at the door of every Christian. As a human concern, development will always be a developing concept, and its shape and contents will always be provisional in relation to the socio-historic circumstances. There are political, cultural, social, economic, spiritual and ecological dimensions of development which are all inter-related, and to which the Christian will need to pay particular regard if an authentic confessional response is to be made. The problem will revolve around definitions and goals. In so far as the Christian is prepared to continually relate developmental goals to the human environment, he will be anxious and ready to review his working definitions of development itself in the light of changing circumstances. For the Caribbean in particular, such goals and definitions will need to emerge out of the actual experiences and aspirations of the people of the region rather than to be imported from external sources. Furthermore, it will be important for Caribbean societies to adopt a mirror image in learning from the experiences of other societies whose conditions and circumstances are not dissimilar. In this respect, more communication between African societies and Caribbean societies will be crucial - for in so many obvious ways these two areas of the Third World share a past of colonialism, a present of neo-colonialism, and a hope of total liberation for self-development. The chances for materializing such a hope may now be greater in Africa than in the Caribbean, but nevertheless there may be so much that both regions can learn from each other in their quest for a better life. Christians will have a part to play in all of this, for it is in the constant appeal to the struggle for human-beings to become who they are - made in the image of God - that the human face of development will constantly be seen.

This has implications for the use that is made of science and technology, and for the way in which technology can become an instrument for human fulfillment rather than for the denial of humanity. It has implications for broadening the horizons of Caribbean people in terms of their search for more appropriate, and less expensive, ways of harnessing and exploiting the resources at their disposal, without underscoring their dependence on the traditional orginators of technology - the metropolitan countries. It has implications for the Caribbean in terms of how they measure development - for one feels less underdeveloped if one recognizes that similar conditions exist in other countries of the Third World. In any event, development is more meaningful if it is seen in terms of a move towards less poverty at a time, rather than a miraculous thrust from poverty to wealth (as measured by metropolitan standards). In the long run, the mature Christian must engage in development as in a struggle for a just and sustainable society. In other words -

> "Society must be so organized as to
> sustain the earth so that a sufficient
> quality of material and cultural life for
> humanity may itself be sustained indefinite-
> ly. A sustainable society which is unjust
> can hardly be worth sustaining. A just
> society that is unsustainable is self-
> defeating". (40)

Such a project will be a continuing challenge for the mature Christian.

Finally, there is the challenge of the f u t u r e . The one dimension of human experience which always seems to reduce mankind to inexplicable fear and confusion of thought is the uncertainty of the future. This is often coupled with an over-riding concern for the indefinite extension of the present. Those who are rich and powerful would seek, as far as possible, to imprison the future by being resistant to change, or by making only such minimal modifications as would suggest change - if only in form. For the poor, the powerless, and the oppressed, the hope for change is often a hope for a less uncomfortable experience of existing circumstances, rather than for a radical transformation that would completely overturn all terms of reference and provide radically new definitions and experiences. For the mature Christian, whether rich or poor, the challenge lies in being open to the future by actively recognizing the provisional and imperfect nature of that which exists in the present, and by actively striving for a better tomorrow as a response to faith. This need to be future-oriented lies deep in the heart of Christianity, for its basic gospel is that the Kingdom of God can be realized on Earth, that it is drawing near but that it has not yet come.

For the Caribbean Christian, whose experience of structured poverty, dependence and alienation would necessitate the advent of a better tomorrow - the imperative is not only to wish or to pray, but t o w o r k

for change. The possibilities of a better tomorrow are real, for if
today does not, it is possible to believe that tomorrow will, belong
to the people. This is the message of A.J. Seymour -

> "Ignorant
> Illegitimate
> Hungry sometimes,
> Living in tenement yards
> Dying in burial societies
> The people is a lumbering giant
> That holds history in his hand.
>
> ....
> ....
>
> "Today they hope
> But to-morrow belongs to the people.
> Tomorrow they will put power behind their brow
> And get skill in their hands.
>
> To-morrow
> They will make a hammer to smash the slums
> And build the schools.
>
> "Like a River, the people hold history in
>   their hands
> And tomorrow belongs to them". (41)

Such a message however can only ring true for the Christian if he holds
firm to the faith that the future belongs to God. "Tomorrow" for Seymour
is but a radical break from "today", but there is no talk of "tomorrow's
tomorrow". All this can only be taken up in the future which belongs not
to the people, but to God. It is this faith which enables the man of faith
to engage in the conflicts and struggles of today as an active response
to God's liberating call in Christ. Christian praxis for liberation in the
Caribbean will face squarely the reality of conflict and confrontation,
pain and possibility, promise and fulfillment. The conflicts of the present are real, the possibility of transformation for the better is also
real. Between conflict and transformation lies the will to be free. That
freedom is assured for the mature Christian in the active translation
of the Exodus event and the Christ event in terms of the historical NOW.

The witness of the CCC between 1971 and 1977 provides one powerful
signal to mature Christians in the Caribbean that the Church can, if
it so wills, make way for new possibilities to displace all that inhibits
human growth, human maturity, and human fulfillment, leaving open
the opportunities for God to influence the course of Caribbean history.
Thus it is in the light of all that has been discussed in these pages that
the following words of a Caribbean Christian, Edmond Desueza, whose
devoted witness to the cause of liberation praxis cost him the joy
of living in his native land (the Dominican Republic), are of profound

value and inspiration for all who would engage faithfully in Christian action for development in the Caribbean -

> "We as Christians must be ready to become
> ourselves in a movement towards a continual
> transformation of the shape and content
> of human beings. Ready to move from exodus
> to exodus; ready to discover for ourselves
> the new experiences that remove the grounds
> of all known security in order to meet those
> realities in which there are better condi-
> tions to release from within us and our ex-
> periences those forces that may lead us to
> become what we are potentially able to become.
> Such a process does not have any end: there
> is no dead end in images of situations that
> transcend our present experience, rather
> there is a process that moves us from the
> hope of one eschatology to another, always
> experiencing, always becoming, never
> achieving total fulfillment". (42)

Appendix 1

CARIBBEAN CONFERENCE OF CHURCHES
CONSTITUTION (REVISED)

1. Preamble

We, as Christian people of the Caribbean, separated from each other by barriers of history, language, culture, class, and distance, desire because of our common calling in Christ to join together in a regional fellowship of Churches for inspiration, consultation, and co-operative action. We are deeply concerned to promote the human liberation of our people, and are committed to the achievement of social justice and the dignity of man in our society. We desire to build up together our life in Christ and to share our experience for the mutual strengthening of the Kingdom of God in the world.

2. Name

The name of the regional fellowship shall be the Caribbean Conference of Churches (CCC).

3. Basis

The Caribbean Conference of Churches is a fellowship of Churches which confess the Lord Jesus Christ as God and Saviour according to the Scriptures, and therefore seek to fulfil together their common calling to the glory of the one God, Father, Son and Holy Spirit.

4. Functions

(a) To serve the Churches of the Caribbean in the cause of unity, renewal, and joint action;
(b) to assist national and local Christian Council in the Caribbean to promote consultations and common action among them;
(c) to provide and stimulate programmes of study, research, and experimentation, so as to help the Churches understand the decisive action of God in Christ in terms of their culture, experience, and needs;

(d)   to provide a service to enable information and insights to be shared by Member Churches and national and local Christian Councils;

(e)   without prejudice to its autonomy, to promote collaboration and co-ordination with agencies of the World Council of Churches, of the Roman Catholic Church, and of other bodies in such ways as may be mutually agreed.

5. Membership

The CCC shall be composed of Churches in the Caribbean region which apply to join the Conference, provided they accept its Basis and satisfy such criteria as the Assembly may prescribe. 'Church' shall mean a national or sub-regional organization of individual Christian communions within the Caribbean.

6. The Assembly

(a)   There shall be an Assembly of the Caribbean Conference of Churches, composed of:
   (i)   voting representatives of the Churches directly appointed by them. For each administrative unit within each denomination representation shall be one member of the clergy, and one lay representative;
   (ii)   one voting representative from each regional body;
   (iii) fifteen voting representatives of women endorsed by their church, due regard being paid to geographical, linguistic, and confessional considerations;
   (iv)   fifteen voting representatives of youth endorsed by their church, due regard being paid to geographical, linguistic, and confessional considerations;
   (v)   official non-voting representatives of National Councils;
   (vi)   such consultant non-voting members and observers as the Assembly or Continuation Committee shall invite;
   (vii) such other non-voting consultants as the General Secretary, in consultation with the officers and executive staff of the CCC, shall invite.

(b)   The Assembly shall elect three Presidents; one of these shall be designated by the Assembly as Chairman of the Continuation Committee.

(c)   The Assembly shall meet once every four years.

(d)   The Assembly shall adopt By-Laws by a two-thirds majority of those present and voting.

(e)   The Assembly shall review the work of the Conference, provide guidelines for its continuing activity, and shall make such statements as it thinks fit; in no case shall such statements be binding on the Churches nor shall the Assembly legislate for the Churches.

(f)   The Assembly shall appoint the Continuation Committee, according to provisions laid down by the By-Laws.

7. The Continuation Committee

(a)   The Continuation Committee shall consist of the three Presidents and of not more than twenty-five members, only voting representatives being eligible for election, due regard being paid to geographical, linguistic, and confessional consideration. For every elected member an alternate shall be elected.

(b)   The Continuation Committee shall meet at least twice between Assemblies. A quorum shall consist of two-thirds of the members.

(c)   Between meetings of the Assembly the Continuation Committee shall be empowered to take decisions in the name, and on behalf, of the Assembly within the framework of the policies, programmes, and budget arrangements approved by the Assembly.

(d)   The Continuation Committee shall elect a Treasurer, shall appoint a General Secretary and two Associate General Secretaries and shall confirm the appointment of all executive staff, including a Financial Comptroller;

  (i)   The General Secretary shall act as Secretary to the Continuation Committee, and shall be responsible to it for implementing the policies and decisions approved by the Assembly and/or Continuation Committee. The General Secretary shall also coordinate the entire programme of the CCC and its Commissions;

  (ii) One Associate General Secretary shall be responsible for coordinating the programmes and agencies of the Commission on Renewal;

  (iii) One Associate General Secretary shall be responsible for coordinating the programmes and agencies of the Commission on Development;

  (iv) The Treasurer shall be responsible for administering the budget of the Assembly and/or Continuation Committee.

  (v)   The Financial Comptroller shall be responsible for coordinating the financial affairs of the CCC and its agencies.

(e)   The Continuation Committee shall act as the Finance Committee of the CCC, formulating its budget and securing its financial support through membership fees prescribed by the Assembly, and through funds obtained from other sources. An audited financial statement shall be prepared annually and circulated to member Churches, Councils, and Associated Organizations.

(f)   The Continuation Committee shall be empowered on behalf of the CCC to appoint trustees; to hold and disburse funds; to negotiate appropriate contracts and agreements; and generally to transact such business as is necessary for the execution of the function of the CCC.

(g)   The Continuation Committee shall apoint an executive Committee, called the General Purposes Committee to act in all matters entrusted to the Continuation Committee in between meetings of the Continuation Committee.

8. Structure

(a)   The Assembly or, between meetings of the Assembly, the Continuation Committee shall establish such commissions, programmes, and agencies as may be needed to execute the functions of the CCC.

(b)   The Continuation Committee shall have general oversight over all commissions, programmes, and agencies and receive regular reports.

(c)   The Continuation Committee shall determine the budget of each Commission, Programme, and Agency and shall ensure that a reasonable proportion of such budget shall be contributed by Member Churches. No Commission, Programme or Agency shall have power to commit funds of the CCC without consent of the Continuation Committee.

(d)   The CCC shall discharge its functions initially through the following Commissions:

(i)   Commission on Renewal, consisting of not more than twenty members;

(ii)   Commission on Development, consisting of not more than twenty members.

These Commissions shall implement their work through different programmes and agencies as they may deem necessary.

9. Officers

The Officers of the CCC shall be the three Presidents, the Treasurer, the General Secretary and the two Associate General Secretaries. They shall hold office for a four-year term, or until the conclusion of the next regular meeting of the Assembly. They shall be eligible for re-election or re-appointment.

10. Associated organizations

(a)   The Continuation Committee shall be empowered on behalf of the
      Assembly to negotiate agreements for co-operation with the CCC
      of other organizations concerned with fields of work within the
      sphere of interest of the CCC.
(b)   The Continuation Committee shall periodically review the relation-
      ship of the Associated Organizations with the CCC.

11. Amendments

Amendments may be proposed by a Member Church and shall be re-
viewed by the Continuation Committee. Notice of all amendments shall
be sent to every Member Church not less than six months before the
meeting of the Assembly. Amendments shall require for adoption a
two-thirds majority of those present and voting.

12. Entry into force of its constitution

The original Constitution became effective on adoption by a two-thirds
majority of the votes of the official representatives of the Churches
present and voting at the first Assembly.

MEMBER CHURCHES OF THE CCC AT THE END OF 1977

1. United Church of Jamaica and Grand Cayman
2. The Jamaica Baptist Union
3. The Disciples of Christ in Jamaica
4. The Presbyterian Church in Trinidad and Grenada
5. The Presbytery of Guyana
6. The Guyana Presbyterian Church
7. The Congregational Union of Guyana
8. The Lutheran Church in Guyana
9. The Caribbean Synod of the Lutheran Church in America
10. The Church of God - Ebenezer - Haiti
11. The African Methodist Episcopal Church - 16th Episcopal District
12. The United Protestant Church of Curacao and Bonaire
13. Iglesia Cristiana Pentecostal - Cuba
14. The Moravian Church - Eastern West Indies Province
15. The Moravian Church - Jamaica Province
16. The Moravian Church - Guyana
17. The Moravian Church - Surinam
18. The Salvation Army in the Caribbean and Central America
19. The Methodist Church in the Caribbean and Americas
20. The Anglican Church in the Province of the West Indies
21. The Antilles Episcopal Conference of the Roman Catholic Church
22. Episcopal Church - Dominican Republic
23. The Presbyterian Reformed Church - Cuba
24. The Ethiopian Orthodox Church of Jamaica
25. The Methodist Church of Cuba
26. The Evangelical United Church - Dominican Republic
27. The Episcopal Church - Puerto Rico

Appendix III

THE CCC HYMN

"The right hand of God"

1.   The right hand of God is writing in our land,
     Writing with power and with love.
     Our conflicts and our fears, our triumphs and our tears
     Are recorded by the right hand of God.

2.   The right hand of God is pointing in our land,
     Pointing the way we must go.
     So clouded is the way, so easily we stray,
     But we're guided by the right hand of God.

3.   The right hand of God is striking in our land
     Striking out at envy, hate and greed.
     Our selfishness and lust, our pride and deeds unjust
     Are destroyed by the right hand of God.

4.   The right hand of God is lifting in our land,
     Lifting the fallen one by one.
     Each one is known by name,
     And rescued now from shame,
     By the lifting of the right hand of God.

5.   The right hand of God is healing in our land,
     Healing broken bodies, minds and souls,
     So wondrous is its touch,
     With love that means so much,
     When we're healed by the right hand of God.

6.   The right hand of God is planting in our land,
     Planting seeds of freedom, hope and love,
     In these Caribbean lands
     Let His people all join hands,
     And be one with the right hand of God.

Appendix IV

A LIST OF THE
MAJOR AGENCIES WHICH SUPPORT
THE CADEC PROGRAMME

1. Inter-Church Co-ordination Committee for Development Projects (ICCO) - Holland

2. Inter-American Foundation (IAF) - U.S.A.

3. Christian Aid - England

4. OXFAM - England

5. Inter-Church Fund For International Development (ICFID) - Canada

6. Church World Service (CWS) - U.S.A.

7. Protestant Central Agency For Development Aid (EZE) - West Germany

8. United Methodist Church Board of Global Ministries - U.S.A.

9. MISEREOR - Catholic Development Agency - West Germany

10. World Council of Churches - Geneva

11. TROCAIRE - Ireland

12. Bread For The World - West Germany

Notes to Chapter I

1   The total population of the entire Caribbean at the beginning
     of the 1970's was in the region of 26,000,000. Our study will
     mainly be concerned with the Commonwealth Caribbean (former
     British territories), the Netherlands Antilles and Haiti, which
     account for some 9,000,000 people.
     Irene Hawkins, The Changing Face Of The Carib-
     bean, (Barbados, Cedar Press, 1976) pp. 19-20

2   Raymond T. Smith, Caribbean Integration, ed. Sybil
     Lewis and T.G. Matthews, (University of Puerto Rico, 1967)
     p. 258

3   Woodville Marshall, "Historical Experience in the Caribbean",
     Caribbean Background Vol. IV 1973, p. 8

4   Alfred Thorne, Politics And Economics In The
     Caribbean, ed. T.G. Matthews and F.M. Andic, (University
     of Puerto Rico, 1971), p. 255

5   Quoted by Alfred Thorne, Ibid.

6   George Beckford, Persistent Poverty, (O.U.P., 1972)
     p. 63-Beckford is a Jamaican economist who teaches at the
     University of the West Indies.

7   Eric Williams, From Columbus to Castro, (Andre
     Deutsch, 1970), p. 447

8   Ibid;

9   Rex Nettleford (ed.), Manley And The New Jamaica,
     (Longmans, 1971) pp. 71-72

10   Irene Hawkins, op. cit, pp. 15-16; Caribbean Contact,
     Vol. V, No. 9, January 1978, p. 1

11   See George Beckford, op. cit, pp. 216-217

12   "The bands of relatively well-dressed, idling youngsters on
     many street corners are a tragically common reminder of this
     lack of opportunities which, throughout most of the Caribbean,
     accompanies a living standard that is comparatively affluent
     for developing countries"
                              (Irene Hawkins, op. cit, p. 16)

13   George Beckford, op. cit, p. 213

14   Rex Nettleford (ed.), op. cit, p. 337

15   Paul G. Singh, "Structured Poverty: Some Conceptual Issues",
     mimeo, (University of Guyana, 1976) p. 6

16   J.S. Furnivall, Colonial Policy And Practice, (New York University Press, 1956) ch. 1
17   George Beckford, op. cit, p. 206
18   Aime Cesaire, Discourse On Colonialism, trans. Joan Prinkham (New York, 1972) p. 21
19   Most of the former British territories have gained their independence, and it is anticipated that by the end of the decade only Montserrat, the British Virgin Islands, the Turks and Caicos Islands and the Cayman Islands will be the remaining British Colonies in the region. The Netherlands Antilles expect to be fully independent in the near future
20   Mary Proudfoot, Britain And The United States In The Caribbean, (Faber & Faber, 1954), pp. 1-2
21   Rex Nettleford (ed.) op. cit, p. 96
22   Rex Nettleford (ed.) op. cit, p. 315
23   Gordon K. Lewis, The Growth Of The Modern West Indies, (New York, Monthly Review Press, 1969), p. 387
24   Gordon K. Lewis, op. cit, p. 388
25   Caribbean Contact, Vol. V, No. 5, August 1977, p. 20
26   See In Search Of Partnership, Report of the First CCC Consortium, Trinidad 1977, (Barbados, CADEC/CCC Documentation Service, 1977) p. 6
27   Eric Williams, op. cit, p. 507
28   William Demas, The Political Economy Of The English-speaking Caribbean, (Barbados, Cedar Press, Fourth Edition, 1976), p. 22
29   See George Beckford, op. cit, pp. 203-214
30   Clive Y. Thomas, The Aftermath Of Sovereignty, ed. David Lowenthal and Lambros Comitas, (New York, Doubleday, 1973), p. 539
31   The question of the Church's dependence on foreign resources is discussed in Chapters 2, 8 and 9
32   James Tucker, Moving Into Freedom, ed. Kortright Davis, (Barbados, Cedar Press, 1977), p. 90
33   Paul Singh, op. cit, p. 9
34   David Lowenthal, West Indian Societies, (O.U.P., 1972), p. 291
35   Ibid.
36   Keith Hunte, "The Social Legacy Of Negro Slavery", Caribbean Backgrounds Vol. IV, 1973, p. 44
37   See Called To Be, (Barbados, CADEC, 1973), p. 23
38   Aime Cesaire, op. cit, p. 21
39   Mary Proudfoot, op. cit, p. 74
40   For example, see Melville J. Herskovits, The Myth Of The Negro Past, (Boston, Beacon Press, 1958)

41   M.G. Smith, The Plural Society In The British
      West Indies, (University of California Press, 1965);
      Kinship And Community In Carriacou, (Yale University
      Press, 1962)

42   Raymond T. Smith, The Negro Family In British
      Guiana: Family Structure And Social Status In The
      Villages, (Routledge and Kegan Paul, 1956)

43   M.G. Smith, Plural Society

44   J.S. Furnivall, op. cit, p. 307

45   M.G. Smith, Plural Society, p. 6

46   Lloyd E. Braithwaite, "Social Stratification And Cultural
      Pluralism", Annals Of The New York Academy Of
      Sciences, Vol. LXXXIII, 1960, pp. 816-31; David Lowenthal,
      op. cit; Gordon K. Levis, op. cit; Raymond T. Smith,
      "Social Stratification, Cultural Pluralism And Integration In
      West Indian Societies", in Caribbean Integration
      (supra. note 2)

47   Raymond T. Smith, Caribbean Integration

48   George Beckford, op. cit, pp. 67-73

49   Aime Cesaire, op. cit, p. 79

50   David Lowenthal, op. cit, p. 93

51   Raymond T. Smith, op. cit, p. 237

52   George Beckford, op. cit, p. 78

53   There is a French Patois spoken in Martinique, Guadeloupe,
      Dominica and St. Lucia, but it is not an official language.
      French Creole is spoken in Haiti, and Papiamento (a mixture of
      Dutch, Spanish, French, Portugese and English) is spoken in
      the Netherlands Antilles - neither of these is the official language
      in their respective territories

54   Kathleen Drayton, Moving Into Freedom, ed. Kortright
      Davis, p. 18

55   William Demas, op. cit, p. 18

56   Eric Williams, op. cit, p. 460

57   Commitment, Skill And Organisation, Presidential
      Statement, Caribbean Development Bank, 1976, p. 15

58   See also Called To Be, (CADEC, 1973), pp. 25-28, 35-6,
      51

59   Philip Mason, Patterns Of Dominance, (O.U.P., 1970),
      pp. 38-47, 288

60   Mary Proudfoot, op. cit, p. 93

61   Rex Nettleford (ed.) op. cit, p. 385

62   Ibid.

63   Eric Williams, op. cit, p. 503

64   Drexel Gomez, Today's Church And Today's Word
      ed. John Howe, (Church Information Office, London, 1977)
      p. 41

Notes to chapter I

65   For more on Marcus Garvey, see E.D. Cronon, Black Moses, (Wisconsin, 1968)

66   Rex Nettleford (ed.) op. cit, pp. 351-6

67   J. Michael Dash, "Marvellous Realism - The Way Out Of Negritude", Caribbean Studies, Vol. XIII, No. 4, 1974, p. 66

68   "CARICOM" means "Caribbean Community And Common Market". It was established in 1973, with headquarters in Guyana, and is comprised of the following member countries: Antigua, Barbados, Belize, Dominica, Grenada, Guyana, Jamaica, Montserrat, St. Kitts-Nevis-Anguilla, St. Lucia, St. Vincent, and Trinidad and Tobago. For more on CARICOM see William G. Demas, West Indian Nationhood And Caribbean Integration, (Barbados, CCC Publishing House, 1974).

69   "ACP" means the African, Caribbean and Pacific countries that are Third World signatories to the Lome Convention establishing trading arrangements with the European Common Market.

70   "IBA" is the International Bauxite Association comprising the world's major bauxite-producing countries. International cartels became more important after the serious effects of the oil crisis of 1973 in which the OPEC (Organization of Petroleum Exporting Countries) was so powerfully placed.

71   Caribbean economists such as George Beckford, Lloyd Best, and Clive Thomas are firmly convinced of this. It must be noted however, that there are others like Bernard Codrington, who see no viable alternative for agricultural production especially in sugar-producing countries like Barbados. Codrington is Head of the Research Division of the Barbados National Bank.

72   See Irene Hawkins, op. cit, pp. 209-211

73   The question of the utilization of surplus labour in the Caribbean has been, and will continue to be, the major problem for economists and the political directorates of the region. For a technical discussion on this issue see W. Arthur Lewis, "Economic Development with Unlimited Supplies of Labour", The Economics Of Underdevelopment, ed. A.N. Agarwala and W.P. Singh (O.U.P., Delhi 1977) pp. 400-49.

74   On the question of divestment, see Edith Hodgkinson (ed), Development Prospects And Options In The Commonwealth Caribbean, (Overseas Development Institute, London, 1976). The aftermath of nationalization in Guyana has not been the happiest of experiences for the people of Guyana, and the social effects have todate been rather counter-productive through the prevalence of deep political divisions at the national level.

75   The call for a socialist transformation is very much in evidence throughout the Caribbean, based on the apparent success of the

210

Cuban revolution, and the attractiveness of Marxism as a
social philosophy. But the recent economic crises in Guyana
and Jamaica, two countries which have chosen the socialist route
(without the radical confrontation of the Cuban situation), have
not filled most people with great confidence or enthusiasm. Each
Caribbean territory will need to work out the most appropriate
form of political transformation for itself, having regard to
the need for all the people to become active and free participants
in the national political process.

76 See Called To Be, pp. 12-15
77 Edward Brathwaite, Contradictory Omens, (Jamaica,
    Savacou Publications, 1974), p. 64
78 Called To Be, p. 23

Notes to chapter II

1 For some (incomplete) statistical information on Caribbean
   Churches, see Joan Brathwaite (ed.), Handbook of Churches
   In The Caribbean, (Barbados, CADEC, 1973) pp. 40-85
2 Such a measure of ecumenical co-operation in those early years
   laid the groundwork for the establishment of the United Theological College of the West Indies in Jamaica, in 1966, sponsored
   by ten denominations - The Jamaica Baptist Union, The Anglican
   Church in Jamaica, The Disciples of Christ in Jamaica, The
   Evangelical Lutheran Church in Guyana, The Methodist Church
   in the Caribbean and the Americas, The Moravian Church in
   Jamaica, The Moravian Church in the East West Indies Province,
   the Guyana Presbyterian Church, The Presbyterian Church in
   Trinidad and Grenada, and the United Church in Jamaica and
   Grand Gayman.
3 In 1937, a Christian Social Council was formed in Guyana; the
   Jamaica Christian Council was formed towards the end of World
   War II; social needs gave rise to the formation of councils in
   Grenada and the Netherlands Antilles in the following decade,
   while the Trinidad Christian Council was formed in the early
   1960's. Thus over a period of thirty years ecumenical structures
   were appearing in Commonwealth Caribbean countries.
4 David Mitchell (ed.) With Eyes Wide Open, (Barbados,
   CADEC, 1973) p. 192
5 Quoted by Victor Hayward, "The Caribbean Conference of
   Churches In Process of Formation", Report 53 - Secretariat For
   Relationships With Christian Councils, mimeo. , (World Council
   of Churches, November 1970), p. 2

6   David Mitchell (ed.) op. cit. , p. 193. The Curriculum was
        designed to relate the teaching of the Christian Faith to the
        Caribbean cultural context, and to make the meaning of the
        Bible 'come alive' in the familiar surroundings of Sunday
        School teachers and students. A great deal of emphasis was
        placed on the use of visual-aids, and on activities by the students.
        Sunday School material had been formerly imported from Eng-
        land and North America.
7   The Rev. J. Leroy Elder, a Trinidadian minister of the Pres-
        byterian Church, had been sent to the USA for special training
        in Leadership and Youth work, and assumed responsibility for
        the Youth Commission on his return to the Caribbean in 1970.
8   This Committee is shortly called "Church World Service"
        (C.W.S.)
9   James Hackshaw, Social And Economic Planning In
        The Leeward And Windward Islands, (New York,
        Church World Service, 1967) p. 5
10   James Hackshaw, op. cit. , p. 6
11   James Hackshaw, op. cit. , p. 17
12   James Hackshaw, op. cit. , p. 25
13   James Hackshaw, op. cit. , p. 29
14   James Hackshaw, op. cit. , p. 30
15   James Hackshaw, op. cit. , pp. 31-32
16   CADEC was first designed to serve the Leeward and Windward
        Islands, and Barbados, but its role was expanded to serve the
        entire region in 1971.
17   Copies of the Reports of the Hackshaw Survey and the St. Vincent
        Consultation were sent to representatives of every government
        in the Eastern Caribbean and to key persons in all Churches and
        ecumenical bodies in the Caribbean.
18   "Report Of The Co-ordinator", November 1969 (CADEC) mimeo.,
        p. 1
19   F.D. Chaplin, "Report On A Meeting Of The Caribbean Steering
        Committee And Ecumenical Consultation In Jamaica, October,
        1970", (Trinidad, WCC Inter-Church Relations Secretariat, 1970)
        mimeo., p. 2 (limited circulation).
20   F.D. Chaplin, "Report", p. 1
21   F.D. Chaplin, "Report", p. 14
22   Ibid.
23   F.D. Chaplin, "Report", p. 15
24   Called To Be, (Barbados, CADEC 2nd ed.), p. 45
        For the Report on the Consultation, see Marlene Cuthbert (ed)
        The Role Of Women In Caribbean Development,
        (Barbados, CADEC, 1971).
25   Called To Be, p. 46

26   See for example, Clarence Asong, "Tourism: A Phenomenon
      Of Our Time", in The Role Of Tourism In Caribbean
      Development, (Barbados, CADEC, 1971) pp. 21-57
27   William Demas, The Political Economy Of The
      English-Speaking Caribbean, p. 9
28   Ibid.
29   See Report of Consultation in The Role Of Tourism
      In Caribbean Development, pp. 1-19
30   See The Role Of Tourism, p. 20
31   CADEC is represented on the Board of Directors of CTRC.
      CTRC has received substantial funding from several North
      American bodies. The Centre has conducted a number of useful
      studies on the effects of tourism on Caribbean communities. It
      continues to monitor the growth of the industry with particular
      regard to the benefits derived by host communities.
32   Called To Be, p. 3
33   Caribbean Contact, Vol. I No. 1, November, 1971, p. 12
34   Called To Be, p. 7
35   Called To Be, p. 14
36   Called To Be, p. 12
37   Called To Be, p. 6
38   Called To Be, p. 10
39   Called To Be, p. 8
40   Called To Be, pp. 14-15
41   Called To Be, p. 15
42   F.D. Chaplin, "Report", p. 1
43   The Rev. F.D. Chaplin returned to Britain to join the staff of the
      Anglican Consultative Council in London. He however attended the
      Inaugural Assembly in Jamaica in November 1973.
44   Called To Be, p. 37
45   Called To Be, p. 38
46   Called To Be, p. 41
47   Called To Be, p. 41-42
48   For a better understanding of this kind of funding relationship,
      see note 56 below.
49   Called To Be, p. 42
50   Kortright Davis (ed.), The Right Hand Of God, (Barbados,
      CCC, 1976) p. 17
51   Offices had already been established in Trinidad, Curacao,
      Barbados, Antigua, and Jamaica. The Guyana Office was establish-
      ed in September 1974. Guyana and Curacao have been closed down.
52   The ARC Programmes are: - Theological Renewal, Theological
      Education, Caribbean Church Women, The Youth Programme
      (CEYA), Home And Family Life, Christian Education, Ecumenical
      Councils, Caribbean Church Music, Caribbean Identity, Caribbean
      Ecumenical Programme, Evangelism And Mission.

53   See Called To Be, p. 41
54   The CADEC Programmes are: - Development Fund, Project Development Programme, Caribbean Community Appeal, CADEC Communications Network, Education For Development, Documentation, DERAW, Land And Food For People, CEDAR PRESS, Human Rights.
55   "Report Of The General Secretariat", CCC Second General Assembly, November 1977, Mimeo, p. 3
56   See Called To Be, p. 8
57   The CCC has used the Consortium mechanism to secure substantial funding support for most of its programmes since 1974. By this method a three-year programme and budget is drawn up by the CCC, and representatives from funding agencies in North America and Europe are invited to a meeting in the Caribbean to discuss the programme and budget. The CCC priorities are thoroughly analysed and discussed, after which funding agencies make indications of what support they are able (or likely) to provide over the three-year period. The emphasis is generally on the CCC's priorities for programming, and consequently on its principles of receiving financial support. These principles are generally in keeping with the expressed concerns and objectives of most funding agencies represented at such meetings. The 1977 Consortium meeting in Trinidad proved to be a difficult exercise however, since both sides failed to agree on what was to be considered a "realistic" budget. The problems were later resolved, and the consortium arrangement continues.
58   "CADEC Development Fund Report 1973-1975", (Barbados, Project Development Department, 1976), p. 1
59   This information has been computed from the Development Fund Reports for 1973 to 1977, produced by the Project Development Department of CADEC in Barbados. (BDS $ 2.00 = US $ 1.00)
60   The figure varies according to the size of the territory.
61   These samples are drawn from CADEC Development Fund Reports.
62   CADEC Development Fund 1976, (Barbados, CADEC 1977) pp. 16-17. The Project received an amount of BDS $ 130,416.
63   Development Fund 1976, p. 16
64   Development Fund 1976, p. 17
65   Ibid. The area was recently devastated by a hurricane "Greta" in September 1978, and the project-carriers have suffered a major disaster.
66   For example, The Salvation Army in Barbados was assisted in acquiring financial support for the construction of a new Church-cum-Community Centre in 1976. They received assistance from the Evangelical Church in Germany.

67   The Chaguaramas Consultation had called for such an
      appointment.
68   This post has been vacant for most of 1978, and the progress
      of the work in the Eastern Caribbean has been halted.
69   Recent indications suggest that this project may not be brought
      to a successful completion due to a lack of metropolitan funding
      support.
70   See Called To Be, pp. 12-13
71   Freire's best-known work is Pedagogy Of The Oppressed,
      (Penguin, 1972)
72   Called To Be, p. 12
73   Ibid.
74   Dora F. Browne, "Report On: The Work of The Education For
      Development Programme, 1973-1977", (Barbados, CADEC,
      1977) mimeo., p. 1
75   They included Dr. David Mitchell, Sister Marthe Vanrompay -
      a Belgian Roman Catholic Nun who had been recruited from
      St. Croix in the U.S. Virgin Islands, and Mr. Owen Baptiste -
      formerly Editor of the Trinidad Express.
76   See pages 57-60
77   Mainly through courses sponsored by the University Of the West
      Indies, and the University of Guyana.
78   The surveys were carried out by Rupert Lake, an Antiguan
      economist.
79   The Consultation on Unemployment chose to make specific
      recommendations to CADEC for action rather than to issue a
      general call for Caribbean governments to take action. CADEC
      had sponsored a survey in the Leeward Islands in 1973 to
      enquire about the motivation among young people to engage in
      agriculture. For the Report on this survey, see Kortright Davis
      (ed.), Voices For Change, (Antigua, CADEC, 1973).
      This Report was also tabled at the Consultation.
80   "CEYA - A Brief History", mimeo, (Trinidad, CEYA, 1977)
      p. 3
81   "CEYA - A Brief History", p. 5
82   Caribbean Contact, Vol. II, No. 10, January 1975, p. 10
83   The CCC still communicates in English throughout its constituency,
      but this will need to be modified if the French- and Spanish-
      speaking member-Churches are to participate more effectively
      in the ecumenical process. English is widely spoken in the Dutch
      territories, but this should not induce the CCC to postpone the
      drive to become a truly multi-lingual organization. The wider
      use of Spanish in CCC activities would appear to this writer to
      be of urgent necessity.

84   These were: Iglesia Reformada Presbiteriana and Iglesia
        Metodista (Cuba), Iglesia Episcopal and Iglesia Evangelica
        (Dominican Republic), Iglesia Episcopal (Puerto Rico). It is
        interesting to note that there is a wider Caribbean fellowship
        of Anglicans (Episcopalians) within the CCC than among the
        Caribbean Anglican Churches themselves - only the Epicopalians
        in the Virgin Islands and Haiti are outside of the CCC.
85   Supra. pp. 50-51
86   See Appropriate Technology And People, (Barbados,
        CADEC Documentation Service, 1976), p. 24
87   Ibid.
88   Supra. p. 46
89   "Communicarib" has become integrated with a new programme
        in Development Studies at Codrington College.
90   The programme is broadcast regularly on 14 Radio Stations in
        the region. For a summary of the Communications Programme
        between 1974 and 1977, see The CCC Communications
        Cluster, (CCC Second Assembly, Guyana, 1977).
91   The CCC Communications Cluster, p. 31
92   These publications have dealt with such specific issues as The
        Role of Women, Law in the Caribbean, Caribbean Economic
        Integration, and Caribbean Church Music.
93   The CCC Communications Cluster, p. 25
94   Caribbean Contact, Vol. I, No. 7, July 1973, p. 2
95   The CCC Communications Cluster, p. 8
96   See Caribbean Contact, Vol. II, No. 1, March 1974
97   See Caribbean Contact, Vol. III, No. 12, March 1976
98   Caribbean Contact, Vol. II, No. 8, November 1974, p. 4
99   The CCC Communications Cluster, p. 26
100   It is significant that Hackshaw had not suggested the mobilization
        of local financial support in his 1967 Report. The Caribbean
        Churches were therefore making a specific move forward
        towards greater self-reliance in their development planning.
101   Called To Be, p. 42
102   Totals for 1974 to 1977 are as follows: (1974) BDS $ 38,702;
        (1975) BDS $ 67,024; (1976) BDS $ 75,256; (1977) BDS $ 73,309.
103   See The Great Shake, (Antigua, CADEC, 1975)
104   Workers Together With Christ, Report Of The
        Second General Assembly, (Barbados, CEDAR Press, 1978)
        p. 43
105   Ibid.
106   Second Assembly Report, p. 51
107   Second Assembly Report, p. 75
108   Ibid.
109   Operation Outreach 1976, (Barbados, CCC 1977
        Assembly Planning Unit, 1976), p. 34

110   "Preliminary Report On Project Five", mimeo, (Assembly Planning Unit, 1977) p. 3
111   Ibid.
112   Supra. p. 25

Notes to chapter III

1   Rex Nettleford, "Caribbean Perspectives - The Creative Potential And The Quality of Life", Caribbean Quarterly, Vol. 17, Nos. 3 & 4, 1971, p. 123
2   Rex. Nettleford is Professor of Extra Mural Studies at the University of the West Indies in Jamaica. He is a Jamaican. He is also Head of the Trade Union Education Institute at Mona, Jamaica, as well as Cultural Advisor to the Jamaican Government and Chairman of the Institute of Jamaica.
3   See Paul Streeten, The Frontiers Of Development Studies, (MacMillan, 1972), pp. 23-24
4   See World Development Report 1978, (Washington, The World Bank, 1978) p. 65
5   Paul Streeten, Frontiers, p. 8
6   Ibid.
7   Ibid.
8   This comment generally refers to the West, since the Soviet Union and China are known to favour progressive regimes, in most instances.
9   Dudley Seers, "Rich Countries And Poor", Development In A Divided World, ed. Dudley Seers and Leonhard Joy, (Penguin, 1971)
10   John Cole, The Poor Of The Earth, (MacMillan, 1977), p. 7
11   This is not to suggest that Development was not a concern before this period. The stark contrasts between the 'developed' and 'developing' countries became a major concern around this period as 'developing' countries began to take more initiatives in moving forward from their state of economic backwardness.
12   Norman T. Uphoff and Warren F. Ilchman (ed.), The Political Economy Of Development, (University Of California Press, 1972), pp. 76-77
13   S. L. Parmar, "Concern For Man In The Quest For Development", Ecumenical Review, Vol. XIX, No. 4, October 1967, p. 353
14   Kenneth Kaunda, "Rich And Poor Nations", Ecumenical Review, Vol. XX, 1968, p. 340

Notes to chapter III

15   Lauchlin Currie, "The Objectives Of Development", World
       Development, Vol. 6, No. 1, 1978, p. 9
16   Peter L. Berger, Pyramids Of Sacrifice, (Penguin,
       1977) p. 210
17   Duncan B. Forrester, "Western Academic Sophistry And The
       Third World", Economic and Political Weekly,
       Vol. IX, No. 40, October 5, 1974, p. 1699
18   Pamela H. Gruber (ed.), Fetters Of Injustice, (Geneva,
       World Council of Churches, 1970), p. 112
19   See pp. 117-170
20   Benjamin Higgins, United Nations And U.S. Foreign
       Economic Policy, (Illinois, Richard D. Irwin Inc., 1962)
       ch. 1
21   W.W. Rostow, The Stages Of Economic Growth,
       (Cambridge, 1968) pp. 166-167
22   See W. Arthur Lewis, The Development Process,
       (New York, United Nations, 1970) p. 1
23   See Max F. Millikan and Donald L.M. Blackmer (eds.),
       The Emerging Nations: Their Growth and United
       States Policy, (London, Asia Publishing House, 1961).
24   Quoted by B.S. Minhas, "The Current Development Debate",
       mimeo, (Sussex, 1977) p. 2
25   Partners In Development, Report Of The Commission
       On International Development, (New York, Praeger Publishers,
       1969) p. 3
26   Partners In Development, p. 22
27   Thomas Balogh, "Failures In The Strategy Against Poverty",
       World Development, Vol. 6, No. 1, 1978, pp. 18-19
28   Thomas Balogh, op. cit., p. 19
29   The recent concern of the USA for the promotion of human rights
       in developing countries is a very strong indication of a new
       approach to international development assistance. Perhaps the
       specific rights of the poor ought to be vigorously pur-
       sued.
30   Charles Elliott, The Development Debate, (S.C.M.
       (Press, 1971) p. 19
       Elliott is an Anglican clergyman and an economist. He is now
       in charge of the Institute of Development Studies at Swansea.
31   Charles Elliott, op. cit., pp. 20-21
32   S.L. Parmar, op. cit., pp. 353-362
33   S.L. Parmar, "The Limits-To-Growth Debate in Asian Per-
       spective", Ecumenical Review, Vol., XXVI, 1974,
       pp. 35-36
34   James Grant, "Can The Churches Promote Development?"
       Ecumenical Review, Vol. XXVI, 1974, p. 24

35   Ibid.
36   See Irene Hawkins, op. cit., p. 29
37   See Edith Hodgkinson (ed.), op. cit., p. 7n
38   Norman Girvan and Owen Jefferson (ed.), Readings In The
      Political Economy Of The Caribbean, (Jamaica,
      New World Group, 1971), p. 214
39   Norman Girvan and Owen Jefferson (ed.), op. cit., p. 215
      Girvan and Jefferson are Jamaican economists, formerly on the
      staff of the UWI.
40   B. N. Y. Vaughan, The Expectation Of The Poor,
      (SCM Press, 1972), p. 23
      Vaughan was formerly Anglican Bishop of Belize.
41   B. N. Y. Vaughan, op. cit., p. 25
42   For an enlightening discussion on developments in Tanzania
      see R. H. Green, Toward Ujamaa and Kujstegemea:
      Income Distribution and Absolute Poverty
      Eradication Aspects of the Tanzania Transition
      to Socialism, (I. D. S. Discussion Paper Nr. 66, Sussex,
      December, 1974), and Budd L. Hall, Participation And
      Education In Tanzania, (I. D. S. Discussion Paper
      No. 86, Sussex, November, 1975)
43   For example, O. Sunkel, C. Vaitsos, and C. Furtado.
44   Norman Girvan and Owen Jefferson (ed.), op. cit., p. 222
45   Eric Williams, op. cit., pp. 511-512
46   Norman Girvan and Owen Jefferson (ed.), op. cit., p. 190
47   Quoted by B. S. Minhas, op. cit., p. 11
48   Norman Girvan and Owen Jefferson (ed.), op. cit., p. 213
49   See Hollis Chenery (et. al) (eds.), Redistribution With
      Growth, (O. U. P., 1974)
50   What Now: Another Development, (Uppsala, The Dag
      Hammarskjold Foundation, 1975)
51   Employment, Growth And Basic Needs - A One-
      World Problem, (Geneva, International Labour Organization,
      1976).
52   R. H. Green, Solidarity, Self Reliance, Basic
      Human Needs, mimeo (Geneva, WCC, Justice and Service,
      1977) p. 20
      Green is an American Professorial Fellow at the Institute of
      Development Studies at Sussex.
53   R. H. Green, "Basic human needs, collective self-reliance and
      development strategy: some reflections on power, periphery
      and poverty", Self-Reliance And Solidarity In The
      Quest For International Justice, (Geneva, World
      Council of Churches, 1976), p. 24
54   R. H. Green, Solidarity, p. 20

55	Employment, Growth And Basic Needs, p. 43
56	Ibid.
57	B.N.Y. Vaughan, op. cit., p. 19
58	Helene Castel (ed.), World Development: An Intro-ductory Reader, (Collier-Macmillan, 1971), p. xv
59	Charles Elliott, op. cit., p. 22
60	S.L. Parmar in Fetters Of Injustice ed. Pamela Gruber, p. 41
61	R.H. Green, Solidarity, p. 22
62	Dudley Seers, "The Meaning Of Development", International Development Review, Vol. XI, No. 4, 1969, pp. 2-6 Seers is an English Professorial Fellow at the Institute of Development Studies at Sessex.
63	Dudley Seers, "The New Meaning Of Development", mimeo., (Institute of Development Studies, Sussex, 1977).
64	Dudley Seers, New Meaning, p. 10
65	Ibid.
66	Dudley Seers, New Meaning, p. 11
67	To Break The Chains Of Oppression, Report of An Ecumenical Study Process on Domination and Dependence, (Geneva, World Council of Churches, 1975), p. 21
68	Ibid.
69	Ibid.
70	Fetters Of Injustice, p. 52
71	B.S. Minhas, op. cit., p. 15
72	Ibid.
73	Charles Elliott, op. cit., p. 35
74	Self-Reliance And Solidarity, p. 72
75	Self-Reliance And Solidarity, p. 23
76	R.H. Green, Solidarity, p. 22
77	R.H. Green, Solidarity, p. 23
78	R.H. Green, Solidarity, p. 22
79	See contributions in Readings, as well as William Demas' writings.
80	Norman Girvan and Owen Jefferson (ed.), op. cit., pp. 87-98
81	Supra. p. 210, note 68.
82	See Commitment, Skill And Organization, (Barbados, Caribbean Development Bank, 1976).
83	It is not unreasonable to suggest, however, that the CARICOM arrangement has not been provided with the minimum amount of support required for it to perform effectively. To a large extent, CARICOM has been like a tool, constructed by partici-pating Governments but devoid of a regional strategy with which to function efficiently. The Governments display a serious lack of political will in this respect, and the fact that it took

15 months to fill the vacant post of Secretary-General is perhaps indicative of a lack of interest. Barbadian-born Dr. Kurleigh King assumed duties as Secretary-General on November 1, 1978, after his predecessor (Alister McIntyre) had taken up an assignment with UNCTAD in Geneva in August 1977. Furthermore, there continues to be a very high turn-over of personnel at the CARICOM Secretariat.

84   CDB: A Bank And A Development Instrument, (Barbados, Caribbean Development Bank, 1977), p. 36
85   Forbes Burnham, A Destiny To Mould, (Longmans, 1970), p. 246
86   Emanuel de Kadt, Church, Society And Development in Latin America, (Sussex, Institute Of Development Studies), Reprint 103 from The Journal Of Development Studies, Vol. 8, No. 1, October 1971, pp. 23-43.
87   Fetters Of Injustice, p. 133
88   David Miller, Social Justice, (O.U.P., 1976), p. 334
89   Fetters Of Injustice, p. 70
90   Fetters Of Injustice, p. 55
91   Employment, Growth And Basic Needs, p. 35
92   Samuel P. Huntingdon and Joan M. Nelson, No Easy Choice, (Harvard University Press, 1976)
93   Samuel P. Huntingdon and Joan M. Nelson, op. cit., p. 4
94   Huntingdon and Nelson, op. cit., p. 29
95   Huntingdon and Nelson, op. cit., p. 40
96   But experience in Latin America and the Caribbean has shown that with charismatic leadership the poor can begin to take political participation seriously.
97   Michael Manley, The Politics Of Change, (Andre Deutsch, 1974), p. 68
98   Michael Manley, op. cit., p. 75
99   Michael Manley, op. cit., p. 60
100   Kortright Davis (ed.), The Right Hand Of God, p. 3
101   C.I. Itty, "Development", Ecumenical Review, Vol. XIX, No. 4, October 1967, p. 351
102   R.H. Preston (ed.), Technology And Social Justice, (SCM Press, 1971), p. 5
103   World Conference On Church And Society, Official Report, Geneva 1966 (Geneva, WCC, 1966), p. 53
104   Denys Munby (ed.) World Development: Challenge To The Churches, (Washington, Corpus Books, 1969), p. 9
105   See Fetters Of Injustice for official Report
106   See Hunger For Justice, Report of The All India Consultation On Development, New Delhi, February 1970, (New Delhi, CASA, 1970)

107   See The Church And Development, (Nairobi, AMECEA, 1971)
108   See Called To Be
109   See Church And Development, Report Of An Ecumenical Consultation on Church And Development In Lebanon, (Beirut, Ecumenical Commission Development Justice & Peace, 1972)
110   See, To Break The Chains Of Oppression
111   See, David M. Paton (ed.), Breaking Barriers, (Michigan, Wm. B. Eerdmans, 1976).
112   "Opening Address by Cde. Prime Minister L.F.S. Burnham at the Second General Assembly of The Caribbean Conference of Churches, at Pegasus Hotel on November 17, 1977", mimeo., (Georgetown, CCC Second Assembly, 1977), p. 7
113   Philip Potter, "Working Together With Christ - For Human Rights", mimeo., (Georgetown, CCC Second Assembly, 1977), pp. 7-10
114   Philip Potter, op. cit., p. 13
115   C.T. Kurien, Poverty And Development, (Madras, 1974), p. 40
       Kurien is an Indian economist at the Madras Christian College.
116   Ibid.

Notes to chapter IV

1   Repoduced on the inside cover of Betting On The Weak, CCPD Document 9, August 1976, (Geneva, World Council of Churches, 1976).
2   Karl Marx - Selected Writings In Sociology And Social Philosophy, ed. T.B. Bottomore and Maximilieu Rubel, (Penguin, 1976), p. 90
3   Ibid.
4   Bottomore and Rubel, (ed.), op. cit., p. 67
5   Cited by Juan Luis Segundo, The Liberation Of Theology, trans. John Drury, (Gill and Macmillan, 1977), p. 10, from Karl Mannheim, Ideology And Utopia (New York: Harcourt, Brace, Jovanovich, Harvest Book, 1936).
6   See Alfredo Fierro, The Militant Gospel, (SCM Press, 1977), p. 243
7   It must however be recognized that the discussion on 'ideology' up to this point deals specifically with some empirical aspects of ideology. Ideology in this sense is determined by the situational context. But Mannheim made a distinction between utopian and ideological ideas, stating that ideas were

utopian when they transcended reality, and were such that "when they pass over into conduct, tend to shatter, either partially or wholly, the order of things prevailing at the time". (Ideology And Utopia, p. 173)

8   Juan Luis Segundo, op. cit., p. 122
9   After faith is dead, however, theology can still live on
10   James H. Cone, God Of The Oppressed, (SPCK, 1977) p. 43
11   Official Report of World Conference On Church And Society, Geneva, 1966, (Geneva, World Council of Churches, 1967), p. 202
12   Charles Elliott, Development Debate, p. 113
13   Gustavo Gutierrez, A Theology Of Liberation, trans. Sister Caridad Inda and John Eagleson, (SCM Press, 1974) p. 11
14   Gustavo Gutierrez, op. cit., p. 13
15   Ibid.
16   See Shoki Coe, "Contextualizing Theology", Mission Trends No. 3 ed. Gerald H. Anderson and Thomas F. Stransky, (Michigan, Wm. B. Eerdmans, 1976), pp. 19-24.
17   Wolfhart Pannenberg, "The Contribution of Christianity To The Modern World", Cross Currents, Vol. XXV, No. 4, 1976, p. 366.
18   Towards A Theology Of Development, Geneva, SODEPAX, 1969)
19   The counterparts which comprise the CCPD Network are: Ethiopia, The Cameroons, Indonesia, and the Caribbean.
20   Denys Munby (ed.), World Development, p. 139
21   Denys Munby (ed.), op. cit., p. 141
22   World Conference On Church And Society - Report (1966), p. 201
23   Church And Society - Report, p. 205
24   B.N.Y. Vaughan, op. cit., p. 142
25   Denys Munby (ed.), op. cit., p. 140
26   Ronald H. Preston (ed.), op. cit., p. 149
27   Ronald H. Preston (ed.), op. cit., p. 151
28   In Search Of A Theology Of Development, (Geneva, SODEPAX, 1969), p. 100
29   Alves, in part, quotes from Murnford; see In Search Of A Theology Of Development, p. 83
30   In Search Of A Theology Of Development, p. 21
31   Ibid.
32   In Search Of A Theology Of Development, pp. 70-71
33   Charles Elliott, The Development Debate, pp. 70-107
34   Charles Elliott, op. cit., p. 79
35   Charles Elliott, op. cit., p. 80
36   Charles Elliott, op. cit., p. 98

37   Charles Elliott, Inflation And The Compromised Church, (Belfast, Christian Journals Ltd., 1975), pp. 140-141.
38   See Ecumenical Review, Vol. XXV, 1973, p. 426
39   Paragraph 46 of the Report of Section III of the Fourth Assembly of the World Council of Churches, Uppsala, 1968.
40   See "Ecumenical Dialogue Of Third World Theologians", LADOC Vol. VII, No. 26, 1976, p. 25
41   Paulo Freire, "Education, Liberation and the Church", Study Encounter, Vol. IX, No. 1, 1973, p. 15
42   LADOC, Vol. VII, No. 26, 1976, p. 28
43   See Hugo Assmann, Theology For A Nomad Church, trans. Paul Burns, (New York, Orbis Books, 1976), p. 73.
      It is important to point out, however, that countries as such do not exercise a prophetic role, this takes place among persons or groups of persons within countries, be they 'developed' or 'developing'. Freire's point is nevertheless a valid one, since prophetic praxis for social change on behalf of the poor and oppressed is more likely to be found where such persons are in the majority.
44   Ibid.
45   Study Encounter, Vol. IX, No. 1, 1973, p. 15
46   Hugo Assmann, op. cit., p. 73
47   "Orthopraxis" denotes the recognition of the "work and importance of concrete behavior, of deeds, of action, of praxis in the Christian life."
      (Gutierrez, op. cit., p. 10)

Notes to chapter V

1   T. B. Bottomore and Maximilieu Rubel (ed.), op. cit., p. 245
2   Self-Reliance And Solidarity In The Quest For International Justice (Geneva, W. C. C., 1976), p. 76
3   Kosuke Koyama, "We Had Rice With Jesus", CCPD Document 6, (Geneva, W. C. C., 1975), p. 5.
4   Hugo Assmann, op. cit.
5   See Anderson and Stransky (ed.) op. cit., pp. 6-18
6   See Idris Hamid (ed.), Troubling Of The Waters, (Trinidad, 1973), p. 55.
7   Idris Hamid (ed.), op. cit., p. 79
8   See Lilith M. Haynes (ed.), FAMBLI, (New York, Church World Service, 1971), pp. 152-172.
9   Idris Hamid (ed.), op. cit., p. 40

10   Idris Hamid (ed.), op. cit., pp. 42-44. Moore is a Guyanese historian, who once served as his country's High Commissioner to Ottawa. His reflections on the role of the Church in Caribbean history, and on the need for appropriate methods for theological reflection are most helpful. See also his contribution in Lilith Haynes (ed.), F A M B L I, and his address to the Second Assembly of the CCC - the full text of which exists only in mimeographed form.

11   Horace Russell is a Jamaican theologian who was formerly President of the United Theological College of the West Indies (UTCWI) in Jamaica. He now serves as a pastor of a leading Baptist Church in Kingston. See his "The Challenge of Theological Reflection In The Caribbean Today" in Idris Hamid (ed.) op. cit., pp. 25-34.

12   Kortright Davis (ed.), Moving Into Freedom, p. 58 Thompson is a Bahamian Anglican who serves as pastor of a leading congregation in Nassau. He is a member of the Board of Governors of Codrington Theological College, Barbados.

13   Kortright Davis (ed.), Moving Into Freedom, p. 59

14   Kortright Davis (ed.), Moving Into Freedom, p. 60

15   See Luis Rivera, "The Mission Of The Church And The Development Of A Caribbean Theology Of Liberation", in Out Of The Depths ed. Idris Hamid, (Trinidad, St. Andrew's Theological College, 1977) pp. 249-261. Rivera is a Puerto Rican theologican who has been active in the cause of social transformation in Puerto Rico. He is a Baptist.

16   Ibid.

17   See Dr. Kenrick R. Khan, "Reflections On The Caribbean Towards A New Hermeneutic", mimeo, (Guyana, CCC Office, 1977).

18   Idris Hamid, In Search Of New Perspectives, (Barbados, CADEC, 1971), p. 8

19   Idris Hamid, New Perspectives, p. 5

20   See David Mitchell (ed.), With Eyes Wide Open, p. 123

21   Ibid.

22   Ibid.

23   David Mitchell (ed.) With Eyes Wide Open, p. 125

24   Ibid.

25   For an informative study of the Vodun Cult, see George Eaton Simpson, Religious Cults Of The Caribbean: Trinidad, Jamaica, And Haiti, (Puerto Rico, Institute of Caribbean Studies, 1970).

26   George Eaton Simpson, op. cit., pp. 234-256

27   George Eaton Simpson, op. cit., p. 253. In a very real sense, the concept of religion as the "opiate of the people" (Marx) - the sigh of the oppressed - finds concrete expression in Vodun.

28   According to Alain Rocourt (a Haitian Methodist minister) (see
        With Eyes Wide Open, pp. 76-77), the majority of the
        masses in Haiti still belong to the Roman Catholic Church.
        The more recently established non-Catholic Churches have
        "ignored" the elite and middle-class and "have gone directly
        to the masses". By these Rocourt is referring to the Pentecostal
        Churches - who now represent about 25 % of the population.
        Thus of the other 75 % most of these are Catholics, while the
        historical Protestant Churches (mainly Methodists, Baptists
        and Episcopalians) would have attracted a significant portion
        of the middle-class. So Rocourt states - "as time went by the
        first Protestant Churches established in the country were
        considered as Churches of the elite, if not of the mulattoes".
29   See George Eaton Simpson, Religious Cults Of The
        Caribbean.
30   George Eaton Simpson, op. cit., p. 110
31   See for example Lucy Mair, New Nations (London 1967),
        Mair also draws on the work of Dr. Muhlmann, and the French
        Sociologist Dr. Balandier. There is also Kenelm Burridge,
        New Heaven New Earth, (Oxford, 1969). The works of
        Cohn and Lanternari are referred to in the text.
32   Norman Cohn, The Pursuit Of The Millenium,
        (Temple Smith, 1970).
33   Norman Cohn, op. cit., p. 282
34   Norman Cohn, op. cit., p. 283
35   Ibid.
36   Vittoric Lanternari, The Religions Of The Oppressed,
        (New York, 1963), p. 322
37   For an illuminating biography of Marcus Garvey, see J. A. Crabb,
        Black Moses: The Story Of Marcus Garvey,
        (University of Wisconsin, 1955).
38   Leonard E. Barrett, The Rastafarians (Puerto Rico,
        Institute of Caribbean Studies, 1968), p. 76
39   See Idris Hamid (ed.), Troubling Of The Waters,
        p. 167
40   Idris Hamid (ed.), Troubling Of The Waters, p. 166
41   Idris Hamid (ed.), Troubling Of The Waters, pp. 167-
        170. See also Joseph Owens, Dread, (Jamaica, 1976).
42   Leonard E. Barrett, op. cit., pp. 175-6
43   Rex M. Nettleford, Identity Race And Protest In
        Jamaica, (New York, William Morrow & Co. Inc.,
        1972), p. 111. Nettleford has also written an excellent introduction
        to Joseph Owen's book, Dread.
44   G. Goring, R. G. Neehall, P. I. Gomes (ed.), Christians
        In Dialogue And Joint Action, Report of A Consultation
        on The Ecumenical Sharing of Personnel, Codrington College,

Barbados, West Indies, January 7-11, 1975, (Barbados, CCC, 1975), p. 30.

45 Louise Bennett, "Back to Africa", Caribbean Voices Volume 2 The Blue Horizons, ed. John Figueroa, (Evans Brothers Limited, 1970), p. 167

46 E. M. Roach, "March trades", John Figueroa (ed.), op. cit., p. 156

47 This is a typical attitude among poor mothers with many children, especially where most of the fathers have failed to provide for the care and sustenance of their offspring.

48 See for example V.S. Naipaul, Mimic Men, (Andre Deutsch, 1967); Derek Walcott, Another Life, (New York, Farrar, Straus & Giroux, 1973); John Hearne, Land Of The Living? (Faber & Faber 1961)

49 Orlando Patterson, An Absence Of Ruins, (Hutchinson, 1967), p. 160.

50 George Lamming, "Birthday Poem for Clifford Sealy", John Figueroa (ed.), op. cit., p. 119

51 See Idris Hamid (ed.), Troubling Of The Waters, p. 200

52 See David Lowenthal and Lambros Comitas (ed.), The Aftermath of Sovereignty, (New York, Anchor Press, 1973), p. 367

53 See C. L. R. James, Beyond A Boundary, (Hutchinson, 1963).

54 See below p. 124-126

55 In the Caribbean experience, social forgiveness is not to be confused with the condoning of evil, or the acceptance thereof. It is rather the acknowledgement of human frailty and imperfection and the recognition that none is "without sin", and that all desire to be given a chance to reach after that which is better and higher. Social forgiveness in the Caribbean is sometimes associated with the claim that Caribbean people have "short memories". In any event, in small, close, islandic societies the consciousness that another man's lot today might be one's own tomorrow is a very powerful motive to do as one would have done to oneself.

56 The 'anger' which is sometimes expressed by Caribbean intellectuals is not typical of the Caribbean personality. The pragmatic approach of accomodation in the Caribbean is by far the normal Caribbean way of life - it more easily ensures survival.

57 See Christians In Dialogue And Joint Action, p. 16

58 Sylvia Wynter rightly speaks of "an underground cultural dynamic; a dynamic which had remained in opposition to the colonial and

neo-colonial superstructure of the society; has remained as
an alternative way of apprehending reality". (Sylvia Wynter,
"One Love - Rhetoric Or Reality? - Aspects Of Afro-Jamaicanism", Caribbean Studies, Vol. XII, No. 3, October
1972, p. 66).

Notes to chapter VI

1   See Ebony, Vol. XXXIII, No. 2, December 1977, p. 76
     (Chicago, Illinois)
2   Charles R. Taber, "Is There More Than One Way To Do
     Theology?", Gospel In Context, Vol. 1, January 1978,
     pp. 4-10 (Abington, Pennsylvania)
3   Exodus 3:9,10.
4   Isaac Watts (1719), Hymn 165, Hymns Ancient & Modern,
     Standard Edition, (William Clowes & Sons Ltd., 1924).
5   Supra. p. 121
6   For the story of the Adulterous Woman, see John 7:53 - 8:11;
     although it should be noted that in the Revised Standard Version
     (RSV) of the Bible it is omitted from the main text. The RSV
     Editors have taken the view that it does not belong to the Fourth
     Gospel originally, although it "appears to be an authentic
     incident in the life of Jesus". (The Holy Bible, The Oxford
     Annotated Bible, ed. Herbert G. May and Bruce M. Metzger,
     (O. U. P. New York 1962), p. 1296).
7   The question might well arise about the place of the middle and
     upper classes in the fellowship of a Church that is fundamentally
     the Church of the poor, down-trodden and oppressed. The clue
     to the answer lies in the importance which such persons of wealth
     and status attach to their possessions and position, since it is
     to be acknowledged with Jesus that a man's life should not be
     measured solely on the basis of what he possesses. The fellow-
     ship of the Church can indeed provide common ground for all
     classes who are equally committed to the elimination of all
     unnecessary poverty, suffering, oppression and de-humanizing
     systems. The wealthier classes are in a better position to bring
     about social amelioration, if they are really committed.
8   See Matthew 27:1-26; Mark 15:1-15; Luke 23:1-5; 13-25; ·
     John 18:28 - 19:22.
9   Acts 12:20-23.
10   Luke 12:15.
11   Matthew 16:26.
12   See below pp. 160-173

13   Fernando Henriques, Family And Colour In Jamaica,
      2nd edition, (Humanities Press, New York, 1969).
14   Dom Basil Matthews, Crisis Of The West Indian
      Family: A Sample Study, (UCWI, Jamaica, 1953).
15   M.G. Smith, West Indian Family Structure,
      (University of Washington Press, Seattle, 1962).
16   Raymond T. Smith, The Negro Family In British
      Guiana, (Routledge and Kegan Paul, 1956).
17   Edith Clarke, My Mother Who Fathered Me: A Study
      Of The Family In Three Selected Communities
      In Jamaica, 2nd edition, (Humanities Press, New York,
      1966).
18   See below pp. 177-197
19   Karl Barth, The Christian Understanding Of
      Revelation, (Bonn University, 1947).
20   Supra. pp. 106-107, 120-123, 128-130
21   Reinhold Niebuhr, Moral Man And Immoral Society,
      (Charles Scribner's Sons, New York, 1960), p. 167
22   Ibid.
23   Ibid.
24   Joseph Scriven (1857) Hymn 779, The Book Of Common
      Praise, (O.U.P., Toronto 1962).

Notes to chapter VII

1   Robert J. Moore, "Caribbean countries just want the chance to
      develop confidence", Canada and the Third World
      What are the Choices, Report of the 44th Couchiching
      Conference of the Canadian Institute on Public Affairs, ed.
      Dean Walker, (Toronto, Yorkminster Publishing Ltd., 1975),
      p. 116.
2   "Report of The General Secretariat", Second General Assembly
      of the CCC, mimeo, (Guyana, CCC), p. 2.
3   The CCC experience in this respect is not surprising. Christian
      activists often claim that praxis is in fact theology. Further,
      prophetic vision often fails to be as creative as it is minatory.
      In any event, it is possible for different theological stances to
      agree on what they consider to be common (or joint) action.
4   P.I. Gomes, J. Massiah, L. Shorey, Internal Evaluation
      of the CCC, mimeo., (Barbados, CADEC, 1975), p. 32
5   "Development A Form Of Ministry", Report of a CADEC
      Consultation December 1975, (newspaper format), (Barbados,
      CCC, 1976).

6   R. Cuthbert, K. Clarke and L. Nurse, Evaluation of CCC
     Programme Integration, (Barbados, CCC, 1976), p. 42
7   Ibid.
8   "Report of The General Secretariat", CCC Second Assembly,
     p. 3. cf. Dr. Philip Potter's statement, supra. p. 98
9   "Programme Report On Human Rights To The General
     Secretary - Towards The Second General Assembly in Guyana,
     November 16-23, 1977", mimeo, (Jamaica, CCC Human Rights
     Bureau, 1977), p. 3
10   Human Rights Bureau 1977 Report, p. 5
11   Human Rights Bureau 1977 Report, p. 6
12   Ibid.
13   Called To Be, p. 7
14   Called To Be, p. 11
15   Ibid.
16   Ibid.
17   Called To Be, p. 13
18   See Appendix
19   The Right Hand Of God, ed. Kortright Davis, (Barbados,
     CCC, 1976), p. 2
20   The Right Hand of God, p. 3
21   The Right Hand of God, p. 6
22   See The Right Hand of God, p. 7
23   The Right Hand of God, p. 8
24   The Right Hand of God, p. 10
25   The Right Hand of God, p. 11
26   The Right Hand of God, p. 20
27   Ibid.
28   "Sermon For Prayer Service Opening The Second Assembly
     of The Caribbean Conference Of Churches - November 16,
     1977 - Georgetown, Guyana", mimeo, (Guyana, CCC Second
     Assembly, 1977), p. 5
29   "Working Together With Christ Proclaiming The Gospel",
     Report of Second Assembly Work Group 1, mimeo, p. 1
     It must be readily agreed that this formulation of the Gospel
     imperative in terms of the rich and the poor is not strong
     enough to deal with the Caribbean realities. The rich indeed
     should not merely be 'challenged' but rather required if
     not forced to share. The poor need more than to be
     'assured' - they need to be helped and mobilized to
     secure for themselves the just rewards of human
     worth and dignity in their socio-historical existence.
30   Report of Second Assembly Work Group 1, p. 2
31   Report of Second Assembly Work Group 1, p. 3
32   Report of Second Assembly Work Group 1, p. 4
33   Report of Second Assembly Work Group 1, p. 5

34 Report Of The Second General Assembly, p. 72.
    This resolution was referred to the Continuation Committee
    for ratification in 1978.
35 Ibid.
36 Report Of The Second General Assembly, pp. 76-77
37 See Called To Be, p. 6
38 This is the burden of the message of the eighth century prophets
    Amos, Hosea and Micah.
39 The Gospel story does of course include rich characters like
    Nicodemus, the Good Samaritan, and the Centurion (whose
    servant was sick), whose wealth did not blur their sense of
    justice, or humility, or commission. Yet Jesus did underline
    the real conflict which the rich would experience, in terms
    of their authentic membership in the Kingdom of God. While
    no attempt is being made here to classify power and goods as
    evil, or to glorify poverty, it remains a Gospel imperative that
    the Kingdom of God should unceasingly confront the poverty
    that results from human injustice in all its forms.
40 Max Weber, The Religion of India, (New York, Free
    Press, 1967) pp. 37-8
41 St. John 10:10
42 P.S. Minear, Images Of The Church In The New
    Testament, (Philadelphia, 1960) See also Hans Kung,
    The Church, (New York, Image Books, 1976).
43 For a comparison between foreign slaves and Israelite slaves
    see "Slave" in W. Corswant, A Dictionary Of Life In
    Bible Times, trans. Arthur Heathcote, (Hodder & Stoughton,
    1960).
44 See St. Luke 16:1-9; 19:11-27
45 See St. Mark 4:30-32
46 See Percy Selwyn, Small, Poor and Remote: Islands
    at a Geographical Disadvantage, Discussion Paper
    123, (Sussex, IDS, 1978)
47 Supra. p. 125
48 Supra. p. 50
49 Richard Dickinson, "Toward A New Focus For Churches' Develop-
    ment Projects", Ecumenical Review, Vol. XXII, 1970,
    pp. 217-218
50 Projects Funded March 1973 - December 1975,
    CADEC Development Fund Report 1973-1975, (Barbados, CADEC,
    1976), p. 1
51 CADEC, Action For Community In The Caribbean,
    (Barbados, CADEC, 1973), p. 36
52 Ibid.
53 CADEC, Action For Community, pp. 37-38

54   CADEC, Action For Community, p. 38
55   Ibid.
56   St. Matthew 24:36-25:13
57   St. Matthew 8:5-13
58   St. Mark 13:13
59   St. Mark 14:36
60   St. John 19:30
61   St. John 15:13
62   Hebrews 12:1-2
63   CADEC, Action For Community, p. 35
64   CADEC, Action For Community, p. 36
65   Singh is currently located in Barbados, and is allowed to function
        on a short-term work permit issued by the national Government.
66   Caribbean CONTACT, Vol. 1, No. 3, February 1973,
        p. 8
67   Hymn 208, Hymns Ancient & Modern, Standard Edition,
        (William Clowes & Sons Ltd., 1924)
68   Hans Kung, On Being A Christian, trans. Edward Quinn,
        (Collins, 1976), p. 469
69   A.J. Van Der Bent, The Utopia of World Community,
        (SCM Press, 1973), p. 131
70   Paulo Freire, Pedagogy Of The Oppressed, trans.
        Myra Bergman Ramos, (Penguin, 1972), p. 41
71   Paulo Freire, Cultural Action For Freedom,
        (Penguin, 1972), p. 83

Notes to chapter VIII

1   Hebrews 5:11b-14
2   Edward Hallett Carr, The Twenty Years' Crisis
        1919 - 1939, (McMillan, 1940), p. 15
3   Ephesians 4:13
4   Daniel Jenkins, Christian Maturity And The Theology
        Of Success, (S.C.M. Press 1976), p. 4
5   Daniel Jenkins, op. cit., p. 75
6   The CADEC Development Fund 1976, (Barbados,
        CADEC, 1977), p. 2
7   "Christian Action Week Sub-Regional Receipts 1974-1977",
        mimeo, Report to CCC Second Assembly, Guyana 1977, p. 1
8   Support Christian Action Week, Promotion Booklet
        from CADEC, (Barbados, CADEC, 1978), p. 6
9   A grant from the Evangelical Church of Germany is slowly being
        exhausted, and the Newspaper has not yet been able to build up

its own financial reserves to pay for itself. Caribbean
CONTACT should become a permanent project for support
by the Development Fund of CADEC, to guarantee its survival.

10   See St. Luke 4:23
11   See Walter J. Hollenweger, "The Church For Others - Ten Years
     After", Research Bulletin 1977, ed. Professor J.G.
     Davies, (Birmingham, Institute For The Study of Worship And
     Religious Architecture, 1977), p. 91
12   Ibid.
13   James Tucker, "The Church And The Management of Change",
     Moving Into Freedom, ed. Kortright Davis, (Barbados,
     CEDAR Press, 1977), p. 97
14   Hans Kung, On Being A Christian, p. 601
15   Other aspects which require serious attention by the Churches
     are: (a) Structures of organization (ministry and leadership);
     (b) Use of Church buildings; (c) Re-appraisal of the role of the
     clergy in raising funds to ensure that their salaries are paid;
     (d) Re-examination of all social privileges and concessions e.g.
     duty-free privileges, 'charitable organization' status.
16   J.G. Davies, Everyday God, (S.C.M. Press, 1973),
     p. 269
17   J.G. Davies, op. cit., p. 282
18   Adrian Cunningham, Terry Eagleton, brian Wicker, Martin
     Redfern, Laurence Bright, Catholic And The Left,
     (Sheed and Ward, 1966), p. 13
19   J.G. Davies, op. cit., p. 282
20   Brian Wicker, First The Political Kingdom, (Sheed
     and Ward, 1967), pp. 83-84
21   See for example D.E. Nineham, Saint Mark, (Penguin
     1977), pp. 176-184; J.C. Fenton, Saint Matthew, (Penguin,
     1976), pp. 241-244.
22   Walter J. Hollenweger, The Pentecostals, trans. R.A.
     Wilson, (S.C.M. Press, 1976), p. 465
23   Walter J. Hollenweger, op. cit., p. 466
24   Walter J. Hollenweger, op. cit., p. 467
25   "Operation Feedback (1976)", Preliminary Report,
     mimeo., (Barbados, CCC Assembly Planning Unit, 1976), p. 7
26   "Operation Feedback (1976)", p. 6
27   Leslie Newbigin, The Household Of God, (S.C.M. Press,
     1964), p. 107
28   Desmond M. Tutu, "Whither African Theology?", Christianity
     In Independent Africa, ed. Edward Fashole-Luke,
     Richard Gray, Adrian Hastings and Godwin Tasie, (Rex Collings,
     1978), p. 367

29   Walter J. Hollenweger, "Intercultural Theology", paper read
      at Annual Conference Of The Society For The Study Of Theology,
      Cambridge, 4-7 April 1978, mimeo., p. 11.
30   The Economist, Vol. 270, No. 7066, February 3, 1979,
      p. 40
31   USPG NETWORK, No: 10 new series, Summer 1978, p. 9
32   Laurenti Magesa, "Towards a theology of liberation for Tanzania",
      Christianity Independent Africa, ed. Edward Fashole-
      Luke at. al., p. 511
33   Andre Dumas, Political Theology And The Life Of
      The Church, trans. John Bowden, (S. C. M. Press, 1978),
      p. 18
34   Andre Dumas, op. cit., p. 134
35   Andre Dumas, op. cit., p. 135
36   Ibid.
37   Andre Dumas, op. cit., p. 138
38   Ibid.
39   Ibid.
40   Faith Science And The Future, Preparatory Readings
      For The 1979 Conference of the World Council of Churches,
      (Geneva, WCC, 1978), p. 5
41   A. J. Seymour, "Tomorrow Belongs To The People", in
      Report of CADEC Consortium, Jamaica, September
      1974, (Barbados, CADEC, 1974), pp. 2-3.
42   Edmond Desueza, "Missiology In The Caribbean Today", Out
      Of The Depths, ed. Idris Hamid, p. 245.

BIBLIOGRAPHY

A. CCC Materials

The Gift of Land, Report of a Seminar sponsored by CADEC in
November 1969 in Barbados, CADEC, 37 pp. (Barbados, 1970)
Early Reports And Circulars from the Co-ordinator of CADEC
(1969-1972)
Report on A Meeting of The Caribbean Steering Committee And Ecumenical
Consultation in Jamaica, October, 1970.
Report On A Consultation For The Planning Of The Caribbean Con-
ference of Churches (CCC), held in Trinidad, November 1971
Report on Caribbean Youth Consultation, Nelson Island, Trinidad,
January 5-9, 1970, (Trinidad, Youth Department, 1970)

The Church And Agrarian Reform in The Caribbean,
Harold Sitahal, 5 pp. (Barbados, 1972)

Called To Be, Report of Caribbean Ecumenical Consultation for
Development, Trinidad November 1971, CADEC, 80 pp.
(Barbados, 1972)

The Role Of Tourism In Caribbean Development,
CADEC, 59 pp., (Trinidad, 1972)

Caribbean Unity Christian Unity, Resolutions of the Caribbean
Ecumenical Consultation On Development, CCCN, 32 pp., (Barbados
1972)

Consultation On Church-Communications-Development,
Barbados 1972 17 pp., (Barbados, 1972)

Handbook Of The Churches In The Caribbean, J. Brathwaite (Ed.) CADEC, 234 pp. (Barbados, 1973)

Action For Community In The Caribbean, CADEC, 44 pp.
(Barbados, 1973)

All A We Is One! One What?, Packet produced by Dr. Joyce
Bailey for CADEC's Education For Development Team, CADEC,
(Barbados, 1973)

Report Of Inaugural Assembly of the CCC, November
1973 143 pp. CCC (Barbados, 1973)

A Chance For A Change, CADEC, 26 pp. (Barbados, 1973)

Voices For Change From CADEC, K. Davis (Ed.) 62 pp.
(Antigua, 1973)

Two Years After, A Progress Report of the CADEC Development Fund to November 1974, CADEC, 78 pp. (Barbados, 1974)

Caribbean Conference of Churches, Report (Decisions) Of Continuation Committee held in Port-au-Prince, Haiti, June 5-11, 1974, CCC 33 pp. (Barbados, 1974)

Report On Evaluation Study Of 1971-1973, Pastors' Courses Sponsored by CADEC, Garth A. Southwell, 17 pp., (Barbados 1974)

Tomorrow Belongs To The People, Report of Consortium meeting in Jamaica, September 1974, 24 pp., (Barbados, 1974)

Programme and Budget of ARC - Renewal Commissions of CCC 1975-1977, CCC, 30 pp., (Barbados 1974)

Report of Educational Strategies and Priorities Workshop, Guyana, April 1974, CCC, 5 pp. (Barbados, 1974)

A List Of Projects Funded March 1973 - October 1974, CADEC, 19 pp. (Barbados, 1975)

Christians In Dialogue And Joint Action, Report of a Consultation on the Ecumenical Sharing of Personnel in Barbados, January 1973, G. Goring, R.G. Neehall, P.I. Gomes (Editors), 40 pp. (Barbados, 1975)

Christian Action Week, A Leader's Guide, Promotional literature for fund-raising Campaign, 1975, 6 pp. (Barbados, 1975)

Thank God I'm A Woman, Joyce Holder (Ed.), 18 pp., (Barbados, 1975)

Come Let Us Reason, A Collection of articles by the General Secretary of the CCC Dr. Roy Neehall, P.I. Gomes (Ed.), 44 pp. (Trinidad, 1975)

Caribbean Women In The Struggle, CCW, 64 pp. (Barbados, 1975)

Women And Development, CCW, 48 pp., (Trinidad, 1975)

Christian Action And The Leewards, Papers from the Leeward Islands Social Action Conference, 1975, K. Davis (Ed.), 76 pp. (Antigua 1975)

"Evangelism And Practice", Idris Hamid, 15 pp., (Trinidad, 1975)

"Preaching - The Proclamation of the World", W. Watty, 24 pp., (Trinidad, 1975)

Draft Report On Internal Evaluation of CCC, P.I. Gomes, J. Massiah, L.S. Shorey 47 pp., (Barbados, 1975)

Relections In Oil & Sugar, A Andrews (Ed.) 104 pp., (Trinidad, 1975)

The Great Shake, (Antigua, CADEC, 1975)

Review Of CCC Administrative Management Seminars,
September & October 1976, M.C.L., Dominica, 6 pp.,
(Dominica, 1976)

"Leisure-Tourism In the Context Of Caribbean Development", L. A.
Nurse - Paper presented at Conference on the Gospel, Freedom
and Leisure, Williamsburg, Virginia September 29 to October 2,
1976; 10 pp., (Barbados, 1976)

A Survey - Education For Development In The Caribbean, James J. And Winnell M. Thomas, 90 pp., CODEL,
(New York, 1976)

The Right Hand Of God, K. Davis (Ed.), Resolutions and Report
of CCC Inaugural Assembly of 1973, 25 pp., CCC (Barbados, 1976)

Development A Form Of Ministry, (Newspaper format),
Report of a Consultation in Barbados December 1975, 4 pp., CADEC,
(Barbados 1976)

We Stand Together, Report On A Consultation On Cirruculum
Development, Trinidad 1976, (Sponsored by Education Renewal
Action of the CCC) 79 pp., CCC (Trinidad, 1976)

Report of Projects Funded by CADEC, March 1973 -
December 1975, CADEC, 16 pp., (Barbados, 1976)
Draft Manual for Scholarships - CCC, 8 pp., (Barbados, 1976)

CADEC, Report On The Urbanization-Unemployment
Programme 1973-1975, K. Davis, 11 pp., (Barbados, 1976)
Project Development Programme And Budget For 1977 (Including
Review of Programme 1976), CADEC, 14 pp., (Barbados, 1976)

"Operation Feedback" 1976 - Preliminary Report,
Assembly Planning Unit of CCC - (Survey of reactions to ecumenism
and the CCC in the Region), 11 pp., (Barbados 1976)

CCC Constitution and By-Laws, CCC, 10 pp., (1976)

The Core Consortium: Dialogue Among Partners,
Report of the Core Consortium held in Barbados, April 1976, 20 pp.,
(Barbados, 1976)

Operation Outreach 1976, K. Davis (Ed.), 37 pp., (Barbados,
1976)

The United Church of Canada And Caribbean Development with CADEC, K. Davis (Ed.), 26 pp., (Barbados 1976)

CADEC Development Fund, A Limited Evaluation of
Its Performance March 1973 to August 1976, CADEC,
35 pp., (Barbados 1976)

Evaluation of CCC Programme Integration, R. Cuthbert,
K. Clarke, L. Nurse, 50 pp., (Barbados, 1976)

Report of Christian Action Week, 1975, CADEC 12 pp.,
(Barbados, 1976)

Education For Development Programme Report
October 1975 - July 1976, CADEC, 15 pp., (Barbados,
1976)
Dossier of Human Rights Seminar, September 1976, CCC, Trinidad
CCW Progress Report, September 1975 - February 1976
Report of Local Councils' Consultations 1976
Progress Reports on ARC Programmes, 1976
Dossier for Theological Education Consultation, October, 1976
(Trinidad)
Development Fund Committee Minutes, 1976

The CCC Conference on Evangelism, A Summary Report, CCC, 18 pp., (Barbados 1976)

Appropriate Technology And People, (Barbados, 1976)

Report Of The Land And Food For People Programme
1976, CADEC, 20 pp., (Barbados, 1977)

In Search of Partnership, (Report of the First CCC Consortium
held in Trinidad February 1977). CADEC/CCC Documentation Service,
55 pp., (Barbados, 1977)

Land, Homes And People: Towards Self-Development
Through Community Action, A First Evaluation and Report
of the Barroualie Glebe Development Project in St. Vincent,
Randolph Cato (prepared by), CADEC, 51 pp., (Barbados, 1977)

Christian Action Week 1976, Report, CADEC, 9 pp.,
(Barbados 1977)
Consultation on Christian Unity, May 24-26, 1977, Papers from, CCC
(Trinidad, 1977)

Documentation: Annual Report 1976, CADEC, 7 pp.,
(Barbados, 1977)
"Human Rights And Institutional Change", Position paper on CCC's
Human Rights Programme, CCC, 17 pp., (Trinidad, 1977)

CADEC 1976 Report, CADEC, 14 pp., (Barbados, 1977)

CADEC Communications Report 1976, CCN, 22 pp.,
(Barbados 1977)
"Communicarib 1976", A Report from the Administrator, CCN, 22 pp.,
(Barbados, 1977)
Report For 1975/76 Of Action For Renewal Of The Churches, ARC,
26 pp., (Trinidad, 1977)

CCC - Report Of First Training And Orientation
Programme, November 1976 - by CADEC Project
Development Programme, CADEC, 58 pp., (Barbados,
1977)

CADEC Programme, Notes to the Budget 1978-1980, CADEC, 19 pp.,
(Barbados 1977)

Together For Change: A Synopsis of the CCC and its Consortium
Agencies, 116 pp., CCC, (Barbados, 1977)

The CADEC Development Fund 1976, CADEC, 21 pp.,
(Barbados, 1977)
Education For Development Programme Report January 1977 to June
1977, M. Cockburn, CADEC, 9 pp., (Barbados, 1977)

CCC Programme & Budget, 1978-1980, CCC, 65 pp.,
(Jamaica, 1977)

Theological Education In a New Caribbean, Report of
A Consultation of Directors of Theological Institutions and Programmes
In The Caribbean, Trinidad, October 1976, 42 pp., (Barbados 1977)
Papers From Second General Assembly, Georgetown, Guyana, November
16-23, 1977
"Preliminary Report On Project Five", mimeo., (Assembly Planning
Unit, 1977)

The First Ten Years, CCC/CADEC/ARC, A Synopsis of The
Movement 1967-1977, (Barbados, Documentation Service, 1977)

Development Fund Report 1977, (Barbados, CADEC, 1978)

CADEC Report 1977, (Barbados, 1978)

Workers Together With Christ, Report Of The Second
General Assembly, (Barbados, 1978)

Support Christian Action Week, Promotion Booklet from
CADEC, (Barbados, CADEC, 1978)

OTHERS

(a) Sample Copies Of Project Proposals To The Development Fund
    Committee
(b) CADEC Report 1978, (Barbados, CADEC, 1979)
(c) Caribbean CONTACT, Vols. 1 to 6 (1973-1979)

B. Unpublished Theses

BRERETON, Bridget Mary, A Social History Of Trinidad
1870-1890, University of the West Indies. Ph.D. 1973
CHEVANNES, Alston B., Jamaican Lower Class Religion:
Struggles Against Oppression, University of the West
Indies. M.Sc. 1972
COYE, R.V. Evadne, Dependence And Foreign Policy:
The Cuban Experience 1961-1971, University of the
West Indies. M.Sc. 1976
DAVIS, D.H. Kortright, Church And Society In Barbados
1870-1890, University of the West Indies. M.A. 1976
EMTAGE, S.E., Growth, Development and Planning in a
Small Dependent Economy, the Case of Barbados,
University of Sussex. M.Phil. 1970
FARQUHAR, D.V., Christian Missions In The Leeward
Islands, University of Leeds. D.Phil. 1971
GILLIES, F., The Eschatological Structures Of Chris-
tianity And Marxism, University of Sussex. D.Phil. 1976
JONES, Edwin S., Pressure Group Politics In The West
Indies, University of Manchester. Ph.D. 1970
KILPATRICK, J.W., Protestant Missions in Jamaica:
A Critical Survey Of Mission Policy from 1754 to
Present Day, University of Edinburgh. Ph.D. 1943/44
McFARLANE, Dennis Homer Clare, Industry And the Process
of Industrial Development In A Situation of Under-
development, University of the West Indies. Ph.D. 1970
PHILLIPS, Peter D., The Political Economy Of Jamaican
Foreign Relations: A Study Of The Orientations Of
National Capitalists To Foreign Relationships,
University of the West Indies. M.Sc. 1977
RYDALL, D.A., The Organization Of Missionary Societies
And The Recruitment Of Missionaries In The Dif-
fusion of British Culture In Jamaica During the
Period 1834-65, University of London. Ph.D. 1959/60
ST.PIERRE, Maurice, The Anatomy Of Decolonization:
A Study of Guyana's Struggle For Independence,
University of the West Indies. Ph.D. 1976

C. Articles, papers and periodicals

ABRECHT, Paul, "Rapid Social Change And Human Need",
Ecumenical Review, Vol. XIII, 1960-61, pp. 180-190

BALOGH, Thomas, "Failures In The Strategy Against Poverty",
World Development, Vol. 6, No. 1, 1978
BIENEFELD, M.A., The Self-Employed Of Urban
Tanzania, D54 (Sussex IDS, 1974)
BRAITHWAITE, Lloyd E., "Social Stratification And Cultural
Pluralism", Annals Of The New York Academy Of
Sciences, Vol. LXXXIII, 1960, pp. 816-31
CARIBBEAN DEVELOPMENT BANK, Annual Presidential Statements
1971-1978
Caribbean Journal of Religious Studies, Vol. 1,
No. 1, 1975 (irregular)
Caribbean Quarterly, Vols. 17 (1971), 18 (1972), 19 (1973),
22 (1976)
CENTRE FOR MULTI-RACIAL STUDIES (Barbados)
Caribbean Background Vol. IV, 1973
CHAPLIN, F.D., "Report on a Meeting of the Caribbean Steering
Committee And Ecumenical Consultation In Jamaica, Ocotber,
1970", mimeo., (Trinidad, WCC Inter-Church Relations Secretariat,
1970). (Limited circulation).
CLIFFE, Lionel, Underdevelopment or Socialism? A
Comparative Analysis of Kenya and Tranzania,
D33, (Sussex, IDS, 1973)
COLLINS, Paul, Decentralisation and Local Administration
for Development in Tanzania, D94, (Sussex, IDS, 1976)
CRUISE O'BRIEN, Rita, Domination And Dependence In
Mass Communications: Implications for the Use
of Broadcasting In Developing Countries, D64,
(Sussex, IDS, 1974)
CURRIE, Lauchlin, "The Objectives Of Development", World
Development Vol. 6, No. 1, 1978.
DASH, J. Michael, "Marvellous Realism - The Way Out of Negritude"
Caribbean Studies, Vol. 13, No. 4, 1974, pp. 57-70
DEMAS, William G., - The Political Economy Of The
English-speaking Caribbean, 4th edition, (Barbados,
CEDAR Press, 1976)
-, "National Policies For Increasing The Utilization of Labour in the
Caribbean", mimeo., (Barbados, 1975)
DICKINSON, Richard, "Toward A New Focus For Churches' Develop-
ment Projects", Ecumenical Review, Vol. XXII, 1970
DORE, Ronald, Underdevelopment In Theoretical Perspec-
tive, D109, (Sussex, IDS, 1977)
Ebony, Vol. XXXIII, No. 2, December, 1977
EDWARDS, P.A., Education For Development In The
Caribbean, (Trinidad, CADEC, 1971)
ELKINS, W.F., "Hercules And The Society Of Peoples Of African
Origin", Caribbean Studies, Vol. 11, No. 4, January 1972,
pp. 47-59

FERNANDES, Angelo, "The Role of the Church in Development",
Ecumenical Review, Vol. XXII, 1970

FORRESTER, Duncan B., "Western Academic Sophistry And The
Third World", Economic and Political Weekly,
Vol. IX, No. 40, October, 1974

FREIRE, Paulo, "Education, Liberation and the Church", Study
Encounter, Vol. IX, No. 1, 1973

GIRVAN, N., "The Development of Dependency Economics in the
Caribbean and Latin America", Social and Economic
Studies, Vol. 22, No. 1, March, 1973

GITTINGS, John, How To Study China's Socialist Development, C117, (Sussex, IDS, 1976)

GODFREY, M., "The International market in skills and the transmission of inequality", Development and Change, Vol. 6,
No. 4, October 1975

GOODRIDGE, Sehon, - Politics And The Caribbean Church,
A Confession of Guilt, (Trinidad, CADEC, 1971)

-, The Church Amidst Politics And Revolution,
(Barbados, CEDAR Press, 1977)

GORMAN, G.E., (Ed.), Development Studies - Register
of Research, In The United Kingdom 1976-77, (Sussex, IDS,
1977)

Gospel In Context, Vol. 1, 1978

GRANT, J., "Can The Churches Promote Development?"
Ecumenical Review, Vol. XXVI, 1974

GREEN, R.H., - Twoard Ujamaa and Kujitegemea: In-
come Distribution and Absolute Poverty Eradication
Aspects Of The Tanzanian Transition to Socialism,
D66, (Sussex, IDS, 1974)

-, Productive Employment In Africa: An Overbiew Of
The Challenge, D87, (Sussex, IDS, 1975)

-, "Toward a transformation of the International Economic Order?
Industrial World Responses," Mimeo., 1976

-, "Basic human needs, collective self-reliance and development
strategy: some relections on power, periphery and poverty," in
Self-Reliance And Solidarity In The Quest For
International Justice, (Geneva, World Council of Churches,
1976)

-, Solidarity, Self-Reliance, Basis Human Needs,
mimeo, (Geneva, WCC, Justice & Service 1977)

GUYANA INSTITUTE FOR SOCIAL RESEARCH AND ACTION (GISRA),
What Colour Is God's Skin? (Guyana, 1971)

HACKSHAW, James, Social And Economic Planning In The
Leeward And Windward Islands, (New York, Church
World Service, 1967)

HALL, Budd L., Participation and Education in Tanzania,
D86, (Sussex, IDS, 1975)

HAMID, Idris, In Search Of New Perspectives, (Trinidad, CADEC, 1971)

HAYWARD, Victor, "The Caribbean Conference of Churches In Process of Formation", Report 53 - Secretariat For Relationships With Christian Councils, mimeo., (Geneva, World Council of Churches, 1970)

HOLLENWEGER, Walter J., - Marxist And Kimbanguist Mission A Comparison (University of Birmingham, 1973)

-, "Marxist Ethics", Expository Times, Vol. 85, No. 10, July 1974

-, "The Church For Others - Ten Years After", in Research Bullentin 1 9 7 7, ed. Professor J.G. Davies, (Birmingham, Institute For The Study Of Worship And Religious Architecture, 1977)

-, "Intercultural Theology", paper delivered at Annual Conference of the Society for the Study of Theology, Cambridge, April 4-7, 1978

IDOC International, The Church At The Crossroads, Europe Dossier 6, 1978

IDS BULLETIN Vols. 7-10

INTERNATIONAL REVIEW OF MISSION, Vol. LXVI, Nos. 261 & 263, 1977

ITTY, C.I., - "Development", Ecumenical Review, Vol. XIX, No. 4, 1967

-, "Are We Yet Awake?", Ecumenical Review, Vol. XXVI, 1974

KAUNDA, Kenneth, "Rich And Poor Nations", Ecumenical Review, Vol. XX, 1968

KHAN, Kenrick R., "Reflections On The Caribbean Towards A New Hermeneutic", mimeo., (Guyana, CCC, 1977)

LADOC, Vol. VII, No. 26, 1976; Vol. VIII, No. 6, 1977

LATEEF, K. Sarwar, China And India: Economic Performance And Prospects, C 118 (Sussex, IDS, 1976)

LEHMANN, David, Optimistic Reflections On A Cuban Fortnight And The Trajectory Of The Cuban Revolution, C 102, (Sussex, IDS, 1970/71)

LIPTON, Michael, Confrontation Versus Co-operation: Poor Countries' Dwindling External Options, 'Bargaining'; and the Case for Multiple Bilateralisms, D47, (Sussex, IDS, 1974)

McCORMACK, Michael, Liberation Or Development, The Role Of The Church in the New Caribbean, (Trinidad, CADEC, 1971)

MAZRUI, Ali A., "From Social Darwinism To Current Theories of Modernization - A Tradition Of Analysis", World Politics, Vol. XXI, No. 1, 1968, pp. 69-83

MINHAS, B.S., "The Current Development Debate", mimeo., (Sussex, IDS, 1977)

NETTLEFORD, Rex, "Caribbean Perspectives - The Creative Potential And The Quality of Life", Caribbean Quarterly, Vol. 17, Nos. 3 & 4, 1971, pp. 114-127

NYERERE, Julius K., "Education For Self-Reliance", Ecumenical Review, Vol. XIX, No. 4, 1967, pp. 382-403

PANNENBERG, Wolfhart, "The Contribution Of Christianity To The Modern World", Cross Currents, Vol. XXV, No. 4, 1976

PARMAR, S.L., " Concern For Man In The Quest For Development", Ecumenical Review, Vol. XIX, No. 4, 1967, pp. 357-62

-, "The Limits-to-Growth Debate In Asain Perspective", Ecumenical Review, Vol. XXVI, 1974

-, "Development: Priorities And Guidelines", Ecumenical Review, Vol. XXVII, No. 1, 1975

POTTER, Philip, "Report Of The General Secretary", Ecumenical Review, Vol. XXV, 1973

RAMPHAL, Shridath S., To Care For Caricom, (Guyana, Caricom Secretariat, 1975)

Savacou, Nos. 5 & 6

SAWYERR, H. & David Mitchell, Workers With Christ, (Barbados, CEDAR Press, 1977)

SEERS, Dudley, "The Meaning Of Development", International Development Review, Vol. XI, No. 4, 1969, pp. 2-6

-, What Are We Trying To Measure? C 106R, reprint, (Sussex, IDS, 1973)

-, Cuba Quizas, D45, (Sussex, IDS, 1974)

-, "The New Meaning Of Development", mimeo., (Sussex, 1977)

SELWYN, Percy, Small, Poor And Remote: Islands At A Geographical Disadvantage, DP 128, (Sussex, IDS, 1978)

SINGH, Paul, "Structured Poverty: Some Conceptual Issues", mimeo., (University Of Guyana, 1976)

SODEPAX, Church Alert, The SODEPAX Newsletter

SMITH, Raymond T., "Social Stratification, Cultural Pluralism And Integration In West Indian Societies", Caribbean Integration, ed. S. Lewis and T.G. Matthews, (Rio Piedras, Institute of Caribbean Studies, University of Puerto Rico, 1967)

WORLD BANK, World Development Report, 1978, (Washington, World Bank, 1978)

WYNTER, Sylvia, "One Love - Rhetoric or Reality? - Aspects of Afro-Jamaicanism", Caribbean Studies, Vol. 12, No. 13, October 1972

D. Books

AGARWALA, A.N., and W.P. SINGH, The Economics Of Development, (Delhi, OUP, 1977)

ALPHONSE, Ephraim S., God On The Bridge, (Barbados, CEDAR Press, 1975)

ALVES, Rubem, A Theology Of Human Hope, (Washington D.C., Corpus Books, 1969)

ANDERSON, Geral H., (ed.) Asian Voices In Christian Theology, (New York, Orbis Books, 1976)
- with Thomas F. Stransky (ed.) Mission Trends No. 1 (1974), No. 2 (1975), No. 3 (1976), (Michigan, Wm. B. Eerdmans)

Arusha Declaration And Christian Socialism, The, (Six Papers at a Seminar at University College, Dar es Salaam, 1967)

ASSMANN, Hugo, Theology For A Nomad Church, trans. Paul Burns, (New York, Orbis Books, 1976)

ATKINSON, John W., Motives In Fantasy, Action And Society, (New Jersey, Van Nostrand Co. Inc., 1958)

AUGIER, F.R. with Shirley Gordon, Douglas Hall, and Mary Reckord, The Making Of The West Indies (Longmans, 1960)

AUGUSTUS, Earl, The Spiritual Quest Of Antillean Man, (Trinidad, Scope Caribbean Publishing Ltd., 1977)

BAËTA, C.G., (ed.) Christianity In Tropical Africa, (OUP, 1968)

BARAN, Paul, The Political Economy Of Growth, (Penguin, 1973)

BARRETT, Leonard E., The Rastafarians: A Study In Messianic Cultism In Jamaica, (Rio Piedras, Institute of Caribbean Studies, University of Puerto Rico, 1968)

BARTH, Karl, The Christian Understanding Of Revelation, (Bonn University, 1947)
-, The Humanity Of God, (Collins, 1967)

BASTON, C. Daniel, with J. Christiaan Beker and W. Malcolm Clark, Comitment Without Ideology, (SCM Press, 1973)

BAUER, P.T., Dissent On Development, (Weidenfeld and Nicholson, 1976)

BECKFORD, George L., Persistent Poverty, (OUP, 1972)

BENNETT, John E., (ed.) Christian Social Ethics In A Changing World, (New York, Association Press, 1966)

BERGER, Peter, The Sacred Canopy, (New York, Doubleday, 1967)
-, Pyramids Of Sacrifice, (Pelican, 1977)
with Brigitte Berger and Hansfried Kellner, The Homeless Mind, (Pelican, 1973)

BIGO, Pierre, The Church And Third World Revolution, (New York, Orbis Books, 1978)

BOFF, Leonardo, Jesus Christ Liberator, (New York, Orbis Books, 1978)

BONINO, Jose Miguez, Doing Theology In A Revolutionary Situation, (Philadelphia, Fortress Press, 1975)

-, Christians And Marxists, (Hodder & Stoughton, 1976)

BOTTOMORE, T.B., and Maximilien Rubel, Karl Marx - Selected Writings In Sociology And Social Philosophy, (Penguin, 1976)

BOWDEN, John, Voices In The Wilderness, (SCM Press, 1977)

BOYD, Robin H.S., India And The Latin Captivity Of The Church, (Cambridge University Press, 1974)

-, An Introducation To Indian Christian Theology (Madras, Christian Literature Society, 1975)

BRATHWAITE, Edward, The Development Of Creole Society In Jamaica 1770-1820, (Oxford, Clarendon Press, 1971)

-, The Arrivants A New World Trilogy, (OUP, 1973)

-, Contradictory Omens, (Jamaica, Savacou, 1974)

-, Our Ancestral Heritage: A Bibliography Of The Roots Of Culture In The English Speaking Caribbean, (Jamaica, Carifesta Committee, 1976)

BREWSTER, H.R., and C.Y. Thomas, The Dynamics Of West Indian Economic Integration, (Jamaica, ISER, UWI, 1967)

BRITISH COUNCIL OF CHURCHES and The Conference of Missionary Societies of Great Britain and Ireland, Community, Work And The Churches, Report of A Working Group, (London, 1976)

BRODERICK, Walter, J., Camillo Torres: A Biography Of The Priest - Guerrilla, (New York, Doubleday, 1975)

BROOKFELD, Harold, Interdependent Development, (Methurin, 1975)

BRUEGGEMANN, W., The Land, (SPCK, 1978)

BURNHAM, Forbes, A Destiny To Mould, (Longmans, 1970)

BURRIDGE, Kenelm, New Heaven New Earth A Study Of Millenarian Activities, (OUP, 1969)

CAIRD, G.B., Saint Luke, (Penguin, 1977)

CALDWELL, Malcolm, The Wealth Of Some Nations, (Zed Press Ltd., 1977)

CAMARA, Helder, Church And Colonialism, trans. William McSweeney, (Sheed & Ward, 1969)

-, Spiral Of Violence, trans. Della Couling, (New Jersey, Dimension Books, 1971)

-, The Desert Is Fertile, trans. Dinah Livingstone, (Sheed & Ward, 1974)

CARDENAL, Ernesto, The Gospel In Solentiname Vols. 1 & 2, trans. Donald D. Walsh, (New York, Orbis Books, 1978)

CARR, Edward Hallett, The Twenty Years' Crisis 1919-1939, (McMillan, 1940)

CASTEL, Helene, (ed.), World Development: An Introductory Reader, (Collier-McMillan, 1971)

CASTRO, Emilio, Amidst Revolution, (Belfast, Christian Journals Ltd., 1975)

CESAIRE, Aime, Discourse On Colinialism, trans. Joan Pinkham, (New York, 1972)

CHENERY, Hollis, with Montek Ahluwalia, Clive Bell, John Duloy and Richard Jolly (ed.) Redistribution With Growth, (OUP, 1974)

Church And Development, Report of An Ecumenical Consultation on Church And Development in Lebanon, 23-27 February, 1972, (Beirut, Ecumenical Commission Development, Justice & Peace, 1972)

CHURCH AND SOCIETY IN LATIN AMERICA, Social Justice And The Latin Churches, trans. Jorge Lara-Braud, (Virginia, John Knox Press, 1969)

CLARKE, Edith, My Mother Who Fathered Me: A Study Of The Family In Three Selected Communities In Jamaica, 2nd edition, (New York, Humanities Press, 1966)

COHN, Norman, The Pursuit Of The Millenium, (Temple Smith, 1970)

COLE, John, The Poor Of The Earth, (MacMillan, 1977)

COMITAS, Lambros, Caribbeana 1900-1965. A Topical Bibliography (Seattle, Washington, University of Washington Press, 1968)

CONE, James H., Black Theology And Black Power, (New York, Seabury Press, 1969)

-, God Of The Oppressed, (SPCK, 1977)

COOMBS, Orde (ed.), Is Massa Day Dead? Black Moods In The Caribbean (New York, Anchor Press, 1974)

COSTAS, Orlando E., The Church And Its Mission: A Shattering Critique From The Third World, (Illinois, Tyndale House, 1976)

CRAGG, Kenneth, Cristianity In World Perspective, (Lutterworth, 1969)

CRONON, Edmund D., Black Moses: The Story Of Marcus Garvey And The Universal Negro Improvement Association, (Madison, University of Wisconsin Press, 1964)

CROSS, Malcolm, (ed.), West Indian Social Problems, (Trinidad, Columbus Publishers, 1976)

CUNNINGHAM, Adrian, with Terry Eagleton, Brian Wicker, Martin Redfern, and Laurence Bright, Catholics And The Left, (Sheed & Ward, 1966)

DA BREO, D. Sinclair, The West Indies Today, (Grenada, 1971)

DAG HAMMARSKJOLD FOUNDATION, What Now: Another Development, (Uppsala, 1975)

DATHORNE, O.R. (ed.), Caribbean Narrative, (Hiennemann, 1966)

DAVIES, J.G., Everyday God, (SCM Press, 1973)

-, Christians, Politics, and Violent Revolution, (SCM Press, 1976)

-, New Perspectives On Worship Today, (SCM Press, 1978)

DAVIS, Kortright (ed.), Voices For Change, (Antigua, CADEC, 1973)

-, Moving Into Freedom, (Barbados, CEDAR Press, 1977)

DE KADT, Emanuel, Patterns Of Foreign Influence In The Caribbean, (OUP, 1972)

-, with G. Williams (ed.), Sociology and Development, (Tavistock, 1974)

DEMAS, William G., The Economics Of Development in Small Countries (with Special Reference to the Caribbean) (Montreal, McGill University Press, 1965)

-, West Indian Nationhood And Caribbean Integration, (Barbados, CCC Publishing House, 1974)

-, Change And Renewal In The Caribbean, (Barbados, CEDAR Press, 1975)

-, Essays On Caribbean Integration And Development, (Jamaica, ISER, UWI, 1976)

DERR, Thomas Sieger, Ecology And Human Liberation, WSCF Book Vol. III, No. 1, 1973, Serial Number 7, (Geneva, 1973)

DOUGLAS, J.D. (ed.), Let The Earth Hear His Voice, (Minnesota, World Wide Publications, 1975)

DUMAS, Andre, Political Theology And The Life Of The Church, trans. John Bowden, (SCM Press, 1978)

DUSSEL, Enrique, History And The Theology Of Liberation, trans. John Drury, (New York, Orbis Books, 1976)

ELLACURIA, Ignacio, Freedom Made Flesh. The Mission of Christ And His Church, trans. John Drury, (New York, Orbis Books, 1976)

ELLIOTT, Charles, The Development Debate, (SCM Press, 1971)

-, Inflation And The Compromised Church, (Belfast, Christian Journals Ltd., 1975)

-, (ed.) Patterns Of Poverty In The Third World, (New York, Praeger Publishers, 1975)

EYRE, Alan, A New Geography Of The Caribbean, (George Philip, 1962)

FANON, Frantz, The Wretched Of The Earth, trans. Constance Farringdon, (Penguin, 1977)

FASHOLE-LUKE, Edward, with Richard Gray, Adrian Hastings, and Godwin Tasie (ed.), Christianity In Independent Africa, (Rex Collings, 1978)

248

FENTON, J.C., Saint Matthew, (Penguin, 1976)

FIERRO, Alfredo, The Militant Gospel, trans John Drury, (SCM Press, 1977)

FIGUEROA, John (ed.), Caribbean Voices, (Evans Brothers Ltd., 1971)

FRANK, Andre Gunder, Latin America: Underdevelopment Or Revolution, (New York, Monthly Review Press, 1970)

FRASER, Ian M., The Fire Runs, (SCM Press, 1975)

FREIRE, Paulo, Pedagogy Of The Oppressed, (Penguin, 1972)

-, Cultural Action For Freedom, (Penguin, 1972)

FURNIVALL, J.S., Colonial Policy And Practice, (New York University Press, 1956)

FURTADO, Celso, Development And Underdevelopment, trans. Ricardo W. De Aguiar and Eric Charles Drysdale, (Berkeley, University of California Press, 1971)

GARAUDY, Roger, From Anathema To Dialogue, (Collins, 1967)

-, The Alternative Future, trans. Leonard Mayhew, (Penguin, 1976)

GARDAVSKY, V., God Is Not Yet Dead, (Penguin, 1973)

GERBER, Stanford N., (ed.), The Family In The Caribbean, (Rio Piedras, Institute of Caribbean Studies, University of Puerto Rico, 1968)

GHEDDO, Piero, Why Is The Third World Poor?, (New York, 1973)

GHEERBRANT, Alain, The Rebel Church In Lation America, trans. Rosemary Sheed, (Penguin, 1974)

GILL, Robin, The Social Context Of Theology, (Mowbrays, 1976)

-, Theology And Social Structure, (Mowbrays, 1977)

GIRVAN, Norman and Owen Jefferson (ed.), Readings In The Political Economy Of The Caribbean, (Jamaica, New World Group Ltd., 1972)

GOLLWITZER, H., The Rich Christians And Poor Lazarus, (Edinburgh, St. Andrew, 1970)

GOULET, Denis, The Cruel Choice - A New Concept In The Theory Of Development, (New York, Atheneum, 1971)

-, The Uncertain Promise: Value Conflicts In Technology Transfer, (New York, IDOS/North America, 1977)

GREEN, Michael (ed.), The Truth Of God Incarnate, (Hodder & Stoughton, 1977)

GUERIN, Daniel, The West Indies And Their Future, (Dennis Dobson, 1961)

GUTIERREZ, Gustavo, A Theology Of Liberation, trans. Sister Caridad Inda and John Eagleson, (SCM Press, 1974)

GUYANA INSTITUTE FOR SOCIAL RESEARCH AND ACTION (GISRA), Caribbean Development And The Future Of The Church, (Guyana, GISRA, 1969)

HAMID, Idris (ed.), Troubling Of The Waters, (Trinidad, 1973)

-, Out Of The Depths, (Trinidad, St. Andrew's Theological College, 1977)

HARE, Nathan, The Black Anglo-Saxons, (Collins, 1970)

HASTINGS, Adrian, African Christianity, (Geoffrey Chapman, 1976)

HAWKINS, Irene, The Changing Face Of The Caribbean, (Barbados, CEDAR Press, 1976)

HAYWARD, Victor, Christians And China, (Belfast, Christian Journals Ltd., 1974)

HEARNE, John, Land Of The Living, (Faber & Faber, 1961)

HENGEL, Martin, Victory Over Violence, trans. David E. Green, (SPCK, 1975)

-, The Son Of God, trans. John Bowden, (SCM Press, 1976)

-, Christ And Power, trans. Everett K. Kalin, (Belfast, Christian Journals Ltd., 1977)

HENRIQUES, Fernando, Family And Colour In Jamaica, 2nd edition, (New York, Humanities Press, 1969)

HERSKOVITS, Melville J., The Myth Of The Negro Past, (Boston, Beacon Press, 1958)

-, The New World Negro, (Indiana, Minerva Press, 1969)

HICK, John (ed.), The Myth Of God Incarnate, (SCM Press, 1977)

HIGGINS, Benjamin, United Nations And U.S. Foreign Economic Policy, (Illinois, Richard D. Irwin Inc., 1962)

HILL, Clifford, Black Churches. West Indian And African Sects In Britain, (London, Community And Race Relations Unit Of The British Council of Churches, 1971)

HODGKINSON, Edith, (ed.), Development Prospects And Options In The Commonwealth Caribbean, (London, Overseas Development Institute, 1976)

HOETINK, Harmannus, The Two Variants In Caribbean Race Relations, (OUP, 1967)

-, Caribbean Race Relations, (OUP, 1971)

HOLLENWEGER, Walter J., The Pentecostals, trans. R.A. Wilson, (SCM Press, 1972)

-, Pentecost Between Black And White, (Belfast, Christian Journals Ltd., 1974)

-, Evangelism Today, (Belfast, Christian Journals Ltd., 1976)

HOOKE, S.H., The Resurrection Of Christ, (Darton, Longman & Todd, 1967)

HOROWITZ, Michael M., (ed.), Peoples And Cultures Of The Caribbean, (New York, National History Press, 1971)

HOWE, John, (ed.), Today's Church And Today's World, (London, Church Information Office, 1977)

HOWES, Barbara (ed.), From The Green Antilles, (Panther Books, 1971)

Human Rights And Development, Report Of A Seminar Organised by ICJ/OCCBA, (Barbados, CEDAR Press, 1978)

Hunger For Justice, Report Of The All India Christian Consultation on Development New Delhi, 23-27 February, 1970, (New Delhi, Christian Agency For Social Action, 1970)

HUNTINGDON, Samuel P., and Joan M. Nelson, No Easy Choice Political Participation In Developing Countries, (Harvard University Press, 1976)

IDOWU, E. Bolaji, African Traditional Religion, (SCM Press, 1977)

ILLICH, Ivan, Tools For Conviviality, (New York, Harper & Row, 1973)

-, Celebration of Awareness, (Penguin, 1974)

INSTITUTE OF CHRISTIAN THOUGHT, Religions And Political Society, (New York, 1974)

INTERNATIONAL LABOUR ORGANIZATION, Employment, Incomes And Inequality A Strategy For Increasing Productive Employment In Kenya, (Geneva, 1972)

-, Employment, Growth And Basic Needs, (New York, Praeger, 1977)

-, Poverty And Landlessness In Rural Asia, (Geneva, 1977)

JAMES, C.L.R., Beyond A Boundary, (Hutchinson, 1963)

JENKINS, Daniel, Christian Maturity And The Theology Of Success, (SCM Press, 1976)

JOHNSON, David (ed.), Uppsala To Nairobi, (SPCK, and New York, Friendship Press, 1975)

JOHNSON, Paul, Enemies Of Society, (Weidenfeld & Nicholson, 1977)

JÜNGEL, Eberhard, The Doctrine Of The Trinity, (Edinburgh, Scottish Academic Press, 1976)

Karl Marx And Frederick Engels Selected Works, (London, Lawrence And Wishart, 1973)

KASEMANN, Ernst, New Testament Questions of Today, trans. W.J. Montague, (Philadelphia, Fortress Press, 1969)

-, Jesus Means Freedom, (Philadelphia, Fortress Press, 1970)

KEE, Alistair (ed.), A Reader In Political Theology, (SCM Press, 1974)

KEGLEY, Charles W., and Robert W. Brettall (ed.), Reinhold Niebuhr - His Religious, Social, And Political Thought, (New York, McMillan, 1961)

KENDALL, Elliott, The End Of An Era, (SPCK, 1978)

KENNER, M., and J. Petras (ed.), Fidel Castro Speaks,
    (Penguin, 1972)
KING, M.L., Chaos Or Community, (Hodder & Stoughton,
    1968)
KOYAMA, Kosuke, Waterbuffalo Theology, (SCM Press,
    1974)
-, No Handle On The Cross, (SCM Press, 1976)
KUNG, Hans, The Church, (New York, Image Books, 1976)
-, On Being A Christian, (Collins, 1976)
KURIEN, C.T., Poverty And Development, (Madras, 1974)
LANTERNARI, Vittorio, The Religions Of The Oppressed
    A Study Of Modern Messianic Cults, (New York,
    1963)
LEHMANN, Paul, The Transfiguration Of Politics,
    (SCM Press, 1975)
LEWIS, Gordon K., The Growth Of The Modern West
    Indies, (New York, Monthly Review Press, 1969)
-, Puerto Rico: Freedom And Power In The Carib-
    bean, (New York, Monthly Review Press, 1974)
LEWIS, S., and T.G. Matthews (ed.), Caribbean Integration,
    (Rio Piedras, Institute Of Caribbean Studies, University of Puerto
    Rico, 1967)
LEWIS, W.A., The Theory Of Economic Growth, (Allen &
    Unwin, 1955)
-, The Development Process, (New York, United Nations,
    1970)
LEYS, Colin, (ed.), Politics And Change In Developing
    Countries: Studies In The Theory And Practice Of
    Development, (CUP, 1969)
-, Underdevelopment In Kenya, (London, 1975)
LICHTHEIM, George, Imperialism, (Penguin, 1977)
LIPTON, Michael, Why Poor People Stay Poor: Urban
    Bias And World Development, (Temple Smith, 1976)
LISSNER, Jorgen, The Politics Of Altruism, (Geneva,
    Lutheran World Federation, 1977)
LOCHMAN, J.M., Encountering Marx: Bonds And Barriers
    Between Christians And Marxists, trans. Edwin
    Robertson, (Belfast, Christian Journals Ltd., 1977)
LOEN, Arnold E., Secularization, trans. Margaret Kohl,
    (SCM Press, 1967)
LOWENTHAL, David, The West Indies Federation:
    Perspectives On A New Nation (New York, Columbia
    University Press, 1961)
-, West Indian Societies, (OUP, 1972)
    with Lambros Comitas (ed.)
-, Work And Family Life
-, Slaves, Free Men, Citizens

252

-, Consequences Of Class And Color
-, The Aftermath Of Sovereignty each with the Subtitle -
    West Indian Perspectives (New York, Anchor Books,
    1973)
LUTHERAN WORLD FEDERATION, Department of Studies, The
    Encounter Of The Church With Movements Of
    Social Change In Various Cultural Contexts, (Geneva,
    Lutheran World Federation, 1977)
McCLEARY, Paul and J. Philip Wogaman, Quality Of Life In A
    Global Society, (New York, Friendship Press, 1978)
McCLELLAND, David, The Achieving Society, (New York,
    Free Press, 1967)
-, with David G. Winter, Motivating Economic Achievement,
    (New York, Free Press, 1969)
-, with Urie Bronfenbrenner, Alfred L. Baldwin, and Fred L. Strodt-
    beck, Talent And Society New Perspectives In The
    Identification Of Talent, (New Jersey, Princeton, 1958)
MACQUARRIE, John, Principles Of Christian Theology,
    (SCM Press, 1966)
-, The Faith Of The People Of God, (SCM Press, 1972)
-, Christian Unity And Christian Diversity, (SCM Press,
    1975)
-, The Humility Of God, (SCM Press, 1978)
MACPHERSON, John, Caribbean Lands: A Geography Of
    The West Indies, (Longmans, 1963)
MAIR, Lucy, New Nations, (London, 1967)
MAIS, Roger, The Hills Were Joyful Together, Brother
    Man, Black Lightning - The Three Novels Of Roger
    Mais, (Jonathan Cape, 1970)
MANLEY, Michael, The Politics Of Change, (Andre Deutsch,
    1974)
-, A Voice At The Workplace, (Andre Deutsch, 1975)
MARSH, John, Saint John, (Penguin, 1976)
MANNHEIM, Karl, Ideology And Utopia, (New York, Harcourt
    Brace, 1936)
MASON, Philip, Patterns Of Dominance, (OUP, 1970)
MATHEWS T.G. and F.M. Andic, Politics And Economics
    In The Caribbean, (Rio Piedras, Institute Of Caribbean
    Studies, University of Puerto Rico, 1955)
MATTHEWS, Dom Basil, Crisis Of The West Indian Family:
    A Sample Study, (Jamaica, UCWI, 1953)
MAUNIER, Rene, The Sociology Of Colonies Vol. I, ed.
    trans E.O. Lorimer, (London, 1949)
MBITI, John, Africans Religions And Philosophy, (Heine-
    mann, 1969)
METZ, J.B., Theology Of The World, (Burns & Dates,
    1969)

MIDDLETON, Neil, The Language Of Christian Revolution,
(Sheed & Ward, 1968)

MILLER, David, Social Justice, (OUP, 1976)

MILLIKAN, Max F., and Donald L.M. Blackmer (ed.), The
Emerging Nations: Their Growth And United States
Policy, (London, Asia Publishing House, 1961)

MILLWOOD, David, The Poverty Makers, (Geneva, World
Council of Churches, 1977)

MINEAR, P.S., Images Of The Church In The New
Testament, (Philadelphia, 1960)

MIRANDA, Jose, Marx And The Bible, trans. John Eagleson,
(SCM Press, 1977)

MITCHELL, David (ed.), With Eyes Wide Open, (Barbados,
CADEC, 1973)

-, New Missions For A New People, (New York, Friendship Press, 1977)

MITCHELL, Sir Harold, Europe In The Caribbean,
(California 1963), or (Edinburgh, Chambers, 1963)

MITCHELL, J.F., Land Reform In The Caribbean,
(Barbados, CADEC, 1972)

MOLTMANN, Jurgen, Theology Of Hope, trans. James W.
Leitch, (SCM Press, 1967)

-, Religion, Revolution And The Future, trans. Douglas
Meeks, (New York, Charles Scribner's Sons, 1969)

-, The Crucified God, trans. R.A. Wilson and John Bowden,
(SCM Press, 1974)

-, The Experiment Hope, (English trans.), (SCM Press,
1975)

-, The Church In Power Of The Spirit, trans. Margaret
Kohl, (SCM Press, 1977)

MOORE, Basil (ed.), Black Theology: The South African
Voice, (C. Hurst and Company, 1973)

MUNBY, Denys (ed.), World Development: Challenge To
The Churches, (Washington, Corpus Books, 1969)

MUNROE, Trevor and Rupert Lewis (ed.), Readings In Government And Politics Of The West Indies, (Jamaica,
Department of Government, University of the West Indies, 1971)

NAIPAUL, V.S., Mimic Men, (Andre Deutsch, 1967)

NIEBUHR, Reinhold, Christian Realism And Political
Problems, (Faber & Faber, 1954)

-, Moral Man And Immoral Society, (New York, Charles
Scribner's Sons, 1960)

NEIL, Stephen, A History Of Christian Missions,
(Penguin, 1977)

NESS, Gayl D., The Sociology Of Economic Development -
A Reader, (New York, Harper & Row, 1970)

NETTLEFORD, Rex, (ed.), Manley And The New Jamaica,
(Longmans, 1971)

-, Identity, Race And Protest In Jamaica, (New York, Wm. Morrow & Co. Inc., 1972)

NEWBIGIN, Leslie, The Household Of God, (SCM Press, 1964)

NINEHAM, D.E., Saint Mark, (Penguin, 1977)

NOLAN, Albert, Jesus Before Christianity, (Darton, Longman & Todd, 1977)

NOTTINGHAM, Elizabeth K., Religion And Society, (New York, Random House, 1954)

NYERERE, Julius, Ujamaa - Essays On Socialism, (OUP, Eastern Africa, 1968)

O'DEA, Thomas, The Sociology Of Religion, (New Jersey, Prentice-Hall, 1966)

OWENS, Joseph, Dread - The Rastafarians Of Jamaica, (Jamaica, Sangster, 1976)

PAINTER, John, John: Witness And Theologian, (SPCK, 1975)

PANNENBERG, Wolfhart, Theology And The Kingdom Of God, English translation, (Philadelphia, Westminster Press, 1969)

-, The Apostles's Creed In The Light Of Today's Questions, trans. Margaret Kohl, (SCM Press, 1972)

-, Jesus God And Man, trans. Lewis L. Wilkins and Duane A. Priebe, (SCM Press, 1976)

Partners in Development, Report of the Commission on International Development, (New York, Praeger, 1969)

PATCHEN, Martin, Participation, Achievement, And Involvement On The Job, (New Jersey, Prentice-Hall, 1970)

PATON, David M., (ed.), Breaking Barriers Nairobi 1975, (SPCK, 1976)

PATTERSON, Orlando, An Absence Of Ruins, (Hutchinson, 1967)

PENDLE, George, A History Of Latin America, (Penguin, 1978)

PITTENGER, Norman, The Christian Church As Social Process, (Epworth Press, 1971)

Plantation Systems Of The New World, (Washington, D.C., Pan American Union, 1959)

PRESTON, Ronald H., Technology And Social Justice, (SCM Press, 1971)

PROUDFOOT, Mary, Britain And The United States In The Caribbean, (Faber & Faber, 1954)

ROBERTS, J. Deotis, Liberation And Reconciliation, (Philadelphia, Westminster Press, 1971)

ROBERTSON, James, The Sane Alternative, (Villiers Publications, 1978)

ROBERTSON, Roland (ed.), Sociology Of Religion, (Penguin, 1972)

ROBINSON, John A.T., The Human Face Of God, (SCM Press, 1974)

-, Can We Trust The New Testament? (Mowbrays 1977)

ROCHE, Douglas, Justice Not Charity, (Toronto, McClelland and Steward Ltd., 1976)

RODMAN, H., Lower-Class Families: The Culture Of Poverty In Negro Trinidad, (OUP, 1971)

RODNEY, Walter, The Groundings With My Brothers, (Bogle L'Ouverture Publications, 1971)

-, How Europe Underdeveloped Africa, (Bogle L'Ouverture Publications, and Dar-es-Salaam, Tanzania Publishing House, 1972)

ROSTOW, W.W., The Stages Of Economic Growth, (Cambridge, 1968)

RUTTER, Owen, If Crab No Walk, (Hutchinson, 1933)

SALKEY, Andrew, Caribbean Essays, (Evans Brothers Ltd. 1973)

SAWYERR, Harry, Creative Evangelism. Towards A New Christian Encounter With Africa, (Lutterworth, 1968)

SCHUMACHER, E.F., Small Is Beautiful, (Abacus, 1977)

SCOTT, Nathan A. Jr., The Legacy Of Reinhold Niebuhr, (University of Chicago Press, 1974)

SEERS, Dudley and Leonard Joy (ed.), Development In A Divided World, (Penguin, 1971)

SEGUNDO, J.L., A Theology For Artisans Of The New Humanity, 5 Vols. trans. John Drury, (New York, Orbis Books, 1973)

-, The Liberation Of Theology, trans. John Drury, (Gill and Macmillan, 1977)

SEYMOUR, A.J., (ed.), New Writing In The Caribbean, (Guyana, 1972)

SHAW, D.W.D., Who Is God?, (SCM Press, 1968)

SHORTER, Aylward, African Culture And The Christian Church, (Chapman, 1973)

SIMPSON, George Eaton, The Shango Cult In Trinidad, (Rio Piedras, Institute of Caribbean Studies, University of Puerto Rico, 1965)

-, Religious Cults Of The Caribbean: Trinidad, Jamaica, And Haiti, (Rio Piedras, Institute of Caribbean Studies, University of Puerto Rico, 1970)

SINGHAM, A.W., The Hero And The Crowd In A Colonial Polity, (Yale University Press, 1968)

SLEEMAN, John F., Economic Crisis: A Christian Perspective, (SCM Press, 1976)

SMITH, Donald Eugene (ed.), Religion, Politics And Social Change In The Third World (A Sourcebook), (New York, Free Press, 1971)

SMITH, M.G., Kinship And Community In Carriacou, (New Haven, Yale University Press, 1962)

-, West Indian Family Structure, (Seattle, University of Washington Press, 1962)

-, Stratification In Grenada, (California, University of California Press, 1965)

-, The Plural Society In The British West Indies, (California, University of California Press, 1965)

SMITH, Raymond T., The Negro Family In British Guiana, (New York, Humanities Press, 1956)

SOBRINO, Jon, Christology At The Crossroads, (SCM Press, 1978)

SODEPAX, Towards A Theology Of Development, (Geneva 1969)

-, In Search Of A Theology Of Development, (Geneva 1969)

-, Partnership Or Privilege? (Geneva, 1970)

SOLLE, Dorothy, Political Theology, trans. John Shelley, (Philadelphia, Fortress Press, 1974)

SOMMER, John G., Beyond Charity, (Washington, Overseas Development Council, 1977)

STONE, Carl and Aggrey Brown, Essays On Power And Change In Jamaica, (Jamaica, Jamaica Publishing House, 1977)

STREETEN, Paul, The Frontiers Of Development Studies, (MacMillan, 1972)

TAYLOR, John W., Enough Is Enough, (SCM Press, 1975)

-, The Go-Between God, (SCM Press, 1976)

The Church And Development, (Nairobi, Kenya and Aachen Germany, AMECEA and MISEREOR, 1971)

THOMAS, Clive Y., Dependence And Transformation, (New York, Monthly Review Press, 1974)

THOMAS, M.M., The Christian Response To The Asian Revolution, (SCM Press, 1966)

TILL, Barry, The Churches Search For Unity, (Penguin, 1972)

TORRES, Sergio, with John Eagleson (ed.), Theology In The Americas, (New York, Orbis Books, 1976)

-, with Virginia Fabella (ed.), The Emergent Gospel, (New York, Orbis Books, 1978)

TRAYNHAM, Warner R., Christian Faith In Black And White, (Massachusetts, Parameter Press, 1973)

UPHOFF, Norman T., and Warren F. Ilchman (ed.), The Political Economy Of Development, (University of California Press, 1972)

VAN BUREN, Paul, The Secular Meanings Of The Gospel,
(SCM Press, 1963)
VAN DER BENT, A.J., The Utopia Of World Community,
(SCM Press, 1973)
VAN LEEUWEN, A. Th., Development Through Revolution,
(New York, Scribner's, 1970)
-, Critique Of Heaven And Earth, (Lutterworth, 1972)
VAUGHAN, B.N.Y., The Expectation Of The Poor,
(SCM Press, 1972)
VIDLER, A.R., The Church In An Age Of Revolution,
(Penguin, 1971)
WALCOTT, Derek, Another Life, (New York, Farrar, Straus &
Giroud, 1973)
WALKER, Dean (ed.), Canada And The Third World What
Are The Choices, Report of the 44th Couchiching Conference
of the Canadian Institute on Public Affairs, (Toronto, Yorkminster
Publishing Ltd., 1975)
WALKER, Derek, Power To End Poverty, (London, Action
For World Development, 1969)
WALLACE, Elizabeth, The British Caribbean From The
Decline Of Colonialism To The End Of Federation,
(University of Toronto Press, 1977)
WALLERSTEIN, Immanuel (ed.), Social Change - The
Colonial Situation, (New York, 1966)
WEBER, Max, The Religion Of India, Eng. trans., (New
York, Free Press, 1967)
-, The Protestant Ethic And The Spirit Of Capitalism,
trans. Talcott Parsons, (George Allen & Unwin, 1976)
WICKER, Brian, First The Political Kingdom, (Sheed &
Ward, 1967)
-, Culture And Theology, (Sheed & Ward, 1969)
-, Culture And Liturgy, (Sheed & Ward, 1970)
WILLIAMS, Eric, Capitalism And Slavery, (New York,
G.P. Putnam's, 1966)
-, Education In The British West Indies, (New York,
University Place Bookshop, 1968)
-, Inward Hunger: The Education Of A Prime Minister,
(Andre Deutsch 1969)
-, The Negro In The Caribbean, (New York, Haskell House,
1970)
-, From Columbus To Castro, (Andre Deutsch, 1970)
WILSON, Bryan, Religion In Secular Society, (Pelican,
1969)
WINTER, Derek, Hope In Captivity, (Epworth Press, 1977)
WOGAMAN, J. Philip, Christians And The Great Economic
Debate, (SCM Press, 1977)
WOOD, Donald, Trinidad In Transition, (OUP, 1968)

E. World Council of Churches materials (Geneva)

Ecumenical Review, Vols. XIII, XIX, XX, XXII, XXV, XXVI

International Review of Mission, Vol. LXVI, (1977)

Study Encounter, Vol. V (1969)

Risk, Vol. 9, (1973)

Dilemmas And Opportunities, Christian Action In Rapid Social Change, (1959)

World Conference On Church And Society, Official Report (1966)

Development Education, Report of the Consultation organized in Geneva in May 1969 by the Secretariat On Development Education of the WCC, (1969)

Fetters Of Injustice, ed. Pamela H. Gruber, (1970)

To Break The Chains Of Oppression, (1975)

Self-Reliance And Solidarity In The Quest For International Justice, (1976)

CCPD Documents:
    No. 2 - Churches On Development
    No. 6 - Justice Rolling Like A River
    No. 7 - Conscientization
    No. 8 - The Quality Of Aid
    No. 9 - Betting On The Weak
    No.10 - In Search Of The New

Faith, Science And The Future, Preparatory Readings For The 1979 Conference of the WCC, ed. Paul Abrecht, (1978)

STUDIEN ZUR INTERKULTURELLEN GESCHICHTE DES CHRISTENTUMS
ETUDES D'HISTOIRE INTERCULTURELLE DU CHRISTIANISME
STUDIES IN THE INTERCULTURAL HISTORY OF CHRISTIANITY

Herausgegeben von/edité par/edited by

Richard Friedli
Université de Fribourg

Walter J. Hollenweger
University of Birmingham

Hans-Jochen Margull
Universität Hamburg

Band 1 Wolfram Weiße: Südafrika und das Antirassismusprogramm. Kirchen im Spannungs-feld einer Rassengesellschaft.

Band 2 Ingo Lembke: Christentum unter den Bedingungen Lateinamerikas. Die katholische Kirche vor den Problemen der Abhängigkeit und Unterentwicklung.

Band 3 Gerd Uwe Kliewer: Das neue Volk der Pfingstler. Religion, Unterentwicklung und sozialer Wandel in Lateinamerika.

Band 4 Joachim Wietzke: Theologie im modernen Indien - Paul David Devanandan.

Band 5 Werner Ustorf: Afrikanische Initiative. Das aktive Leiden des Propheten Simon Kimbangu.

Band 6 Erhard Kamphausen: Anfänge der kirchlichen Unabhängigkeitsbewegung in Süd-afrika. Geschichte und Theologie der äthiopischen Bewegung. 1880-1910.

Band 7 Lothar Engel: Kolonialismus und Nationalismus im deutschen Protestantismus in Namibia 1907-1945. Beiträge zur Geschichte der deutschen evangelischen Mission und Kirche im ehemaligen Kolonial- und Mandatsgebiet Südwestafrika.

Band 8 Pamela M. Binyon: The Concepts of „Spirit" and „Demon". A Study in the use of different languages describing the same phenomena.

Band 9 Neville Richardson: The World Council of Churches and Race Relations: 1960 to 1969.

Band 10 Jörg Müller: Uppsala II. Erneuerung in der Mission. Eine redaktionsgeschichtliche Studie und Dokumentation zu Sektion II der 4. Vollversammlung des Ökumenischen Rates der Kirchen, Uppsala 1968.

Band 11 Hans Schoepfer: Theologie der Gesellschaft. Interdisziplinäre Grundlagenbibliogra-phie zur Einführung in die befreiungs- und polittheologische Problematik: 1960-1975.

Band 12 Werner Hoerschelmann: Christliche Gurus. Darstellung von Selbstverständnis und Funktion indigenen Christseins durch unabhängige charismatisch geführte Gruppen in Südindien.

Band 13 Claude Schaller: L'Eglise en quête de dialogue.

Band 14 Theo Tschuy: Hundert Jahre kubanischer Protestantismus (1868-1961). Versuch einer kirchengeschichtlichen Darstellung.

Band 15 Werner Korte: Wir sind die Kirchen der unteren Klassen. Entstehung, Organisation und gesellschaftliche Funktionen unabhängiger Kirchen in Afrika.

Band 16 Arnold Bittlinger: Papst und Pfingstler. Der römisch katholisch - pfingstliche Dialog und seine ökumenische Relevanz.

Band 17 Ingemar Lindén: The Last Trump. An historico-genetical study of some important chapters in the making and development of the Seventh-day Adventist Church.

Band 18 Zwinglio Dias: Krisen und Aufgaben im brasilianischen Protestantismus. Eine Studie zu den sozialgeschichtlichen Bedingungen und volkspädagogischen Möglichkeiten der Evangelisation.